Transgender on Screen

Transgender on Screen

John Phillips

palgrave
macmillan

First published 2006 by
PALGRAVE MACMILLAN
Houndmills, Basingstoke, Hampshire RG21 6XS and
175 Fifth Avenue, New York, N.Y. 10010
Companies and representatives throughout the world

PALGRAVE MACMILLAN is the global academic imprint of the Palgrave Macmillan division of St. Martin's Press, LLC and of Palgrave Macmillan Ltd. Macmillan® is a registered trademark in the United States, United Kingdom and other countries. Palgrave is a registered trademark in the European Union and other countries.

ISBN-13: 978-1-4039-1242-8   hardback
ISBN-10: 1-4039-1242-4   hardback
ISBN-13: 978-1-4039-1243-5   paperback
ISBN-10: 1-4039-1243-2   paperback

This book is printed on paper suitable for recycling and made from fully managed and sustained forest sources. Logging, pulping and manufacturing processes are expected to conform to the environmental regulations of the country of origin.

A catalogue record for this book is available from the British Library.

Library of Congress Cataloging-in-Publication Data

Phillips, John, 1950-
    Transgender on screen / John Phillips.
        p. cm.
    Includes bibliographical references and index.
    ISBN 1-4039-1242-4 (cloth) – ISBN 1-4039-1243-2 (paper)
        1. Transvestism in motion pictures. 2. Transsexuals in motion pictures. 3. Internet pornography. I. Title.

PN1995.9.T69P35 2006
791.43'653–dc22   2006043198

10   9   8   7   6   5   4   3   2   1
15   14   13   12   11   10   09   08   07   06

The woman shall not wear that which pertaineth unto a man, neither shall a man put on a woman's garment; for all that do so are abomination unto the Lord thy God.

(Deuteronymy, 22:5)

... there is no way to think dominant culture without transgender ... To cross from one gender to another may suggest that those genders are in place, have their place, prior to the possibility of crossing. But there is no acquisition of gender without such a crossing, a dangerous crossing into cultural norms that brings both pleasure and fear.

(Judith Butler, Afterword, *Sexualities* Vol. 1(3), 355, 359)

Contents

Acknowledgements   *viii*

1   Introduction   1

2   Transgender in the Historical Imagination   30

3   Cross-dressing in Film Comedy   51

4   Psycho–Trans   85

5   Drama Queens and Macho Men   115

6   Walking on the Wild Side: Shemale Internet
    Pornography   147

7   Representation and Reality   165

Notes   *174*

Bibliography   *184*

Index   *192*

Acknowledgements

This book was completed with the aid of an Arts and Humanities Research Council award, which matched funding from my employers, London Metropolitan University, to give me a six-month sabbatical leave in 2005. I am grateful to both institutions for their support.

A longer version of Chapter 6 first appeared in *International Exposure. Perspectives on Modern European Pornography, 1800–2000*, edited by Lisa Z. Sigel (New Brunswick, NJ: Rutgers University Press, 2005). My thanks to Lisa Sigel and the publishers for permission to reproduce this essay here with some revisions.

Nearly fifteen years ago, Camille Paglia (1992: 99) wrote 'The time is right for a major scholarly book on transvestism that would speak in lucid, sensible language to a general audience.' I am far from sure that this modest contribution to the subject lives up to Paglia's high standards, but I have tried to make it readable for the general audience she rightly identifies as the only one that really matters.

1
Introduction

This first detailed study of screen representations of transgender has the following main aims:

- To demonstrate that perceptions of transgender are mediated by culturally constructed images.
- To explore these cultural representations of transvestism and trans-sexuality in modern (late twentieth century) screen media (film, Internet), against the historical background of the evolution of such representations.
- To identify and account for the ambivalence that underlies the depiction of transgender in modern film.
- To reposition and redefine sexual desire against sexual fascination with transgender.

Not merely a topic of intellectual debate in universities and academic writings, transgender has become a major preoccupation in western culture. In the mid-1970s, *The Rocky Horror Picture Show* (Lou Adler, 1975), a drag version of earlier science-fiction films, stimulated a fash-ionable interest in cross-dressing that influenced rock-stars and other icons of popular culture in the 1980s and 1990s, from David Bowie and Boy George to Divine, Ru Paul, and many others. This trend has continued into the new millennium. Among recent instances, an Israeli male-to-female transsexual, Dana International won the Euro-vision Song Contest in 2001, a Spanish male-to-female transsexual, Nadia, won the UK reality TV show, *Big Brother* in 2004, the UK's lead-ing TV soap-opera, *Coronation Street* has for several years featured a male-to-female transsexual character, and 'trannie' porn is said to be the fastest growing type of pornography on the Internet and DVD markets. More surprisingly, perhaps, this preoccupation is not entirely new. Since the eighteenth century, many writers of fiction have focused their attention on the subject, and representations of transgender in religion, philosophy and mythology date back to the ancients. In the second half of the twentieth century, there was a growing cinematic interest in representations of cross-dressers, and occasionally, of transsexuals.

Critical background

The quest to know oneself is both as old as narrative and a fundamental part of it. For the Paris school of semiotics, the resolution of enigmas is an essential objective in all narrative structure, while Roland Barthes emphasises the role of the hermeneutic (or enigmatic) code in the reading process (see Barthes, 1990). Given their mass audiences, screen representations of transgender play a significant role in this wider narrative quest for the identity of a self no longer definable in terms of the 'grand narratives' that have conditioned our thinking over previous centuries, and of which gender and sexuality are primary components. Unsurprisingly, therefore, these representations are at the very heart of current debates about gender and sexuality. Images of cross-dressing in particular have been argued to reveal the constructedness of gender (as opposed to its biological naturalness), and to open up its categorisation along a continuum, as against the conventional fixed positions of masculine and feminine, dictated by religious approaches to the human experience. This process began with Simone de Beauvoir's *Second Sex*, and was continued in Michel Foucault's work on sexualities.

Yet, although gender theorists have made passing reference to the portrayal of transgendered people in the novel and cinema, the significance of transgender for the wider debate around gender and sexuality has not been given the attention it deserves.

Marjorie Garber's lengthy and comprehensive study, *Vested Interests: Cross-dressing and Cultural Anxiety*, is a notable exception, and has had much influence in this area. I shall be referring to it throughout the book, but a brief summary of her arguments may be found useful here. Garber regards cross-dressing as focusing cultural anxiety and challenging the vested interests of a society that depends on the clear separation of genders:

> What this book insists upon ... is that transvestism is a space of possibility structuring and confounding culture: the disruptive element that intervenes, not just a category crisis of male and female, but the crisis of category itself.
>
> (Garber, 1993: 17)

> one of the most consistent and effective functions of the transvestite in culture is to indicate the place of what I call 'category crisis', disrupting and calling attention to cultural, social, or aesthetic dissonances ... putting into question the very notion of the 'original' and stable identity.
>
> (Ibid.: 16–17)

In addition to the binarism of male/female, by 'category crisis' Garber means 'a failure of definitional distinction, a borderline that becomes permeable, that permits of border crossings from one (apparently distinct) category to another: black/white, Jew/Christian, noble/bourgeois, master/servant, master/slave' (ibid.: 16).

However, Garber shows little interest in the erotic implications of gender-play, seeing the transvestite as a useful theoretical figure for the expansion of gender beyond the binary structure of male–female, nor is she especially interested in transsexuality, as opposed to transvestism, for reasons which will be explained below. She also makes the astonishing and novel claim that 'there can be no culture without the transvestite, because the transvestite marks the entrance into the Symbolic' (ibid.: 34). Garber's entire book is, in a sense, designed to demonstrate the validity of this claim, and there is not space here to debate it in the detail it requires. However, this quotation does illustrate Garber's reliance on Lacanian psychoanalysis and raises the problem of associated terminology. As I shall be exploiting the same methodological models, a brief explication of Jacques Lacan's theory of the 'Real', the 'Imaginary' and the 'Symbolic' realms, and his key concept of the 'Father's Law' are given below in the section on methodology.

Garber's book has not been positively received in all quarters. In a swingeing critique, Camille Paglia, for example, describes it as 'stunningly disorganised', 'inadequately researched', 'lumpish' and 'tedious'.

Although such criticisms are perhaps unnecessarily scathing, I agree with Paglia when she says that 'Forever reducing transvestism to politics or vaudeville, Garber never catches its uncanniness, its dangerous magic' (Paglia, 1992: 96–100). My own overarching hypothesis is at once more far-reaching and more modest than Garber's: the crossing of genders (not restricted to cross-dressing) will prove to be the most significant single cultural challenge in the first decades of the new millennium, largely because of the redefinition of sexes and sexualities that necessarily accompanies it. Representations of transgender are already leading the way towards new conceptions of a self increasingly defined in terms of the images that popular culture reflects back to it.

Garber's work is important, and packed with fascinating detail, but her book contains no in-depth analysis of individual texts. *Vested Interests's* encyclopaedic survey of the phenomenon since Elizabethan times is necessarily more limited than this more focused study. Moreover, half of the films analysed here postdate Garber's book (1992), which also contains no discussion of the Internet.

Apart from Garber, very little has been published on screen representations of the subject, and few of those academic articles that have appeared on the films in my corpus take transgender as their central focus. Even the cross-dressing comedies have tended to attract attention from critics who are more interested in the representation of gender in general, and of women in particular, than of transgender per se. This book is designed to fill the gap.

Corpus

Fiction, television, cinema, pop music and the Internet are all media that have, in one way or another, represented transgendered people in recent times. This profusion of images, coupled with the relative dearth of critical writing on such representations, makes the choice of corpus for a book on the subject a challenging and hazardous undertaking – hazardous because there will be some who will wish to draw conclusions of a political or ethical nature from whatever choice is made, especially with regard to what is left out. Other than to insist that my corpus is in no conscious way dictated by political or ethical considerations, I make no apologies for my selectivity, unavoidable in a study of such modest dimensions. My selection is intended, however, to be broadly representative of the treatment of transgender on screen in the second half of the twentieth century and at the start of the twenty-first.

This is a book about representations of transgender in popular entertainment, in particular about the images that serve these representations, images in the poetic but also in the strictly visual sense of the word, and it seemed appropriate to focus on the most commonly and easily accessible forms of these visual images. My film corpus is therefore limited to a dozen 'mass audience' films, all relatively well known and successful. I have divided the films into comedies, thrillers, and mixed genre films – three separate categories that overlap only occasionally. Comedies and thrillers are examined separately because they exhibit entirely different responses to transgender: comedies almost exclusively represent cross-dressers, exploring temporary transformations of gender in a largely playful manner, while thrillers deal with the frightening prospects of a more serious threat to gender identity. The mixed genre films, as this category title suggests, contain examples of both.

All of these filmic works are examples of the mainstream, and although there are significant differences between the 'Hollywood' and 'non-Hollywood' productions in my corpus in terms of the treatment of the subject, this division cannot be taken to imply a judgement as to quality or value, or even as to 'political correctness'.

In the penultimate chapter, I consider the very recent phenomenon of 'shemale' Internet pornography, as a coda to my study of film. Belonging to neither of the traditional genres, such images (and the porn movies from which they are frequently taken) speak openly and directly to the spectator of an eroticism that remains largely covert, even disavowed in mainstream cinema.

Methodologies

Like Garber's, my approach presupposes an unconscious sub-text which is accessible to psychological and psychoanalytical investigation. Hence, the application of Freudian and Lacanian theory – essential tools in the exploration of a powerful textual unconscious. My avowed bias towards a psychoanalytical approach is not out of place in film criticism in which Lacanian theory in particular abounds. Lacan's theories of the three orders of human culture, and his rereading of Freud's Oedipal phase according to which the 'Father's Law' is established have become frequent references in film analysis. Bice Benvenuto and Roger Kennedy (1986) offer the clearest definitions of these difficult, and at times, rather elusive concepts:

> perhaps the best definition of the orders is that they are different conceptual categories which aim to cover the functions and activities of the psychoanalytic field ... The Imaginary Order includes the field of phantasies and images ... The Symbolic Order is easier to grasp, being concerned with the function of symbols and symbolic systems, including social and cultural symbolism. Language belongs to the Symbolic Order, and in Lacan's view, it is through language that the subject can represent desires and feelings, and so it is through the Symbolic Order that the subject can be represented, or constituted. The Real Order, on the other hand, is the most elusive of these categories, and is linked to the dimensions of death and sexuality ... Basically, it seems to be the domain outside the subject ... it sometimes seems to refer to the domain that subsists outside symbolization.
>
> (Benvenuto and Kennedy, 1986: 81)

'The Father's Law' refers to Lacan's notion that the human subject must renounce the mother's body, pass successfully through the oedipal phase, and accept his place in the family triad, if he is to be assimilated into the the Symbolic Order, and the system of language upon which it depends, on pain of 'symbolic castration' by the father.

> (Ibid.: 133 ff.)

Despite this methodological bias towards the psychoanalytical, eclecticism is the key word throughout the book. Each film in the corpus is a separate work of art, and certain analytical tools were found to be better suited to teasing out meanings than others; in some cases, more than one tool was found appropriate. Thus, alongside a more general, less theoretical interpretation, I have at times adopted a broadly psychoanalytical approach (as in my analysis of *Dressed to Kill*, *Cherry Falls*, and shemale Internet porn), a Freudian/Jungian study of castration fear (*Boys Don't Cry*), a structuralist focus on binarism in the text (oppositions in *Midnight in the Garden of Good and Evil*, a Barthesian study of the signifier in *Victor/Victoria*), while at other times a post-structuralist methodology proved more productive (Lacanian psychoanalysis and Butler's Queer Theory for *Psycho*, *Silence of the Lambs*, shemale porn, and the remaining comedies), and in my concluding chapter, the future of gender in relation to desire is explored through the perspective of Jean Baudrillard's postmodern theories of the real and the imaginary. All of these theories will be elaborated, as and when appropriate, in the chapters that follow, with the exception of Queer Theory which is of direct relevance to all of the screen texts discussed, and so will be briefly outlined below. First, though, some key terms need to be defined.

Sex, Gender, Sexuality

The British video version of *The Adventures of Priscilla, Queen of the Desert* begins with an advertisement for Levi jeans. A beautiful and shapely young black girl climbs into a New York cab. The driver is visibly turned on, his excitement accompanied and troped by hyperbolic images – water-hoses spraying the street and the driver's own perspiration. Then, in his rear-view mirror, he catches sight of the young 'woman' shaving. Conscious of the cabbie's realisation of her 'true' sex, the transvestite/transsexual laughs with glee, producing a sense of deflation in the man (and no doubt equally in the male spectator) a feeling that he has been 'had' and rightly punished for his lustful thoughts.

This ad possesses many of the features of those films I shall be discussing in this book: an ironic self-awareness associated with postmodern representation, notions of 'passing' and deception, the eroticisation of transgendered people, a sense of danger that is simultaneously disturbing and thrilling, undertones of castration anxiety, generated here by the woman's laughter.[1] It also illustrates a confusion commonplace in the media between transsexuals, hermaphrodites, transvestites and drag-queens, not to mention 'sex', 'gender' and 'sexuality'. The confusion of these latter terms is a 'key misunderstanding' for Garber, but as she points out, the distinction between gender and sexuality is not always an easy one to make:

> the borderline between gender and sexuality so important to much recent feminist and gender theory is one of the many boundaries tested and queried by the transvestite. The cultural effect of transvestism is to destabilize all such binaries: not only 'male' and

'female', but also 'gay' and 'straight', and 'sex' and 'gender'. This is the sense – the radical sense – in which transvestism is a 'third'.

(Garber, 1993: 133)

For the purposes of this book, 'sex' is to be understood as rooted in anatomical differences, specifically in the nature of the reproductive organs, while 'gender' is a social and ideological construct. We should also consider here the related but distinct concept of 'sexuality' or 'sexual preference', conventionally reduced to the binarism of heterosexual/homosexual, which to a large extent is dependent on and reinforces the male/female binarism of sexual difference. The transgender phenomenon explodes all of these binaries. Medical science is itself beginning to support the concept of a continuum in relation to sex differences: 'Recent research in the biology of sex has shown that "biological" sex encompasses chromosomal and hormonal makeup as well as internal and external genitalia, all of which can appear in combinations that defy a simple binary sex system' (Handler, 1994: 42 n.10).

Hermaphrodites are individuals with both male and female genital characteristics. True hermaphroditism, where the individual has both sets of genital organs, is extremely rare; most people with this condition sharing the other sex's anatomical characteristics to a varying degree. Medical science has termed this majority 'pseudo-hermaphrodites'. Stephen Whittle (2000: 17) distinguishes hermaphroditism from intersexuality, which he defines as a much wider condition in which 'the physical attributes of chromosomes, gonads (testicles or ovaries) and genitals (penis or vagina) do not coincide in the manner we expect'. Since hermaphroditism is an anatomical condition, it has been known since ancient times. Whittle argues that intersexuality and hermaphroditism are different matters from transgender (ibid.: 18), but in the context of a study of representations which are in part determined by attitudes deriving from perspectives that have evolved historically, these conditions are not without importance as instances of what was known in earlier cultures, such as those of Ancient Greece and Rome, as androgyneity or bisexuality (see Chapter 2).

Transvestites, or cross-dressers, have also existed throughout known history. The term denotes people of either sex who derive erotic pleasure from cross-dressing. Magnus Hirschfeld (1868–1935) coined the term, publishing a book about transvestism, *Die Transvestiten* in 1910. It was Hirschfeld who first separated transvestism and transgender generally from homosexuality. The vast majority of male-to-female transvestites are heterosexuals who enjoy a fetishistic pleasure in dressing in women's clothes, especially female lingerie. Transvestism, then, is quite distinct from sexual orientation. In later years, researchers have tended to confirm this judgement, although their work has revealed a broad spectrum of cross-dressing behaviours. Richard F. Docter (1998: 9, quoted by Garber, 1992: 132), for instance, identifies 'five heterosexual behaviour patterns involving cross-dressing: fetishism, fetishistic transvestism, marginal transvestism, transgenderism, and secondary transsexualism (TV type)' and 'four homosexual behaviour patterns involving cross dressing: primary transsexualism, secondary transsexualism, so-called drag queens, and female impersonators'.

Drag-queens, or female impersonators, are biological males who wear women's clothing, usually excessive in character, and often for the purposes of entertaining in public. Drag-queens do not necessarily dress in women's clothing for erotic reasons, and there is wide variation in their motives and styles: 'There are gays who dress as women, male prostitutes who are trying to pass as female, and others who find the character change cathartic, challenging, amusing, or entertaining' (Love, 1999: 90). For the most part, however, drag-queens do not succeed as 'passable' females and remain recognisably male. Drag, in other words, is a masculine display.

Whittle defines transsexuals as persons who 'experience a profound sense of incongruity between his/her psychological sex and his/her anatomical sex. Transsexual people wish to change the anatomical sex, through hormones or surgery, to match the internal perception of their bodies' (Whittle, 2000: 66). Garber's definition is somewhat broader, and in my view more accurately reflects the reality of transsexualism today: 'The term "transsexual" is used to describe persons who are either "pre-op" or "post-op" – that is, whether or not they have undergone penectomy, hysterectomy, phallo- or vaginoplasty. Transsexualism is not a surgical product but a social, cultural, and psychological zone' (Garber, 1993: 106). The medical term for this clash between sex and gender is 'gender dysphoria'.

Until the end of the nineteenth century, those who felt trapped in the wrong body could do no more than cross-dress, living their lives in some cases as a member of the other sex. The rupture between cross-dressing and transsexuality came with the development of new medical technologies. Transsexuality originated about a hundred years ago, following the discovery by scientists in the late nineteenth century of sex hormones identifiable as male or female. In the early twentieth century, it became possible to isolate the specific effects of 'male' and 'female' hormones. By the 1910s European scientists had begun to publicise their attempts to transform the sex of animals, and by the 1920s some doctors, mostly in Germany, had agreed to alter the bodies of a few patients who longed to change their sex. It was not until after World War II, however, that the issue of sex-change was seriously addressed in the United States, and in 1949, Dr David O. Cauldwell, an American psychiatrist, was the first to use the word 'transsexual' to refer to people who sought to change their sex. By the end of the 1950s, there was already a clear scientific distinction between 'hermaphrodites', or people who had both male and female gonads, 'transsexuals', whose gender identities did not correspond with their physical sex, and 'homosexuals', who were sexually attracted to their own sex but had no desire to change sex. Although some surgery and hormone treatment had been practised since the 1920s, it was not until the postwar period that new advances in plastic surgery and the invention of synthetic hormones made sex change more freely available.

The first widely publicised case of male-to-female sex change occurred in 1953. Christine Jorgensen, a former American GI, returned from Denmark where she had undergone the first of several operations as part of what became known as gender reassignment, and, given her film-star looks (she was blonde, beautiful and chic) and gift for self-publicity, she quickly became a media sensation. In what was probably the first public demonstration of erotic interest in a transsexual, there was clearly a large measure of titillation in the media coverage of Jorgensen's case. Her experience blazed a trail for others, however, and thanks to the media publicity, almost at once her psychiatrist in Denmark, Dr Christian Hamburger, started receiving requests from others for advice and treatment, leading in 1953 to the publication of a paper, 'The Desire for Change of Sex as Shown by Personal Letters from 465 Men and Women' (see Meyerowitz, 2002: 40). The medical profession suddenly realised that large numbers of people wished to change their biological sex and gender role, and clinics were set up, first in New York and San Francisco, then, gradually, in many other western cities, to respond to this demand. When the endocrinologist, Harry Benjamin published the first major textbook on the subject in 1966 (*The Transsexual Phenomenon*), gender reassignment was still the subject of extensive social stigma both publicly and in the medical world.[2] Nearly forty years later, some of the stigma remains, but most now accept that transsexuals should be allowed access to hormone therapy and surgical reassignment.

While hermaphrodites and cross-dressers have been around since the ancients and probably earlier, then, transsexuals and drag-queens are relatively recent arrivals on the transgender scene, at least as far as there has been a name for them. In the 1990s, the word 'transgender' was coined to denote all of the above and to include anyone oppressed because of their gender identity or gender presentation: 'Individuals may identify as transgender because they cross-dress some of the time, because they cross-gender live much of the time, because they undergo gender reassignment, or just because their gender identity or gender role is not conventional' (Whittle, 2000: 16). For Judith Butler, however, the term more narrowly denotes only cross-dressers and drag-queens, excluding transsexuals who are perceived as toeing the binary line and thus as reinforcing gender polarities (see below). Butler's objections notwithstanding, I shall follow Whittle in using 'transgender' in its literal linguistic sense as an umbrella term to cover all crossings of gender and sex boundaries, whether temporary or permanent, vestimentary or anatomical.

These are all questions of gender or sexual identity, and have no direct link with sexual orientation. However, one could say that sexuality is as much a continuum as gender, and that in neither case are conventional binary categories (male/female, hetero/homo) adequate or even appropriate.[3]

Queer Theory

Queer Theory, associated mainly with the work of Judith Butler and Eve Kosofsky Sedgwick derives much of its thinking from post-structuralist ideas of identity as decentred and unstable, in particular from Jacques Lacan's model of the subject as structured by the unconscious, from Jacques Derrida's deconstruction of binary concepts and of course, from Michel Foucault's model of subjectivity as the product of discourses.[4] By far the most important work in this area has been Judith Butler's *Gender Trouble* (first published in 1990), which aimed at the 'political convergence of feminism, gay and lesbian perspectives on gender, and poststructuralist theory' (Butler, 1999: xxxii). Strongly influenced by post-structuralist views of human subjectivity as shifting and contextual, Butler concludes that gender 'does not denote a substantive being, but a relative point of convergence among culturally and historically specific sets of relations' (ibid.: 15). Echoing Simone de Beauvoir's famous maxim that one is not born but rather *becomes* a woman, Butler claims that gender identities are a 'doing' not a 'being' (see ibid.: 43), the result of a performative effect: 'gender proves to be performative – that is, constituting the identity it is purported to be. In this sense, gender is always a doing' (ibid.: 33).[5] Borrowing the logic of Nietzsche's claim that the subject does not pre-exist the deed, or as Nietzsche puts it, that 'the doer is merely a fiction added to the deed – the deed is everything' (Nietzsche, *On the Genealogy of Morals*, quoted by Butler, ibid.), she then applies this notion to gender: 'There is no gender identity behind the expressions of gender; ... identity is performatively constituted by the very "expressions" that are said to be its results.' There is no reason to assume, Butler argues, that genders should remain as two, and she questions the immutable character of sex: sex, in fact, she maintains, turns out to have been 'gender all along', or in other words, may it not after all be as culturally constructed as gender? (ibid.: 10). There is, therefore, no such thing as a specific female or male identity. Sexuality, too, is just as much a construct, although in our normative cultures, what Butler calls 'the heterosexual matrix' generates the illusion that like gender and sex, heterosexuality is natural.

Butler is indebted to the work of Monique Wittig, who maintains that not only are gender and sex cultural constructs but that the body itself is never just a given, that, like notions of masculinity and femininity, it is also constructed. Butler follows Wittig in acknowledging that this construction is primarily linguistic: 'That penis, vagina, breasts, and so forth, are *named* sexual parts is both a restriction of the erogenous body to those parts and a fragmentation of the body as a whole' (ibid.: 146). In this emphasis on the link between naming and the creation of a concept, both Butler and Wittig are influenced by Austinian speech-act theory, according to which a number of verbs in our language are not merely 'constative' (descriptive statements) but 'performative' (performing an act) (see Austin, 1962). In her preface to the 1999 edition of *Gender Trouble*, Butler specifically relates the linguistic construction of gender to the case of the transsexual:

> What about the notion, suggested by Kate Bornstein, that a transsexual cannot be described by the noun of 'woman' or 'man', but

must be approached through active verbs that attest to the constant transformation which 'is' the new identity or, indeed, the 'in-betweenness' that puts the being of gendered identity into question?

(Ibid.: xi)

In this passage, Butler acknowledges the transitional nature of the transsexual, implicitly recognising the latter's place outside conventional sex and gender categories and therefore the threat (s)he represents to the heterosexist hegemony; some have questioned why Butler took so long to recognise the significant role of the transsexual in undermining binary norms.[6] On the other hand, a number of paragraphs in *Gender Trouble* are devoted to drag which, Butler maintains, illustrates this performativity of gender well: 'In imitating gender, drag implicitly reveals the imitative structure of gender itself – as well as its contingency' (Butler, 1999: 175). The theatricality of the drag-queen clearly lends itself to an illustration of performativity, but there are political reasons why Butler did not have recourse to the transsexual to illustrate her theory, reasons deriving from Queer Theory's initial hostility to transsexuality. Jay Prosser (1998: 6) explains this blind spot as a rejection of embodiment:

the transgendered subject has typically had center stage over the transsexual: whether s/he is transvestite, drag queen, or butch woman, queer theory's approbation has been directed toward the subject who crosses the lines of gender, not those of sex. Epitomizing the bodiliness of gender transition – the matter of sex the crossdresser has been applauded for putatively defying – the transsexual reveals queer theory's own limits: what lies beyond or beneath its favored terrain of gender performativity.

Although Prosser is highly critical of Queer Theory's position on transsexuality, Prosser's use of the term 'transgendered subject' clearly excludes transsexuals in line with that position. In that the post-op transsexual is widely seen as the product of medical technology, (s)he is definable in terms of a *physically* transformed sex, rather than a linguistically or theatrically determined gender. As such, (s)he is also vulnerable to attack as perpetuating conventional sex binaries, and as complicit with patriarchy.[7] The transsexual, then, brings sex back into the equation, subverting Butler's theory of performativity. It is, above all, the post-op transsexual who disturbs the performativity theory, in that (s)he has undergone a transformation, not merely of gender, but of sex – physical changes that impact permanently on the body. Thus, the transsexual is a 'limit case' for queer theory, refocusing attention on the materiality of the body (see Prosser, 1998: 58). While gender can be read at the surface of the body, in gestures and appearance, sex is an inescapably physical (somatic) dimension that extends throughout both mind and body (ibid.: 43). Because screen images focus particularly on external surfaces, however, film must deal less effectively than the novel, say, with the transsexual condition, and so the four films in our corpus that feature transsexuals who wish to undergo reassignment surgery (*Dressed to Kill, Silence of the Lambs, Priscilla, Queen of the Desert* and *Boys Don't Cry*) fail to convey what Prosser calls 'the logic of transsexuality'. As for Internet shemale pornography, the prè-op transsexuals represented are designed to create a visual illusion that appeals to the viewer's desires, and my analysis will therefore concentrate on the meanings and effects of this essentially 'surface-bound' phenomenon which has less to do with transsexual subjectivity than with the shemale as erotic object. (I am using 'shemale' to denote the male-to-female pre-op transsexual who is deliberately and indefinitely suspended between the masculine and the feminine: see Chapter 6.) Hence, Butler's performativity theory will be found relevant, not only to representations of cross-dressing, but to these 'surface' images of a transsexuality incomplete, frozen in the process of becoming.

Common ground

A number of hypotheses and presuppositions form the basis of my approach throughout this study.

Sexuality as well as gender

These films are not just about gender, but also about sexuality, and it is the very repression of the sexual that makes these films thrilling. As Jean Baudrillard observes, 'Sexual discourse is invented through repression, for repression speaks about sex better than any other form of discourse. Through repression (and only through repression), sex takes on reality and intensity because only confinement gives it the stature of myth' (Baudrillard, 1987: 36–7). Much like the films themselves, most previous criticism has focused on questions of gender, while repressing the sexual undercurrents.

The normativity of popular culture

In the broadest of terms, this book is a study of modern myths which, as Marina Warner says, 'offer a lens which can be used to see human identity in its social and cultural context – they can lock us up in stock reactions, bigotry and fear, but they're not immutable, and by unpicking them, the stories can lead to others' (Warner, 1994: 14). That cinema, especially, is an important site of modern myth is emphasised by Baudrillard who claims that while cinema is being 'contaminated' by television, and is itself moving toward increased hyper-realism, it continues to be predominantly a vehicle of image, myth and the imaginary (see Kellner, 1989: 225 n.13). Since the place of modern myth is predominantly the various forms of popular culture, these are the sites in which these responses are most strongly registered and most clearly perceptible.

Western popular culture is heavily normative, so that sexual perversions and gender deviations of all kinds are routinely demonised. The UK TV soap-opera *Coronation Street* provides a good example of the failure of even well-intentioned popular entertainment to produce wholly positive representations. The character of Hayley Cropper in *Coronation Street* is a post-op male-to-female transsexual, played by a biologically female actress. Shortly after the character's introduction, Hayley falls in love with an established character, Roy Cropper. Whilst the initial problems of a sexual relationship between a heterosexual male and a male-to-female transsexual are sympathetically explored, there is never any sense that gender binaries are being seriously challenged. As Hayley and Roy go upstairs to bed for the first time, we hear in the background the strains of Aretha Franklin's 'You make me feel like a natural woman', reminding the audience that she is anything but natural.[8] Moreover, the principal dramatic interest surrounding Hayley gradually changes from social concern to comedy. In fact, the character has comic potential from the outset. Hayley is played as a warm, friendly but idiosyncratic individual with just a touch of oddity and an old-fashioned taste in clothes and hairstyles. Although her voice is acceptably feminine in pitch (the actress playing her is, after all, a biological female), her diction and tone possess a jauntiness that suggests caricature rather than realism. Despite the politically correct intentions of the programme's producers (see programme website), there is something of the tomboy in this portrayal. While real trans-sexuals aim to be as feminine as possible in their dress, gait and gestures, Hayley is represented as somewhat mannish: hair cut boyishly short, and possessing no erotic interest whatever for the heterosexual male spectator, she waddles comically across the set. Like her partner, Roy, Hayley's interests are represented as deeply eccentric (as suggested by the red anorak she always wears), an eccentricity that leads both characters into comic situations. Roy and Hayley have become the Laurel and Hardy of the programme, and consequently, the serious issue of Hayley's gender has been progressively eroded, overshadowed by her potential as comic relief from the darker scenarios that increasingly dominate *Coronation Street*'s story-lines. Thus is the sexual/gender otherness of Hayley Cropper displaced onto a more anodine eccentric other, and as in all the examples of comedy we shall be examining in this book, the threat of transgender is similarly defused by a comic treatment that is ultimately just as mocking and dismissive of the subject as pantomime.

The centre and the margins

It is not original to label popular TV or Hollywood cinema as normative, but I shall attempt to analyse and explain a normativity which is always accompanied by a prurient fascination. Baudrillard makes the acute observation that the natural condition of our whole culture is obscenity, by which he means the exhibition of our abjection: 'Ours is a culture of "monstration" and demonstration, of "productive" monstrosity' (Baudrillard, 1987: 22). This exhibitionism of contemporary culture, evident in the current obsession with 'reality' television, fosters a preoccupation with all forms of what this culture regards as deviance. The culture thus satisfies a sexual curiosity, at the same time as it distinguishes itself from deviance, constantly redrawing the line between normality and perversion, as if to reassure itself that the line exists at all. The centre necessarily defines itself in opposition to the margins, without which it would have no meaning.[9]

Temporary and permanent change

The notion of temporary change is tolerated by patriarchy and capitalism partly because it is reversible – an allowed transgression that can be playful and erotically exciting; a site from which to champion subversion and transformation (transvestism, drag). On the other hand, the notion of permanent change of sex/gender (transsexualism, hermaphroditism, intersexuality) is perceived as threatening by a work-oriented culture which in many crucial respects depends on binary fixity. In Bakhtin's (1984) terms, transvestism may be seen as a form of inversion, and transsexuality as hybridisation. While inversion, for Bakhtin, does not change the binary system, hybridisation fundamentally threatens it:

> Hybridization, a second and more complex form of the grotesque than the simply excluded 'outside' or 'low' to a given grid, produces new combinations and strange instabilities in a given semiotic system. It therefore generates the possibility of shifting the very terms of the system itself, by erasing and interrogating the relationships which constitute it.
>
> (Stallybrass and White, 1986: 58)

All of the comedies in my corpus represent the temporariness of transvestism and not the permanence of transsexuality, while the reverse is true of the thrillers, confirming the hypothesis that transsexuality is feared and demonised in our cultural imaginary, while transvestism is regarded as innocuous and playful.

An ambivalent space

Representations of both temporary and permanent transgender reflect widely varying attitudes and perspectives, but responses to both manifest profound ambivalence, from fear and repulsion on the one hand to fascination and the thrill of eroticisation on the other. The former emotions are prompted in part by an anxiety that fixed binary models of gender and sexuality might be threatened, and that the breaking down of boundaries between self and other is a potentially dangerous process. This anxiety is unconsciously associated with what Julia Kristeva calls the 'abject', and which she relates to physical matter that normally provokes reactions of disgust: the human corpse, but also bodily excreta such as urine, faeces, menstrual blood, sperm, vaginal fluid and breast milk – even the skin on the surface of milk offers an instance of the abject. However, abjection is not necessarily related to a lack of cleanliness or of health, it is rather 'what disturbs identity, system, order. That does not respect borders, positions, rules. The in-between, the ambiguous, the composite' (Kristeva, 1982: 3–4). In every sense perceivable as a manifestation of abjection, the transgendered body inspires horror precisely because it threatens those boundaries that protect our identities, drawing us outside the symbolic order into the realm of the unnameable. (Kristeva associates the abject with the maternal and therefore with the imaginary.) Underlying this fear, too, in the unconscious of the viewer, is a castration complex that can be found expressed in the images and motifs of all my chosen films.

While comedy, thriller and Internet genres each in their different ways exploit the exciting ambivalence of transgender, films of greater sophistication, which may also be more politically aware, are interested in depicting transgender as a potentially revolutionary position from which to critique fixed boundaries, normalising discourses, and the hegemony of heterosexuality.

The imaginary and catharsis

As we shall see in Chapter 2, transsexuality in modern culture appears to elicit responses similar to those provoked by hermaphroditism throughout history, from fear and revulsion on the one hand to erotic fascination on the other. This similarity of responses is due to the characteristic of physical permanence which both share, in contrast to the temporariness of cross-dressing. However, these are repressed in the imaginary of art, rationalised as philosophy, religion or symbolism. The horror provoked by real hermaphrodites proves that the phenomenon of transgender is deeply disturbing for western culture. This angst is neutralised, displaced, and exorcised in myth, given more acceptable meanings. At times, the erotic asserts itself more (from the Renaissance on, for example), but such moments are usually followed by greater repression.

The veiling and unveiling of truth

Certain identifiable motifs run throughout the corpus, whether comedy or thriller, revealing an underlying collective angst and/or ambivalence. Of these, castration motifs are the most common. In addition, motifs specific to the comedy and thriller genres will be addressed in chapters 3 and 4 respectively. Practically all of the films I examine, however, follow a structure of disguise/deception and unveiling/revelation that can be traced back to ancient representations (see Chapter 2), and so it seems useful to examine these in some detail here as a prelude to further discussion in the context of individual chapters/films.

The theme of deception is a central and recurring one in both ancient and modern representations of transgender. At the level of plot, this theme clearly serves the hermeneutic code well, the code which Roland Barthes associates with the posing and resolution of a mystery in narrative.[10] There would seem to be two main models for this:

1. One or more characters is/are deceived as to the gender/sex of (an)other character(s), and the audience are similarly deceived. The shock of revelation is then followed by the pleasure associated with discovery and with admiration for the deceiver (in this case, the film-maker and/or actors): *Psycho, Dressed to Kill, The Crying Game*.
2. As with (1), except that the audience are in on the deception. The spectator here derives pleasure from observing the deception's success or failure: *Some Like it Hot, Tootsie, Mrs Doubtfire, Victor/Victoria, Priscilla, Queen of the Desert, Midnight in the Garden of Good and Evil, Boys Don't Cry*. In comedy, there are frequently added complications where the deception is a successful one.

The exceptions are *Silence of the Lambs* and *Cherry Falls* in which the mystery concerns the identity of the killer generally, and the cross-dressing aspect of this identity is revealed at the same time. This is an unusual deviation from the norm, according to which gender-switching offers clear dramatic opportunities for comedy or terror.

Intradiegetic deception is thus common to almost all of the films in my corpus, but this device has a variety of different aims.[11] In the comedies, the aim by and large is a comic one, so that the audience enjoy watching other characters being taken in by appearances, often with embarrassing consequences. The audience is not deceived in any of the comedies, which therefore rely for much of their humorous impact on dramatic irony. This genre, in other words, tends to exploit the cross-dressing phenomenon as a means to amuse, although this does not preclude an educative function (for instance, in *Victor/Victoria*, which highlights identity (mis)recognition to expose and ridicule bigotry and homophobia). In all of the thrillers, deception as to the killer's identity and gender occurs intradiegetically, as required by the genre itself. The audience, too, is intentionally misled as to both for at least some of the time in all four of the films I analyse. In each case, audience deception serves the broader objective of maintaining mystery and suspense, while the revelation of a transgendered murderer adds a touch of bizarreness and monstrosity to the killings, trading on the otherness of transgender to engender fear and loathing.

There is a variable pattern in the mixed genre films. Of these, only one, *The Crying Game*, goes out of its way to deceive the audience as to the gender of a leading character. All four films in this category, however, concentrate on the effects of intradiegetic deception, either for comic or shock purposes (*Midnight, Crying*) or, like the comedies, to highlight homophobia and discriminatory attitudes (*Boys, Priscilla*). As one might expect, then, these films are less concerned with playing games with the spectator than with foregrounding issues of sexual politics.

In all of the comedies and mixed genre films, name-change plays an important role in the game of deception. In *Psycho, Dressed to Kill* and *Silence of the Lambs*, however, the 'truth' unveiled is that of the killer's identity, which is always a truth of psychology and not of naming since the audience already know or will have guessed who the killer is in advance of the dénouement. Thus what is revealed are the psychological motivations that led the murderer to commit the crime (motivations that refer back to cross-dressing in a circle of evil): in *Psycho*, the love-hate-guilt relation with the mother, in *Dressed to Kill*, the schizophrenic character within, who wants to be a woman and punishes women for arousing the man, and in *Silence of the Lambs*, the desire to clothe himself in the skin of real women. The murderer is here named in terms of the illness that defines him.

Deception is, in all cases, eventually followed by revelation of the transgender character's 'true' gender and identity. Again, this convention has a long history in literature and myth (see Chapter 2), and in their different ways, both Foucault and Barthes point out that what is hidden is often assumed to be the truth. As Foucault argues, it is in the area of sex that we search 'for the most secret and profound truths about the individual, that it is there that we can best discover what he is and what determines him' (Foucault, 1980: x). In contemporary western culture, Foucault wrote in 1978, 'the idea that one must indeed finally have a true sex is far from being completely dispelled' (ibid.). Foucault points to psychoanalysis and psychiatry as being responsible for the perpetuation of this idea: 'Sexual irregularity is seen as belonging more or less to the realm of chimeras' (ibid.). Foucault claims that we cannot rid ourselves of the belief that these are fictions – we should wake up, we tell ourselves, and remember that we each have a 'true sex' (ibid.). The belief in the existence of a true sex, a true gender and a true sexuality is, then, deeply rooted in western popular culture. We shall see how, to a greater or lesser extent, this belief underlies all filmic representations of transgender. All the narratives we are examining are thus analysable in terms of a quest for truth, through revelation of the hidden.[12] By insisting on the closure that truth or resolution brings, conventional narratives dealing with this subject reassure the audience by returning to normality. The transgender experience/experiment is thus ultimately brought to an end. Those few narratives that approach the transgender issue with the sophistication it deserves avoid the death of closure, making them postmodern narratives: in the case of *The Crying Game*, the enigma to be resolved is the nature of Fergus's passion for Dil which remains unfulfilled; in the case of *Victor/Victoria*, it is the ambivalent nature of Victor's and King Marchan's relationship; for Brandon Tina in *Boys*, it is her 'true' gender which the narrative leaves unresolved (for the audience, it is the outcome of her passion for her girlfriend).

Roland Barthes establishes a general link between unveiling and the restoration of the masculine and the Father's Law in the context of the realist narrative. The progressive unveiling that defines the dissolution of narrative suspense, which he likens to the act of striptease, is always a *mise en scène* of the 'absent Father':

> All the excitement is found in the *hope* of seeing the genitals (schoolboy fantasy) or of knowing the outcome of the story (pleasure of novel-reading) ... oedipal pleasure (stripping, discovering, knowing the beginning and the end), if it is true that all narratives (all unveilings of the truth) are a *mise en scène* of the Father (absent, hidden or hypostasised) – which would explain the consistency of narrative forms, of family structures and nudity prohibitions, all of which are combined in our culture in the myth of Noah covered up by his sons.
>
> (Barthes, 1973b: 20; my translation)

The unveiling of 'truth' in the imagery of art carries unavoidably erotic connotations associated with the denuding of the female body, and thus resembles striptease. To unveil therefore suggests a forbidden gesture, the act of looking at the forbidden in a sexual sense, an Oedipal transgression of the mother's body laid bare. What are the implications of this line of associations for the unveiling of the cross-dresser, who, except in *Victor/Victoria*, reveals himself to be a man? The act would thus appear to reverse the erotic laying bare of the female/mother's body, to parody it through the very process of inversion. At the same time, what is actually unveiled is not the original taboo object but the hidden yet familiar phallus, an erotic parody of the conventional act of striptease, designed to amuse and reassure the male spectator, hitherto beset by castration anxiety. If the man in a frock still has the phallus, then so does he. What was lost is found, and all is right with the world. The revelation of truth is hence inextricably linked in our collective unconscious to the Father's Law and the restoration of normality.

A psychoanalytical reading of the deception and unveiling theme might suggest another deep-seated human imperative. Freud's *Fort!da!* game which symbolically re-enacts the presence and absence of the mother is also a game of concealment and revelation which expresses the need to master the anxiety associated with the mother's absence. Anika Lemaire explains:

> Let us recall the child's game recounted by Freud in *Beyond the Pleasure Principle*, where he shows how a child succeeds in dominating the cloudy lived experience of his mother's absence by replacing that experience with a symbol ... The child, whose favourite game is recounted by Freud, had a cotton-reel with a piece of string tied around it. Holding the string, he would throw the reel over the edge of his curtained cot. While doing so he uttered a prolonged 'ooh', which was easily interpreted as being an attempt at the German *fort*, meaning 'gone' or 'away'. He would then pull the reel back into his field of vision, greeting its reappearance with a joyful *da* ('there'). It should be noted that the child's mother, busy outside, was in the habit of leaving her son alone for long periods. The game thus had the significance of a renunciation. It allowed this 18-month-old child to bear without protest the painful lived experience of his mother's alternating disappearance and reappearance. By means of this game in which he repeated with an object – the reel and the string – the coming and going of his mother, the child assumed an active part in the event, thus ensuring his domination of it ...
>
>   In a first act of symbolization, the child removes himself from the urgency of an event – his mother's disappearance and

reappearance – by replacing it with a symbol – the appearance and disappearance of the reel.

By their alternation, the two phonemes O and A (*ooh* and *da*) will in turn symbolize the disappearance and reappearance of the reel. The distancing of the lived experience is effected in two stages: the child moves from the mother to the reel and finally to language. Such an experience may be considered the inaugural moment of all future displacement, all metaphors and all language.

This game showed that language detaches itself from the Real and allows the subject to register himself by distancing himself from the lived Real.

(Lemaire, 1977: 51)

The game thus enables the infant to deceive himself as to this absence by symbolically substituting the cotton-reel for the mother's physical presence. In a transgender context, such deception links with both the pleasure of the imaginary (eroticism and play) and with the anxiety of an insecurity, generated by the threat of ambiguity and the sense of being cheated, but also with the reassurance brought by the illusion of control. This notion is explored further in Chapter 6.

Language, then, reproduces reality, indeed, there is no thought without language for Lacan. The *Fort!da!* game illustrates the supremacy of the signifier in all representation, and helps us to understand the metaphoricity of our perceptions of transgender and their detachment from the real.

Language acquisition in this Lacanian scenario is an inescapably *binary* process (*Fort!da!*) and the universe is thus defined for the child in *binary* terms: presence/absence, positive/negative and so on. However, the repeated movement between the two poles suggests a desire to push against this binarism, to test it to breaking-point by the violence of the act, and to explore the territory between each extreme.

In the case of those narratives featuring the serious identity issues faced by transsexuals (*Boys, Crying, Priscilla*), such 'truth' is an empty signifier in Barthes's terms. As with La Zambinella in Balzac's story, *Sarrasine*, the only 'truth' discoverable is the 'nothing of castration', whether actual or intended:

Continually undressing his model, the sculptor Sarrasine antici-pates Freud, who (apropos of Leonardo) identifies sculpture with

analysis: each is a *via di levare*, or clearing away ... the sculptor
tears off La Zambinella's veils to get at what he believes to be the
truth about her body; for his part, the subject Sarrasine, through
repeated snares, proceeds ineluctably toward the real condition of
the castrato, the void which is his center. This dual movement is
that of the realist ambiguity. The Sarrasinean artist tries to undress
appearance, tries always to get *beyond, behind*, according to the ideal-
istic principle which identifies secrecy with truth: one must thus
go *into* the model, *beneath* the statue, *behind* the canvas ... The
same rule holds for the realist writer (and his critical posterity): he
must go *behind* the paper, must know, for example, the exact relationship between Vautrin and Lucien de Rubempré (though what
is behind the paper is not reality, the referent, but the Reference,
the 'subtle immensity of writings'). This impulse ... leads to a failure ... *beneath* La Zambinella (and therefore inside her statue)
there is the *nothingness* of castration, of which Sarrasine will die
after having destroyed in his illusory statue the evidence of his
failure: the envelope of things cannot be authenticated, the
dilatory movement of the signifier cannot be stopped.

(Barthes, 1990: 122–3)

Comedies like *Victor/Victoria* play with the notion that the hidden *is*
the true. In the stage-act, Victor plays a woman, the hidden allegedly
being a man, but the hidden is not the 'truth' of the performance,
since the hidden is also a woman. In *The Crying Game*, the hidden is
apparently true (Dil's real sex), but actually only half-true, since her
gender is female. In *Boys Don't Cry* the main character's female sex is
as much an empty signifier as the male sex of Dil in *Crying* or of
Bernadette in *Priscilla*.

The incessant movement of the signifier

The truth of meaning, in a postmodern perspective, is thus unattain-
able, because the signified is out of reach of a signifying process that
never leaves the realm of the signifier. The dominance of the signifier,
its incessant movement within the circularity of language as a closed
signifying system, and its relevance to the 'unveiling' is underlined
by Jacques Lacan's well-known example of 'urinary segregation',
which in turn is best explained with the aid of an example from
popular television.

Let us return to the character of Hayley Cropper. The character was treated sympathetically when she first appeared in *Coronation Street*. There were the usual bigoted reactions by neighbours and workmates (Hayley became one of the machinists in the local clothing factory), one of which is a stereotype that crystallises both the dilemma facing the new or pre-op transsexual and the prejudices of others: the question of what Jacques Lacan calls 'urinary segregation'. When Hayley attempts to go to the Ladies on her first day at the factory, an especially narrow-minded and hostile work-colleague, Karen MacDonald, rounds upon 'Harold' (Hayley's former name as a man), refusing to let 'him' enter female space. For Lacan, this arbitrary polarisation of toilet spaces is linked to the dominance of the signifier in the symbolic:

> We see that, without greatly extending the scope of the signifier concerned in the experiment, that is, by doubling a noun through the mere juxtaposition of two terms whose complementary meanings ought apparently to reinforce each other, a surprise is produced by an unexpected precipitation of an unexpected meaning: the image of twin doors symbolizing, through the solitary confinement offered Western Man for the satisfaction of his natural needs away from home, the imperative that he seems to share with the great majority of primitive communities by which his public life is subjected to the laws of urinary segregation.
>
> (Lacan, 1977c: 151)

In Saussurian terms, the signifier is thus split into the Ladies/Gentlemen difference, which in turn determines a difference of signifieds, that is the twin doors as representing the law of sexual segregation. Lacan draws a diagram showing signifiers (Ladies/Gentlemen) above signifieds (identical doors), emphasising that it is the signifier that articulates the difference and not the signified. Moreover, for Lacan, there is no Saussurian unity of signifier and signified to make the sign, as the twin doors example illustrates, and indeed, the signified constantly slides under the signifier.

The scene from *Coronation Street* bears out Lacan's theory of the dominance of the signifier: for Karen, what matters is observance of the word (Ladies/Gents), in accordance with the name that she gives Hayley (the masculine signifier, Harold). The signified of urinary segregation is less at issue for her than the fixity of binary gender division, represented by the Ladies/Gents signifiers which she perceives as under threat. Although the scene encourages the audience to sympathise with Hayley and not Karen, by representing the former as reasonable and mild-mannered and the latter as unreasonable and aggressive, its focus on this particular expression of binary polarisation exemplifies a concern with gender spaces that the viewing public would undoubtedly share. Although the surface message of the scene is 'understanding for transsexuals', its underlying theme is an acknowledgement of the social and psychological needs associated with the spatial segregation of men and women, needs satisfied at the level of the signifier and not the signified.

The popular film comedy and thriller genres of the last few decades have been marked by an increasing self-referentiality. This self-reflexivity itself further exemplifies the incessant movement of the signifier which never reaches the ultimate or transcendental signified of truth. Just as there is nothing inside Sarrasine's statue, except the emptiness of castration, equally in these films, there is no real behind the representation. *Tootsie* and *Mrs Doubtfire* refer back to a whole tradition of cross-dressing in comedy since ancient times in which the truth unveiled in the dénouement is always another signifier, another representation: that is, what is revealed is the truth of a performance, or a deception (not for the audience who know but for other characters who are fooled); what is revealed is the stock responses of others within the diegesis (amazement, humour, anger, relief and so on). Thus is the comedic tradition itself referred to in both performance and act of unmasking. As we have seen, this self-reflexivity is well brought out in Barthes's analysis of *Sarrasine*. All is representation and reference, there is no real. Beauty and love are trapped in the self-referential circularity of language:

> By declaring La Zambinella adorable, Sarrasine establishes one of the three proofs (narcissistic, psychological, aesthetic) he will continually use in order to deceive himself about the castrato's sex: I am justified in loving her because she is beautiful, and if I love her (I who cannot be mistaken), it is because she is a woman.
>
> (Barthes, 1990: 144)

Similarly, many of the protagonists of our corpus refuse at first to believe in the 'truth' revealed, precisely because of the circularity of the signifier. In *The Crying Game*, Fergus loves and desires Dil because he reads her in terms of the cultural codes of femininity: lustrous long hair, svelte and graceful body, smooth hairless skin, child-like face, higher-pitched voice. In *Victor/Victoria*, this process is ironically inverted as King Marchan reads Victor as a woman *in spite of* his masculine appearance. Like Sarrasine, he cannot believe that the object of his desire is *not* a woman since he is attracted to her. In *Boys Don't Cry*, the girl is equally convinced that Brandon is a man because she is sexually aroused by him and does not identify herself as a lesbian. It is the circularity between cultural codes that persuades all these protagonists of the attractiveness of the opposite sex and the well-foundedness of their own desire. (See Chapter 3 for more detailed discussion of the circularity of codes in the case of *Victor/Victoria*.)

Representation and the real: a postmodern perspective

This book is about screen representations of transgender, not about the various manifestations of transgender in 'real life', and my primary focus will be on the objectification of the cross-dressing and pre-op transsexual subject on screen. On the other hand, is it even possible to distinguish the real from its representation in any meaningful way? Indeed, as Louis Althusser has shown, all social reality is mediated through representation (see his influential essay, 'Ideology and Ideological State Apparatuses'). Given the inescapability of this process of mediation of the real, and the circularity of the signifier within a self-referential system, how are we to think about reality? And what is the relevance of such a distinction in the context of our subject?

Michel Foucault argued that the human body (and the self) are not universal but cultural constructions that change over time. Such a slippage of meanings is gradually moving us away from the fixed binaries that have structured western thinking and social organisation over the last two millennia, and this process is part of a continuum of sliding definitions affecting all aspects of our lives, including the very notion of reality itself. This development manifests itself in popular culture in an increasing elision between the representation of reality and reality itself (if indeed that distinction still has meaning or value). We live in a society obsessed with immediate communication. People walk along the street talking into their mobile phones, or sit in trains, buses and the underground earnestly scanning them for text messages.

Emailing can occupy many hours in the day. Clothing is selected for the brand name (which must be prominently displayed for others to see) rather than for quality or even style. The communication media mark almost every feature of our lives in the west. Life, it seems, will once again very soon imitate art, as ads are set to 'call out' to passers-by, a scenario that appears directly inspired by the scene in Steven Spielberg's futuristic vision, *Minority Report*, in which shoppers in a mall are recognised by their retinal images and then hailed individually with marketing messages that are tailor-made for them. (Althusser's 1971, theory of interpellation seems directly illustrated in this scene.) As the imaginary and the real move ever closer together in a culture in which the sending of images by cell-phone compensates for physical presence, 'postmodern' increasingly describes society itself and not simply the art it produces. For our dependence on messages is a refuge from the real in representation, or rather, it generates situations in which representation *is* the real. At the very least, like a nervous actor who is lost without a script, reality takes its cue from representation. The working-class young of London and the South-East increasingly copy the language and speech patterns of their rap idols, while both working- and middle-class people of nearly all ages pepper their conversations with words and expressions learnt from American soaps and sitcoms. What matters in this universe of simulacra is the imaging of self through a variety of media and in a multiplicity of ways. Much of this imaging process turns upon sex: girls and boys send each other coded *billets doux*, girls wear designer jeans low-slung to reveal a brand, colour and type of underwear – usually a sexy thong. Sartorial and other details of appearance also send out messages about gender and sexuality. All of these representations are audio or visual, and like it or not, their influence is infinitely more powerful than anything in print. This is one reason for the visual focus of this book.

The tension between a desire to escape the symbolic in an imaginary in which all conventional boundaries and taboos dissolve, and a normatising pressure to conform to the symbolic and the Father's Law manifests itself in practically all the films of my corpus through castration anxiety and its consequences. Along with their intertextuality, self-referentiality, parodic elements and emphasis on performance, all of the films and the Internet material examined here illustrate this tendency for the imaginary to stand in for the real, identified by Jean Baudrillard as a defining feature of the postmodern. I shall return to these issues in my concluding chapter.

Before beginning a detailed analysis of these twentieth-century images, however, we need to look at the long history of such representations in western literature and myth. This is the subject of my next chapter.

2
Transgender in the Historical Imagination

Human beings have been fascinated by images of bisexuality and the androgyne since ancient times. The statues of ancient Greece and Rome, and the cults which they represent reveal a particular preoccupation with hermaphroditism, as we shall see later, but cross-dressing, too, has a long and complex history of representation in western culture. The main purpose of this chapter, in the context of a study of the modern imaginary, is precisely to demonstrate the deep-rootedness in the human psyche of these two aspects of what we now call transgender, and the cultural representations that give it expression. This survey will also reveal on the one hand an unchanging hostility towards any real and permanent threat to gender, and on the other, an erotically motivated fascination with transgender which expresses itself in our similarly unchanging myths and narratives.

In this historical perspective, we are concerned only with representations of the androgyne, of cross-dressing and of hermaphroditism. Transsexuality is a modern phenomenon, and so is not discussed here. On the other hand, although the hermaphrodite does not appear in any of the filmic or Internet material the book examines, it is nonetheless, as already indicated, a major figure of the transgender phenomenon in western cultural history and demands attention in any historical review of transgender. This survey is also limited to western culture, from its origins among the ancient Greeks and Romans to twentieth-century Europe and America, a limitation explainable in terms of the focus of this book.

There are two main and connected reasons for including a historical perspective in a book on cultural representations of the late twentieth and early twenty-first centuries. First, the present is in every respect inescapably a product of the past. Nothing in the present can be properly understood in isolation from, or without reference to an evolving historical process. That the reverse is equally true – the past can be viewed only through the lenses of the present – should caution us against falling into the common trap of interpreting the past in terms of modern values and perspectives. As Michel Foucault demonstrates, the medico-legal terminology of gender and sexuality currently in use and determining the rigidity of society's thinking in these areas did not come into existence until the mid- to late nineteenth century (see Foucault, 1978). Thinking about sexuality and gender is always largely determined by temporal and cultural contexts. It would be anachronistic, therefore, to apply this terminology and the concepts it represents to earlier periods when neither existed. Nevertheless, we shall see that, at the level of what Jung terms our collective unconscious, some basic attitudes have persisted for millennia. The detail may vary, and there are, certainly, notable exceptions, but three main tendencies stand out:

1. A clear separation between the real and the imaginary, and at the same time, currents of influence between them.
2. An anxiety in relation to hermaphroditism, accompanied by a fascination which often assumes an erotic character.
3. A playful and at times erotic response to acts of cross-dressing.

Second, in many significant ways, the modern images of transgender which are discussed in subsequent chapters, while embracing a wide variety of themes and forms, can be said to repeat (without being identical to) earlier representations. The drive to repeat is, as Freud observed, ubiquitous in human culture, and is partly motivated by a need to master that which is repeated. Questions of identity, of which gender is an essential component, have preoccupied human beings since the beginning of recorded history, a persistent questioning at the heart of all religions and philosophies. From the Renaissance on, the narrower question of the identity of the self has come increasingly to the fore. The seventeenth-century French philosopher, René Descartes was the first western thinker to focus attention on the identity of the individual as opposed to that of humanity in general. Descartes's famous dictum, 'cogito ergo sum' (I think, therefore I am) has influenced thinking about identity issues right up to our own times. Transgender, as we shall see, has been a dominant feature of this problematic since the ancients, as humans have repeatedly attempted to master it through the representations they have produced.

While this chapter does not set out to be a historical account of real transgender phenomena (any more than this book is about 'real' transgendered people), reality and representations of it cannot so easily be separated. At the most fundamental of levels, as we argued in Chapter 1, 'real' behaviour is clearly influenced by what one reads and sees. Nevertheless, the focus of this and all other chapters will be on how transgender has been and continues to be represented in the imaginary of our culture, rather than on the behaviours of real individuals or groups within it.

Attitudes to hermaphroditism on the one hand and cross-dressing on the other have generally speaking elicited quite different responses throughout known history, and consequently, the evolution of their representation in literature, theatre and culture has followed different trajectories. Before examining these separate trajectories, however, we need to look briefly at how the androgyne, which in a sense links both of them, was represented in the myths and artistic images of the ancient world.

The androgyne

One of the most extensive studies of the androgyne in artistic, religious and philosophical representations of the ancient period was conducted by Marie Delcourt in the early 1960s, a study that has not been surpassed in extent or quality since, and I shall be making frequent reference to this below (see Delcourt, *Hermaphrodite: Myths and Rites of the Bisexual Figure in Classical Antiquity*). One of Delcourt's principal hypotheses is that the horrific reality of the hermaphrodite contrasts sharply and is seemingly incompatible with the ubiquity of images of the androgyne in classical myth. Delcourt sees this representational use as asexual symbolism, but offers no real explanation for this dichotomy between the real and the imaginary, a problem which in my view can be resolved only in terms of a repressive process.

Binary thinking has its roots in prehistory. In every religion, the beginning of creation is conceived as a primeval confusion that needs to be separated for creation to take place. For Plato, heaven and earth were themselves born from chaos, like two sexes seen as issuing from a primitive *utrumque*. Notwithstanding the verse of the

Bible, 'Male and female created he them', the Talmud, on the other hand, contains the doctrine of primitive humanity as bisexual, which passed into Jewish mysticism, as well as into Arabic esotericism, in which the unity Adam-Eve represents universal man. Other religions and philosophies have in their different ways privileged the androgynous character of origins: the Chinese synthesis of the yang and the yin, the two principles held in balance; the Hindu couple Purusha-Prakriti, 'as big as a man and woman enclasped'; the bisexual character of infinite Time in the teaching of the Zervanist magi (see Delcourt, 1961: 72). All these images form part of our common unconscious.

Greek examples of what Delcourt terms 'symbolic androgyny' are the most numerous, but the Latin world soon followed the Greek example. The Romans saw their gods as of indeterminate sex (Venus, for example). Oriental religions also have numerous bisexual figures, but these have had little or no influence on modern western attitudes and concepts, and so are not relevant here.

Orphic poets attributed bisexuality to many divine beings, of whom Dionysus is probably the best example. Eros was always represented by artists and poets as androgynous, and Hera, goddess of marriage appears first as androgynous. 'The androgynous deity of Cyprus had a woman's body and clothing, but the beard and sexual organs of a man; ... To do sacrifice to it, men dressed as women, and women as men' (ibid.: 27).

The androgynous character of the phoenix was well known to the ancients. In this case, bisexuality is a sign of immortality. Itself a symbol of eternity, the moon, too, was seen as having an androgynous character (ibid.: 38). Even the Christian God was conceived as both male and female in the early years of Christianity. At the beginning of the fifth century, Bishop Synesius apostrophised the Almighty thus: 'Thou art father and thou art mother, thou art male and thou art female' (quoted by Delcourt, ibid.).

Delcourt (ibid.: 67–8) argues that underlying the ancient philosophical myths was the ideal of unity:

A dream of primordial unity, of regeneration and return to unity, is expressed by the image of the bisexual being divided into two, of the egg breaking to give birth to the world, of the cauldron-matrix in which the members of Zagreus, hewn in pieces by the Titans, are boiled to be born again, of the pyre which consumes the Phoenix: all symbols which were to dominate the mysticism of waning Antiquity.

For Plato, we were all originally double beings whom Zeus decided to cut through the middle as a punishment for pride. Each of us, therefore, is the half of a whole, and, consequently, we spend our lives constantly searching for our complementary half. Jung has shown that the medieval alchemists were influenced by the same images of a primordial unity of soul, matter, striving to unite animus and anima to produce a balanced psyche (ibid.: 75).

As far from real experience as possible, then, such symbolism was reassuringly asexual, and indeed, asexuality was valorised in ancient times as fostering spiritual purity, associated, as we have seen, with immortality: 'The bisexuality of the philosophers amounts to asexuality: spiritual man is completely freed from the bonds of the flesh' (ibid.: 101). For the ancients, bisexuality became synonymous with asexuality early on (ibid.: 31). For them, there is no erotic component in the myth; bisexuality was symbolic, expressed in rites, cults and legends. For Delcourt, eroticism played no part in the androgynous gods imagined by the Greeks (ibid.: 52–3). Dionysus, Apollo, Aphrodite and Hermaphrodite were all 'indeterminate deities': 'Greek art from its archaic period onwards ... dwells as little as possible on the differences of structure between the male and female body' (ibid.: 56–8). Some Greek legends talk of beings who passed through both sexes, for example, Tiresias who was born a boy, became a woman and died a man. In this successive androgyny, Delcourt does not see an account of concrete experience but of myth (ibid.: 33–4).

In her own study of bisexuality among the ancients, Eva Cantarella draws attention to a similar absence of eroticism in Roman culture, in which cross-dressing was not seen in sexual terms (see Cantarella, 2002: 179–80, and below, 'Cross-dressing').

Does this relentless pursuit of the asexual not suggest an unconscious desire to repress the fears and sinful thrills that a sexualised version of bisexuality arouses? Myth neutralises these fears by transforming the sexual into the sacred. Seeking refuge in symbolism is a strategy designed to contain the dangerously bisexual in the safety of the mythical and the spiritual. Even Delcourt concedes that the asexual character of such representations is a retreat into symbolism:

> Androgyny is at the two poles of sacred things. Pure concept, pure vision of the spirit, it appears adorned with the highest qualities. But once made real in a being of flesh and blood, it is a monstrosity,

and no more; it is proof of the wrath of the gods falling on the unfortunate group in which it is manifested, and the unhappy individuals who reveal it are got rid of as soon as possible.

(Delcourt, 1961: 45)

In ancient times, then, androgyny is associated with the repression of an erotic fascination with the mixing of genders.

Hermaphrodites

Historically, hermaphrodites represent the most extreme case of ambivalence towards transgenderism, but true hermaphroditism is extremely rare, existing only in individuals who have both sets of organs complete or, at least, one set complete with, in addition, characteristics of the other sex: 'What the Ancients termed androgyny is apparent hermaphroditism, or hypospadias, where only the external organs are abnormal' (Delcourt, 1961: 44). However, while there have certainly been some cases of true hermaphroditism in history, the point is worth making here that the real significance of the phenomenon lies in the (imaginary) perception by society and its institutions of a being that could not be assimilated into society's norms. There are strong political motivations behind the ostracisation of hermaphrodites throughout history. The hermaphrodite does not easily fit into a social model. But there are other, more deep-seated reasons for the ambivalent mix of horror and fascination that these beings encountered: the threat of disintegration of the self and its boundaries, which also fascinates because it takes us back to a pre-Oedipal state of fusion with the mother before differentiation assigned to each of us our allotted place.

In its ancient origins, hermaphroditism is an instance of pure myth, more an idea than a person. Delcourt's analysis here itself tends towards the prurient, as she argues that sculptors 'brought into the world of forms what should have remained in the world of the imagination' (that is, they eroticised the pure idea of myth) (ibid.: xi).

Attitudes to real hermaphrodites in the ancient world and throughout the Middle Ages remained largely negative:

the ambivalence of sacred things is nowhere so clearly revealed as in the realm of bisexuality. An abnormal formation of the generative organs seemed to the Ancients the extreme of monstrosity. When a child was born bearing real or apparent signs of hermaphroditism, the whole community felt itself threatened by the anger of the gods.

(Ibid.: 43)

According to Livy, hermaphrodites were held in such horror that they were thrown into the sea in Athens and the Tiber in Rome (see Graille, 2001: 102; Delcourt, 1961: 43). In Greece, many children were killed because their sex was ambiguous at birth or because it seemed to change at puberty (Delcourt, 1961: 45).

In the realm of the imagination, however, in the artistic and religious representations of the ancient world, hermaphrodites were a persistent model. The god, Hermaphrodite is the most obvious example here:

When we see with what care [the Greeks] exterminated miserable children with ill-defined organs, we wonder that a god called Hermaphrodite should have been able to appear in their midst. Or, in more exact terms, we can measure the growing strength of the myth of bisexuality which was able, by about the fourth and third centuries, to overcome a repugnance probably never completely uprooted in the conscience of many men.

(Ibid.: 46)

However, the eroticisation of the hermaphrodite is not always or entirely expunged, and in certain images of Hermaphrodite himself, the repressed returns in the sensual detail that the sculptor has incorporated, perhaps in spite of himself. A number of statues of the god Hermaphrodite have been preserved, some overtly mixing male and female characteristics (see the Marquis de Sade's description of one such statue below). Statues of a dormant Hermaphrodite reflect a combination of sensuality with the need to represent these figures as tamed, safe, unthreatening in their phallicness. At the same time, there is a process of striptease or unveiling as the viewer moves around these statues and finally comes upon the shocking revelation of male genitals in a statue that from the reverse side has the form of a woman. This gradual unveiling serves to focus attention on the unveiled part or parts of the body.

As Delcourt herself concedes, the Hermaphrodite figure slowly becomes eroticised over time: 'All the evidence is that paedophilia strongly influenced all Greek art, from its archaic phase to the turn of the fourth century ...' (ibid.: 65). Hermaphrodite is simply the final development of this trend. And yet, the Greeks and Romans would have been horrified by the sight of a genuinely bisexual being, and may well have ordered their execution. What occupied a central place in the mythical beliefs of the ancients continued to be unacceptable in their social reality.

We can summarise the reasons for the repression of the erotic in the production of bisexual figures in Greek and Roman art as follows. First, hermaphroditism and the androgyne were perceived as a threat to the binarism that structured human society and the myths that it produced and that in turn conditioned its ways of thinking about the human condition. Second, at a profound level, knowledge of other is regarded as a source of potential danger, experience of both sexes being linked to superior knowledge, and so perceived as threatening. Delcourt explains this aspect of the mythical figure of Tiresias:

> Only one anecdote relates to his feminine experience. One day Zeus and Hera were discussing the pleasures of love, and consulted Tiresias, who knew both aspects. He replied that the woman experiences nine times more pleasure than the man. The writers who tell of this episode add that the goddess was so angered by this disclosure that she, not Athena, struck Tiresias blind in retaliation.[1]
>
> (Ibid.: 37)

Third, asexuality and spiritual purity are seen as synonymous (see ibid.: 93).

The legal persecution of real hermaphrodites continued until the Enlightenment. The mixture of horror and contempt that such creatures inspired, and the legal constraints imposed upon them (which included a ban on marriage and reproduction) can be explained by a desire to prevent contamination of the species. A superstitious fear that the birth of a hermaphrodite was an ill-omen sometimes drove parents to kill the baby at birth. Throughout the medieval period, according to Foucault, the hermaphrodite was regarded as a monster sent by the devil and to be burnt as Satan's spawn (Graille, 2001: 105). In *Les Anormaux*, Foucault recounts the case of Antide Collas, a woman denounced and prosecuted at the end of the sixteenth century. Doctors who examined her concluded that her condition was the consequence of commerce with demons, that the devil had given her a male sex alongside her female sex. Collas was put to the question, confessed to intercourse with the devil, and was burnt alive in 1599 (see Foucault, 1999: 105). From this case, Foucault deduces that from the beginning of the seventeenth century, hermaphrodites were not persecuted for anatomical but for moral reasons. Though based on a single case, Foucault's insight is, nevertheless, a valid one: in the modern era, society's fear and loathing of the hermaphrodite stems from an underlying envy, as well as from a belief that a doubling of sexual equipment inevitably led to moral turpitude. From this point on, the hermaphrodite was required to choose one gender and one sexuality. Any use of the superfluous sex was prohibited, transgression of this prohibition amounting to the crime of sodomy (see Graille, 2001: 106).[2]

The fear of a departure from gender fixity in the mixing of sexes that the hermaphrodite embodied continued into the modern period. This fear meant that hermaphrodites had to be assigned a sex at birth. Later, when adults, they might choose to be reassigned to the other sex. However, writing of the case of a nineteenth-century French hermaphrodite, Foucault observes:

> The only imperative was that they should not change it again but keep the sex they had then declared until the end of their lives, under pain of being labelled sodomites. Changes of option, not the anatomical mixture of the sexes, were what gave rise to most of the condemnation of hermaphrodites in the records that survive in France for the period of the Middle Ages and the Renaissance.
>
> (Foucault, 1980: viii)

These measures, which find their modern counterpart in the surgical treatment of intersex babies, also seem to have their origins in a deep-seated anxiety about difference and excess, and a deep-seated fear of sexual promiscuity. It has been commonplace since the 1970s in both the USA and Europe for doctors and parents to decide whether what is now called an 'intersex' child will be a boy or a girl, leading to 'appropriate' surgical procedures. This practice is based on the assumption that gender identity depends on socialisation, on being reared as one sex or the other. Most intersex babies are assigned a female sex, because it is easier to construct a vagina than a penis. The practice of gender assignment was developed by John Money, a researcher at Johns Hopkins University. Not all of these assignments have been successful. Some individuals, unhappy with their assigned gender to the point of being suicidal, have undergone reverse procedures in adulthood. There have consequently been calls to end the routine surgical alteration of intersex children. 'How we treat intersexuals is not a medical matter,' says one victim of this procedure, 'It's a political and social issue. The surgery that disfigured me, that left me inorgasmic and with a profound sense of shame, was politically motivated' (see 'Why should a John be a Joan?', *The Times Higher*, 19, 8 October 1999).

Above all, then, it is uncertainty and ambivalence that is found intolerable and that the requirement of gender choice is designed to dispel. If the modern citizen is to fit into the social, legal and moral categories created for him/her by modern societies, (s)he is required to be unambiguously male or female.

The role of the imaginary in the shaping of all these attitudes, positive and negative, is underlined by Patrick Graille, who notes that of the ten articles on the subject found in the eighteenth-century French *Encyclopédie*, eight are concerned with mythology (Graille, 2001: 17).[3] Moreover, many leading eighteenth-century authors, notably Casanova and the Marquis de Sade, wrote at length about gender ambivalence which became a part of their imaginary world.

The Marquis de Sade had wholly different views on the two separate phenomena of cross-dressing and hermaphroditism. While his depictions of the former are playful and parodic in character (see below), Sade's fascination with the hermaphrodite figure suggests a more overt eroticism. The closest Sade comes to representing hermaphroditism in his novels is the portrayal of sexually voracious women, such as Volmar and Durand in *Juliette*, who have clitorises as long as penises and are said to ejaculate like men. While the three-inch clitoris described by Sade may owe more to wishful thinking than to reality, female ejaculation is a very real phenomenon, one in ten women being capable of ejaculating copious amounts of fluid on climax. In a sense, Sade is simply exploiting a symmetry between male and female genitals perceived in medical discourses of the time, according to which the clitoris was seen as a miniature penis. Masculinised women rather than feminised men, Sade's 'chicks with dicks' are the negative photographic image of the hormonally and surgically altered male-to-female transsexuals of today. Both, however, retain the all-important phallus. Both may be sodomites but both exhibit a masculine virility.

For Sade's views on the hermaphrodite per se, we must turn to his autobiographical account of travels through Italy. In Florence, Sade sees a statue of the god, Hermaphrodite in a museum, and describes it for his wife as follows:

> You are aware, Madame la Comtesse, that the licentiousness of the Romans dared to seek out pleasure even in these sorts of monstrosities. This one is life-size, lying on its stomach, although very slightly on one side; it is resting on its arms in a posture that permits one to see a beautifully feminine bosom; its thighs are somewhat crossed and thoroughly conceal the other feature of the female sex; while the masculine feature is quite vividly revealed; the body is beautiful and its sublime proportions appear with absolute verisimilitude.
>
> (*Voyage d'Italie*, 156; quoted by Shaeffer, 2001: 200)

When he comes upon another statue of Hermaphrodite in Rome, Sade complains that religious piety had driven the owner to break off 'the masculine part'. Sade actually managed to acquire his own Hermaphroditic statue which he had sent back to his home in Provence. Sade's interest in the Hermaphrodite statue derives in part from his profound belief in the power of the imagination, but we also need to understand the transgressive force of this figure for the eighteenth-century French libertine. Sade draws upon this personal experience when he comes to write *Juliette*, in which the eponymous heroine describes her reactions to the Florence statue in similar, if rather more graphic terms. In passing from a factual to a fictional account, the erotic attraction of the figure has become explicit:

> My eyes fell next upon 'The Hermaphrodite'. As you know, the Romans, who all had a special fondness for these monsters, welcomed them into their saturnalian assemblies; the one represented here was probably among those whose lubricious reputation was outstandingly notorious and hence deserved commemoration; but its legs are crossed, which is a pity, for the sculptor

should have displayed what characterized its double sex and singular amenities: it is shown reclining upon a bed, exposing the most tempting ass in all the world ... a voluptuous ass which Sbrigani coveted, telling me he had once bum-fucked a similar creature and had never been able to forget the delight it had given him.

(*Juliette*, 614)

As this passage suggests, Sade's fascination with the statue can partly be understood as a delight at the excess of sexual possibilities available to hermaphrodites. My argument here directly contradicts Philippe Roger's view of a horror on Sade's part incited by the hermaphrodite as an instance of asexuality (see Roger, 1976: 104–6). This horror is in my view associated not with the hermaphrodite but with the castrato, a figure which is described by Sade only a few pages later in *Voyage d'Italie* and which elicits a strong repulsion. Unlike the plenitude offered by the hermaphrodite, the castrato is described as a 'half-man' and so is defined in terms of a physical absence, which the Sadean hero appears to read as the metaphor of a metaphysical void. In Sade's *The 120 Days of Sodom*, a boy is surgically transformed into a girl, conveying a horror that is similarly provoked by absence. This brief description of a gruesome act, which uncannily foreshadows modern realignment surgery for male-to-female transsexuals, is monstrous because it is a form of castration that creates a sexual void:

After having sheared off the boy's prick and balls, using a red-hot iron he hollows out a cunt in the place formerly occupied by his genitals; the iron makes the hole and cauterises simultaneously: he fucks the patient's new orifice and strangles him with his hands upon discharging.

(Sade, *The 120 Days of Sodom*: 655–6)

Paradoxically, it is the absence of the phallus in the female body that Sade represents as troubling, and not its presence in the hermaphrodite.

The Sadean case is worth mentioning at length, in part because of Sade's enormous influence on subsequent writers, artists and thinkers. Foucault sees Sade as standing between the classical and the modern era, and however we might think of his obscenity or the moral dimension of his work, Sade's influence on our thinking about sexuality and gender in the twentieth and twenty-first centuries is undeniable.[4] It is also significant because Sade's texts bring to the surface an eroticisation of the hermaphrodite that hitherto had largely remained covert.

Another eighteenth-century author, Giacomo Casanova, in his autobiography, *Histoire de ma vie*, emphasises the erotic thrill mixed with anxiety and confusion, associated with the perception of gender-mixing. Casanova recounts how, in 1745, he met Bellino, a young castrato soprano. Enraptured by the castrato's charms, but convinced that he was a woman, Casanova made repeated attempts to see Bellino naked. When at last he succeeded in this, he glimpsed what looked like a penis, and was plunged into confusion regarding his own sexuality. However, Casanova had in fact seen a codpiece or false penis, worn so that the young singer could pass as a castrato in the Papal State, where women were not permitted on stage.[5] Nevertheless, the ambivalent source of Casanova's sexual responses is clear.

In the nineteenth century, the case of the French hermaphrodite, Herculine Barbin, as recounted by Michel Foucault and by Barbin's own diary entries, similarly repeats earlier responses: the incongruous mixture of horror and erotic fascination, underpinned by a strongly normatising impulse (see Foucault 1980: xvii). For Foucault, the nineteenth century was 'powerfully haunted by the theme of the hermaphrodite – somewhat as the eighteenth century had been haunted by the theme of the transvestite' (ibid.). In spite of the very real nature of her medical condition, the literariness of Barbin's autobiographical account makes her case as much part of the imaginary as a novel.

Foucault provides a useful summary of Barbin's life in his introduction (ibid.: xi–xii):

> Brought up as a poor and deserving girl in a milieu that was almost exclusively feminine and strongly religious, Herculine Barbin, who was called Alexine by her familiars, was finally recognised as being 'truly' a young man. Obliged to make a legal change of sex after judicial proceedings and a modification of his civil status, he was incapable of adapting himself to a new identity and ultimately committed suicide.

Foucault refers to numerous medical and legal documents touching upon Barbin's life that form an important part of the imaginary corpus. Herculine's story coincided in the late nineteenth century with a new impetus in the medical sciences to classify 'perversions', or in other words, to identify and sanctify the sexual and gender norms:

> The years from around 1860 to 1870 were precisely one of those periods when investigations of sexual identity were carried out with the most intensity, in an attempt not only to establish the true sex of hermaphrodites but also to identify, classify, and characterize the different types of perversions.
>
> (Ibid.: xii)

Foucault points out the reluctance of doctors to see Herculine Barbin as a case of true or complete hermaphroditism: 'This collection of observations would also show clearly – if it was still necessary to demonstrate it – the fact that hermaphroditism does not exist in man and the higher animals' (ibid.: 139). This reluctance on the part of the medical authorities is evidence of the need to believe in binary difference. A third position would undermine the entire social position based on it.

In a typical Foucauldian linking of knowledge and power, Foucault also draws attention to fears relating to the dangers of knowledge of the other gender. Barbin knows both sexes – this is perceived even by her as dangerous:

> I, who am called a man, have been granted the intimate, deep understanding of all the facets, all the secrets, of a woman's character. I can read her heart like an open book. I could count every beat of it. In a word, I have the secret of her strength and the measure of her weakness, and so I would make a detestable husband for that reason. I also feel that all my joys would be poisoned in marriage and that I would cruelly abuse, perhaps, the immense advantage that would be mine, an advantage that would turn against me.
>
> (Ibid.: 107)

Thus, superstitious stereotype joins dubious medical diagnosis to reaffirm hostility to the condition. As we have seen above, the privilege and dangers of insider knowledge of the other sex is an ancient theme. It is also a particular feature of the comedies in our corpus (see Chapter 3, 'Forbidden knowledge').

The case of Herculine Barbin inspired a number of late nineteenth-century works, in particular, Dubarry's *The Hermaphrodite* (Dubarry was a writer of popular adventure stories and medico-pornographic novels), and Panizza's *A Scandal at the Convent*.

Panizza's short story, which can be found as an appendix to the Barbin diaries in the Foucault edition, concerns a young girl named Alexina who develops a close and loving friendship with another girl, Henriette at the convent school they both attend. Wholly ignorant of sex, and uncomprehending of her anatomical abnormalities, Alexina is portrayed as a confused and innocent victim of the repressive forces of religion. One morning, the other girls at the convent are revolted to discover Alexina and Henriette in bed together, and 'what they saw was horrible'. In Panizza's narrative, hermaphroditism is literally demonised, regarded as a monstrosity, spawned by the devil himself, and the repressive forces of religion are implicitly held to account for the barbaric treatment subsequently meted out to the unfortunate Alexina.

If, as Foucault maintains, the nineteenth century was obsessed with the hermaphrodite, the twentieth century became increasingly preoccupied with transsexualism, as we shall see presently. First, however, we need to retrace our steps to the ancients to examine historical attitudes to transvestism.

Cross-dressing

Western culture has a long history of cross-dressing. Ancient Greek and Roman writers refer to young men who wanted to live their lives as women. Throughout history, cross-dressing has been permitted during ritualistic events in some cultures, although this has been a temporary relaxation of gender barriers (see Bakhtin's view of temporary transgression in carnival, discussed in Chapter 3). Such cross-dressing rituals may well have carried erotic as well as symbolic meanings. In ancient Rome, ambivalent attitudes to cross-dressers once again suggest guilt in relation to an underlying eroticism: 'This habit, while not exceptional, was not necessarily exempt from all social disapproval. Undoubtedly, cross-dressing showed a tendency towards "softness". Quintillian writes, for example, that dressing as a woman betokens a lack of virility' (Cantarella, 2002: 177).

The influence of Christianity led cross-dressing to be viewed from the Middle Ages on as a taboo (and therefore eroticised) activity. The

Malleus Maleficarum (The Witches' Hammer), for example, associated cross-dressing with satanism. For the early medieval church, cross-dressing was nothing less than a heresy, although there are many medieval accounts of cross-dressed female saints. The heresy of wearing men's clothes was a strong contributory factor in the sentencing to death of Joan of Arc. There is much evidence, too, of the medieval and Renaissance male cross-dresser, especially among male prostitutes and actors. From the Restoration on, much more documentary evidence exists of transgender behaviour: for instance, in the Netherlands between 1550 and 1839, 119 women are known to have lived as men (see Whittle, 2000: 35).

There is also evidence during this period of men who lived as women. Stephen Whittle quotes evidence of a cross-dressing culture developing in the latter half of the seventeenth century alongside the homosexual scene in London taverns. These taverns became known as 'molly houses' ('molly' was originally a term for a female prostitute and, like the word 'queen', became a term for the effeminate male homosexual). The image of the 'molly' gave rise to a distinctive homosexual culture.[6]

In the nineteenth century, cross-dressing fell prey along with other sexual freedoms to the new puritanism of the Victorian era. In 1885 the Criminal Law Act made all homosexual behaviour illegal in the United Kingdom, and cross-dressers became easy targets for the police because they were associated in the public mind with the homosexual subculture. This law led some members of the medical establishment to campaign to change the view of homosexuality from that of a crime to that of an illness that might be cured, and in response, a whole new medical field developed: sexology. Sexologists such as Richard von Krafft-Ebing (1840–1902) (the first to take a special interest in the sexual impulses of individuals) discovered through extensive case-studies that homosexuals were not always the same, but were, in fact, diverse in history, practices and desires. After Krafft-Ebing, the German scientist, Magnus Hirschfeld (1868–1935) was the next most influential voice in sexology. It was Hirschfeld who in the early years of the twentieth century finally separated transgendered behaviour from homosexuality, allowing the medical profession to regard the former as treatable.

Although sexologists opened up this field to serious study, they were also guilty of evolving normatising discourses on sexuality and gender that persist to the present day.

Transvestism on stage and in literature

From the medieval and early modern periods, there is a growing separation between the perception of cross-dressing in society and cross-
dressing in the imaginary of art, theatre and literature. While the
former is demonised, as we have seen, the latter is accepted as an
amusing entertainment, although underlying this amusement is an
increasingly overt eroticism. This dichotomy between the imaginary
and the real arises from the same ambivalent mixture of fear and fascination identifiable in the ancient Greek and Roman responses to
real hermaphroditism and artistic representations of it.

In medieval and early modern drama it was not considered fitting
for women to appear on stage, and in England male actors always
played women's roles, at least until the Restoration in 1660. In the literature of this period, too, gender-switching was a major theme, from
Ariosto's (1474–1533) poetic masterpiece, *Orlando Furioso*, to the *Arcadia*
of Sir Philip Sidney (1554–86) and to many of the plays of Shakespeare
(for example, *As You Like It*, *The Merchant of Venice*, *Twelfth Night*,
Cymbeline). In spite of the dual anxieties over gender and status existing in Elizabethan England, then, actors were allowed to violate the
laws governing dress and social station on the 'safe' space of the
stage, which was a privileged site of transgression in the Bakhtinian
sense (see Garber, 1993: 35).

The sexual and erotic elements of cross-dressing were a common feature of sixteenth- and seventeenth-century European theatre. Cross-
dressed acting was one reason why puritans attacked the stage as
immoral, attacks that betrayed deep-seated anxieties that identity may
not be fixed (ibid.: 32). One can see why the puritans were disturbed by
the theatre: as the very site of the confusion of genders, the stage even
allowed men (and more disturbingly still, boys) to dress in women's
clothes. In this context, the boy is 'a provoker of category crises, a
destabilizer of binarisms, a transgressor of boundaries, sexual, erotic,
hierarchical, political, conceptual. The changeling boy ... significations
of change ... figures for something that is not there' (ibid.: 90–2).

As Jan Clarke has shown, cross-dressing disguise was also a regular
feature of both French and Italian comedies performed in France
in the seventeenth and eighteenth centuries (see Clarke, 1999: 238).
Italian authors ignored official warnings against indecency issued in
1688, 1690 and 1694 to eroticise their cross-dressing plays (ibid.: 249
n.13), while on the French stage alone between 1673 and 1715, around

thirty female cross-dressing plays have been identified (ibid.: 240). On the English stage, it is estimated that a quarter of all plays performed between 1660 and 1700 featured the device (ibid.: 239 and 249 n.8). Clarke concedes that female-to-male cross-dressing can serve a variety of dramatic purposes, from the satiric to the purely ludic, but she demonstrates that cross-dressing disguise is frequently used on the Early Modern stage to create sexual innuendo: 'Contemporaries referred to such suggestiveness as "équivoque", and it would seem to have been one of the principal motivations for the inclusion of cross-dressing' (ibid.: 238). The ambivalence pointed to by Clarke has a strongly erotic flavour, although as Clarke points out, the erotic dimension is closely linked to the comic and satiric: audiences wanted to laugh 'while enjoying a certain sexual thrill' (ibid.: 242). The eroticism is partly based on the exploitation of the female form to attract audiences and on the 'frisson of forbidden homosexuality' (ibid.: 246).

Of the many examples quoted by Clarke, one will suffice here as illustration of an overtly lesbian component in the representation of female-to-male cross-dressing:

> In [*Isabelle médecin*], Colombine, not knowing that her doctor is a woman, succeeds in tricking Isabelle into massaging her breasts to her evident satisfaction. She even claims particularly to appreciate a man's touch as opposed to the caresses of women that are all that are normally available to her.
>
> (Ibid.: 242)

As Clarke points out, the act of unveiling is as important in this theatre as in all of the film narratives we shall be examining in this book:

> The enjoyment of such scenes by members of the audience would have been complex. First, they see the attempted seduction of a man by a woman or vice versa, itself somewhat unusual in such explicit terms on the seventeenth-century stage. Then, they enjoy the dramatic irony of the knowledge of the protagonists' true genders.
>
> (Ibid.: 247)

The theatrical cross-dressing of this period, then, exhibits many of the features that we shall identify in the modern films that treat the subject: the thrill of transgression disguised in comedy, flirtation with homosexuality, and the pleasures of a play between concealment and revelation.

Cross-dressing is also a recurrent motif in the eighteenth-century novel, carrying both erotic and transgressive connotations. In Matthew Lewis's best-selling Gothic novel, *The Monk*, Mathilda, who is an emissary of the devil, adopts the disguise of a man named Rosario in order to enter a monastery where she can seduce the proud Ambrosio. Cross-dressing for the purposes of seduction is an ancient classical theme, but here it is clearly both erotic and diabolical in nature. This story-line uncannily resembles an incident in the life of the Marquis de Sade, whose wife Renée dresses as a man in order to gain access to her outlaw husband who has been temporarily imprisoned in a monastery. In both cases, cross-dressing is associated with criminal activities.

Both passive sodomy and transvestism in Sade's novels are temporary forms of gender-switching, and while both have erotic dimensions, cross-dressing in particular is a predominantly ludic activity. In either case, gender is never seriously threatened. For Sade, the theatricality of cross-dressing is a superficial exchange of identities that is not anatomical. This playfulness is also a feature of Sade's switching of 'status' identity with his valet on the occasion of a famous trip to Marseilles in search of prostitutes – such a switch can be pleasurable only if it is easily reversed.

In descriptions of orgies in *Juliette*, boys are frequently presented as girls for erotic purposes: 'On hand as well were six youths ranging in age from fifteen to twenty; naked, their hair arranged in feminine style, they served the table' (*Juliette*: 214). The novel also contains the description of a cross-dressed double wedding that reads now like a parody of gender-roles to a dizzying degree. The male libertine, Noirceuil dresses as a woman to marry a man, then dressed as a man, marries a catamite dressed as a girl, while Juliette dressed as a man marries a lesbian, then dressed as a woman, marries a lesbian dressed as a man. This switching of genders is to some extent practised in the orgies, with men adopting the 'female' position in sodomy and dildoed women playing the active 'male' role.

Nineteenth-century European literature is somewhat restrained by the sexual repression of the Victorian era, but literary fascination with transgender still finds ways of expressing itself, sometimes by disguising itself as comic or tragic confusion. Camille Paglia traces transsexual identification in Wordsworth, Coleridge, Whitman, Henry James, Balzac's 'The Girl with the Golden Eyes', and self-hermaphrodisation in Emily Dickinson (Paglia, 1991), while mistaken gender is the intriguing theme of Gautier's *Mademoiselle de Maupin* (1835), in which the hero is attracted to a beautiful young man who eventually turns out to be a woman in disguise. We note here the normatising effects of a dénouement that reaffirms the hero's heterosexuality. At the same time, there is no getting away from the fact that he has been aroused, albeit unwittingly, by the sight of a cross-dressed woman. And of course, Balzac's short story, *Sarrasine*, reverses this situation, so that a young man falls for a castrato whom he first believes to be a woman. To this fictional list, we can add the names of two well-known French authors, George Sand who frequently enjoyed dressing as a man in society, and Rachilde who did so to walk the streets of Paris in safety.

In the second half of the twentieth century, representations of transgender in literature and film focus on both cross-dressers and transsexuals. The films discussed in subsequent chapters demonstrate and are typical of a roughly equivalent public interest in both, but for entirely different reasons, as we shall see.

It is hard to discern any specific trends in the evolution of representations of transgender over the past few millennia. A case could be made for seeing the boundaries between the real and the imaginary as gradually lessening, if not dissolving completely, as art and literature have become less tied to myth and the supernatural and more reflective of human realities, especially since the Renaissance, although such an argument would be clearly speculative and vulnerable to the accusation of simplistic generalisation. (The question of the relationship between the real and the imaginary is explored in greater depth in Chapter 7.) It will also become clear from reading chapters 3 to 6 that the ambivalence underlying these representations has not fundamentally changed: in varying degrees, depending on type and context, reactions to images of transsexuality are informed at unconscious levels by the same archaic mixture of fear and fascination, eroticism and disgust, as reactions to hermaphroditism were in ancient times, while transvestism continues to be a subject for comedy. The broadly unchanging nature of these responses may be taken to imply a fixity of human nature which Foucault, queer theorists and feminists have in their different ways strongly challenged, as we saw in Chapter 1. How can gender and sexuality be liberated from their traditional binary poles, if the human imagination itself is shown to exhibit the same basic anxieties, and the same erotic thrill in relation to the transgression of norms at any given point in the history of western culture? I shall return to these crucial questions in my concluding chapter.

3
Cross-dressing in Film Comedy

In the west, the postwar period has seen an increasing social accept-
ance of homosexuality, which has consequently been represented in
the media as less deviant from the norm. From the 1990s, this development accelerated, as political correctness gained ground. The ridi-
culing of gays in the entertainment media had become unacceptable.
The role played by such figures was now assigned to cross-dressers who
fulfilled the same comic function as the effeminate gay, but without
the now unfashionable character of direct ridicule of a sexual minority. Audiences laughed at men in tights thinking that the butt of the
joke was a heterosexual male who looked ridiculous in women's clothes,
whereas the excessive display of the cross-dressing man, the bizarre
juxtaposition of masculine body traits and feminine attire are always
inescapably a parody of women. Real transvestites, too, might have
felt that they were being held up to ridicule. These media cross-dressers
were sometimes also gay, although this aspect of their representation
was not the central focus. Society still needed representations of figures outside the norm (especially the sexual norm, given our culture's
obsession with sex); women are other to men's self, and transvestites
represent a comically inadequate copy of women's otherness, a failed
simulacrum, both figures that challenge and threaten the male norm,
but only transvestites were now politically acceptable targets. Cross-
dressing, after all, was in the public perception only a temporary performance, not a permanent identity, and as such could not need
protection. (Comedy since the war has tended to gravitate away from
the centre to the edge: in the UK, the 'Beyond the Fringe' comedians
of the 1960s typify this trend.) Audiences of light entertainment and

comedy who, before the war, had openly laughed at effeminate homosexuals, ridiculed on stage or in films, now took a similarly subversive pleasure in seeing conventional gender roles held up to mockery. Comic depiction circumscribes a potentially threatening deviance which is defused in a safe and controlled way. Creatures of the periphery, cross-dressers are nonetheless subsumed by the dominant popular culture, neutralised and transformed into lovable everyday figures of fun (in both the active and the passive sense: emanating fun but also objects of a gentle mockery). With the substitution of cross-dressers for gays, homophobic laughter is rendered politically correct by being displaced onto the act of transvestism as if this were a politically and ethically more acceptable target.

These developments can be traced through the British and American comedies of the postwar years. The four comedy films discussed below exemplify this trend well, although they were produced in wholly different historical and cultural circumstances which impact on the particular ways in which cross-dressing is represented in each film. In addition, these films share a number of other important themes and motifs, all of which in one way or another help to explain the political acceptability of comic cross-dressing, and I shall briefly summarise these too before discussing each film separately.

Deception in the progress narrative

According to Marjorie Garber's category definition, all the films discussed below are 'progress narratives' in which a principal protagonist

> is 'compelled' by social and economic forces to disguise himself or herself in order to get a job, escape repression, or gain artistic or political 'freedom'. Each, that is, is said to embrace transvestism unwillingly, as an instrumental strategy rather than an erotic pleasure and play space; in each of the instances I have cited, indeed, heterosexual desire is for a time apparently thwarted by the cross-dresser's assumed identity, so that it becomes necessary for him or her to unmask. The ideological implications of this pattern are clear: crossdressing can be 'fun' or 'functional' so long as it occupies a liminal space and a temporary time period; after this carnivalization, however ... the cross-dresser is expected to resume life as he or she was,

having, presumably, recognized the touch of 'femininity' or 'masculinity' in her or his otherwise 'male' or 'female' self.

(Garber, 1993: 69–70)

For Garber, the vast majority of cross-dressing stories in literature – virtually all those in Shakespeare, for instance – fall into this category. Thus, the cross-dressers do so in *Some Like it Hot* to escape the mob and secure employment, in *Tootsie*, to get an acting job, in *Victor/Victoria*, to get a singing job, and in *Mrs Doubtfire*, to gain access to children following a marital separation.

Garber rightly regards these progress narratives as both unconvincing and ideologically problematic:

Unconvincing, because they ignore the complex and often unconscious eroticism of such self-transformations and masquerades ... and because in doing so they rewrite the story of the transvestic subject as a cultural symptom. Problematic, because the consequent reinscription of 'male' and 'female', even if tempered (or impelled) by feminist consciousness, reaffirms the patriarchal binary and ignores what is staring us in the face: the existence of the transvestite, the figure that disrupts.

(Garber, 1993: 70)

Cross-dressing is therefore a necessary deception, leading to comic misunderstandings, often involving unwelcome male attentions. The audience are not deceived, only other characters in the diegesis, and so audience pleasure derives in part from watching the deception process unfold. The sharing of the secret with the audience creates endless possibilities for dramatic irony, which depends crucially on the audience knowing something that one or more protagonists do not know. (See Chapter 1 for a more detailed view of the role of deception in transgender narratives.)

Unveiling

Garber calls this 'dewigging': 'The Lord Chamberlain in England has insisted that drag shows end with the obligatory removal of wigs, a convention that ... appears in theatrical and cinematic representations of cross-dressing from Ben Jonson's *Epicoene* to *Some Like it Hot, Victor/Victoria*, and *Tootsie*' (Garber, 1993: 213). We can add *Mrs Doubtfire* to the list of films in which the act of unveiling occurs in a final revelatory scene. For Garber, the wig is 'the very sign of female impersonation'. What Garber does not say is that the removal of wigs (or in the case of *Mrs Doubtfire*, of a facial mask – the effect is the same) plays an essential role in the dénouement in which the world is set to rights. In *Victor/Victoria*, the doubly-eponymous hero(ine) reverses the significance of this gesture of unveiling by incorporating it into the drag act itself, revealing her apparent male identity at the end of the act, whilst her 'true' gender as a biological woman remains hidden, except to the cinema audience. Victor's gesture may perhaps be read as a parody of such scenes in earlier cross-dressing comedies from Shakespeare onwards. With the exception of *Silence of the Lambs*, all of the thrillers we consider in this book also contain 'dewigging' scenes; in these cases, the gesture serves to underline the killer's monstrosity, while dispelling any residual doubt in the spectator's mind as to the killer's 'real' gender and identity.

Absence of eroticism

Overt eroticism is entirely lacking, partly because the cross-dressing is portrayed as a purely pragmatic act, as a temporary solution to a problem. Comic cross-dressing parodies the feminine, acting as a barrier behind which erotic interest hides, is repressed. The parody of drag tames the androgynous, neutralises a threat to individuated gender identity.

Performance

In all our chosen films, the cross-dressers are performers: singer (*Victor/Victoria*), actor (*Tootsie*), voice-over artist (*Mrs Doubtfire*), musicians (*Some Like it Hot*). In addition to serving the needs of the plot in all of these cases, this aspect foregrounds the whole question of performativity in relation to gender, and in the four films we shall be looking at in this chapter, cross-dressing (in contrast to transsexuality) certainly does appear to support Butler's view of gender as performative (see Butler, 1999).

Forbidden knowledge

The cross-dresser gains a privileged insider knowledge of the way women think; in *Some Like it Hot*, for example, Sugar tells Joe/Josephine what turns her on in a man (tenor sax players!). This theme, which suggests essentialist thinking about gender, is given ironic treatment in *Tootsie* in which such insight rebounds on the cross-dressed man. It reflects what has been considered since Plato to be a universal unconscious desire: to know and thus, in the most meaningful sense, to be reunited with the other sex.[1]

Compulsory heterosexuality[2]

The cross-dressers are without exception represented as rabidly heterosexual: from *Some Like it Hot* to *Tootsie* and *Victor/Victoria*, the cross-dressing is seen as solving one problem but creating another, in all cases, raising an obstacle to the pursuit or courting of an individual of the opposite sex. These comedies all address in this way the web of sex, gender and sexuality, and with few exceptions appear to reinforce assumed normative links between them. Except in *Tootsie*, all of the cross-dressers display an unease about the sexual attentions of men. In *Tootsie*, this homophobic tendency is displaced onto the men that Dorothy comes into contact with (such as Michael's agent whom he teases in a restaurant by flirting with him). This homophobia is also related to an anxiety about the permanent loss of a male identity, expressed through motifs of castration. Even in *Tootsie*, which is relatively progressive in terms of its sexual politics, for example, Dorothy pulls a guy out of a taxi when he jumps the queue; she slams her lascivious fellow-actor, Van Horn on the head when he tries to kiss her on set; and brings her knee up into a man's groin when he makes a drunken pass at her. When Dorothy reveals herself to be a man in the dénouement, Julie punches him in the groin, symbolically punishing him for being a man by physically attacking his manhood.

Urinary segregation

In *Some Like it Hot*, *Tootsie* and *Mrs Doubtfire*, the practical difficulties encountered by the cross-dresser are illustrated by the 'toilet gag', whereby the dilemma of which toilet to use in public generates comic situations (see discussion of this motif in Chapter 1 and below in the *Mrs Doubtfire* section).

A temporary transgression

All of these comedies represent cross-dressing and not transsexuality. They thus contain the transgender phenomenon by representing it as harmless, temporary, comic, pragmatic, and fundamentally without any influence on sex or sexuality. There is therefore no serious or permanent threat to gender identities, and indeed, the scripts are punctuated with reassuringly essentialist moments. Traits of masculinity (hairy legs, awkward gait in high heels, low voice) at times betray the 'real' gender of the cross-dressing men. For instance, in *Some Like it Hot*, Lemmon's character is ironically, and in spite of some critical opinions to the contrary, more obviously 'drag' than Curtis's, who, with his 'pretty boy', screen-idol good looks, appears as more passable than Lemmon, while in *Victor/Victoria*, Victoria's femininity at times threatens to give the game away.

Some Like it Hot (Billy Wilder, 1959)

The title of Billy Wilder's comedy of cross-dressing errors is explained in the dialogue itself: 'hot', it seems, denotes jazz as opposed to classical music, but the word also has inescapably sexual connotations, and might be taken to refer to 'kinky' sex or behaviour. This second-level interpretation would imply that 'some' is implicitly opposed to 'most' or 'the majority' who would adhere to the norm – a fitting title, then, for a narrative about two cross-dressing men and their amorous adventures.

This film is an early (possibly the earliest) filmic example of 'the progress narrative'. In this classic Hollywood comedy, set in the Prohibition years of the late 1920s, a pair of out-of-work musicians who accidentally witness a mob killing are obliged by poverty and self-preservation to disguise themselves as women in order to get jobs with an all-female jazz band about to leave Chicago for a three-week booking in Florida. The musicians, Joe played by Tony Curtis and Jerry by Jack Lemmon, assume the names Josephine and Daphne respectively. Critics have found the choice of names significant. Daniel Lieberfeld and Judith Sanders consider Josephine 'a conservative choice that indicates the transience of [Joe's] transgression', while Daphne is 'more flamboyant' (Lieberfeld and Sanders, 1998: 4 (online version)), and Garber sees the latter name as 'metamorphic' (Garber, 1993: 6). Garber does not elucidate this observation, but presumably is referring to the name's mythological origins. In Greek mythology, Daphne was the goddess of music and poetry who refused to requite Apollo's love; as she fled from his embrace, she was saved by the earth-goddesses who transformed her into a tree. In harmony with the connotations of their chosen pseudonyms, Josephine and Daphne do indeed react differently to their cross-dressing experience, for while Joe retains a sense of himself as male, assuming a second disguise as a man for the purposes of seducing Sugar Kane (Marilyn Monroe), the band's voluptuous singer, Jerry allows himself to be seduced, in a metaphorical if not literal sense, by a yacht-owning millionaire named Osgood. The narrative is here at variance, however, with each actor's representation of transvestism. Lemmon is a drag-artist as we have defined the term in Chapter 1, and ironically, it is the more confidently male and heterosexual Joe who appears more passable as a woman, partly thanks to Curtis's screen-idol good looks, but also to his wholly uncomic performance. While Daphne totters self-consciously along in her high-heeled shoes, and complains that Joe has burst her artificial bosoms, Josephine maintains an equanimity throughout, and indeed attracts the unwelcome attentions of a young bell-boy (cocky and impishly cute, not the 'dwarfish' figure that Lieberfeld and Sanders claim him to be).

The film is typical of Garber's 'progress narrative' in appearing to challenge and undermine gender binaries on the one hand, while reinforcing them on the other. Annette Kuhn recognised this as characteristic of cross-dressing narratives generally twenty years ago:

> If cross-dressing narratives always in some measure problematise gender identity and sexual difference ... many do so only to confirm finally the absoluteness of both, to reassert a 'natural' order of fixed gender and unitary subjectivity.
>
> (Kuhn, 1985: 57)

In contrast, Maria Jesus Martinez argues that the film expresses a more serious threat 'to subvert the typically patriarchal construction of gender relations and gender difference', basing her argument on the questionable premise that Jerry and Sugar in their different couples manifest homoerotic tendencies (Martinez, 1998: 143). Similarly, Jennifer Wicke shows herself blind to the humour in her earnest reading of the film (see Wicke, 1997: 363–70). While gender boundaries are temporarily transgressed in the film, it seems to me a case of over-interpretation to read homoeroticism into what are essentially comic moments, as these critics do. When Jerry calls his alter ego, Daphne 'the lesbian inside me', Wicke concludes that this is the start of an exploration of lesbian eroticism (367), utterly failing to see that Jerry is wittily commenting on his attraction to Sugar while cross-dressed as Daphne. Daphne's apparent eagerness to marry Osgood is again read literally by this critic as 'a homosexual awakening' (369). When Joe asks Jerry why a guy would want to marry a guy, and Jerry replies 'Security', it is not, as Wicke suggests, because Jerry has discovered the inequalities of marriage thanks to her experience of femininity (ibid.). The suggestion of a gender-schizophrenia in Daphne is admittedly an interesting one, but Jerry's apparent gender confusion serves wholly comic purposes. In fact, Jerry is seduced, not by the septuagenarian and 'satchel-mouthed' Osgood (the bell-hop refers to him as such) who is an unlikely partner for any young person, man or woman, but by the prospect of the millionaire lifestyle. After all, Jerry, like Joe, is an out-of-work musician in a depressed economy, with no future prospects. In this light, the humour of Jerry's line, 'I'll never find another man who's so good to me!' lies in its transparent ambiguity: is he talking about love or money? When interrogated by Joe as to his motives in accepting Osgood's marriage proposal, he admits that he would disclose his true gender after the wedding and apply immediately for an annulment. But this entirely reasonable 'gold-digging' strategy is overshadowed by a comic bewilderment on the part of Joe. Jerry's earlier self-instruction, 'I'm a girl, I'm a girl!' has now become 'I'm a boy, I'm a boy!' which reads almost as a parody of gender confusion. The prospect of Jerry's and Osgood's coupling on their wedding night is even more ludicrous than the comic tango danced by the couple at the hotel. It is, indeed, the very comic nature of the Daphne/Osgood pairing, together with Daphne's and Josephine's farcical antics, that encourages the audience not to take cross-dressing seriously. The duo in drag are either too masculine (as when they are seen abseiling down the hotel balcony by the mob) or too excessively feminine to the point of parody (as exemplified by Daphne's mannered ladylike expressions and gestures) to be viewed as positive role models of transgender. The impression of Jerry as the feminine foil to Joe's more masculine performance is more reminiscent of Stan Laurel's relationship with Oliver Hardy, or Dudley Moore's with Peter Cook than to any polarisation of gender norms.

There would appear to be a strong current of anxiety running through *Some Like it Hot* in relation to gender instability which expresses itself mainly in castration motifs. However, here again, a closer analysis of these motifs reveals an essentially comic frame which defuses the threat, releasing the tension associated with it. When Osgood offers Daphne his mother's wedding-dress, Jerry nervously exclaims 'She and I ... are not built the same way!'; 'We can have it altered,' suggests Osgood. Jerry's horrified response, 'no you don't!', is a comic play on the ambiguity of Osgood's suggestion – what exactly can be altered? (Lieberfeld and Sanders, 1998: 7 n.2, point out that the script was written shortly after male-to-female reassignment surgery first came to wide public attention.) Such anxieties are similarly mocked in metaphors of violence and threats of violence by the mob that a comic vehicle prevents us from taking seriously. Jerry's woman-shaped double bass has already been shot full of holes in Chicago. Again it is Jerry who is distressed, less by the prospect of being murdered than by the thought of ending up in the 'ladies morgue', or in other words, being permanently feminized: 'I'm going to die of shame!' he sardonically tells Joe (Lieberfeld and Sanders make this point). These castration motifs may be the vicarious expression of a fear shared by the male spectator, but Joe's and Jerry's eventual escape from the castrating mob reassures this spectator that they were never a serious threat.

The film's humour and ironies are themselves sometimes over-interpreted by critics, anxious to read every moment in the narrative as positively linked to transvestism. For instance, when Jerry finally tells Osgood that he is a man, the latter retorts, 'Well, nobody's perfect!' Lieberfeld and Sanders (ibid.: 7) see this as an acknowledgement that 'humans conform only imperfectly to bounded identity categories', whereas the line may be more reasonably construed as a self-conscious denigration of the masculine. After all, it is the men and not the women who throughout the film have behaved badly, from the mobsters Spats Columbo to Little Bonaparte, and including the cross-dressed men who have both used their disguises to achieve selfish ends, sexual seduction in Joe's case and financial extortion in Jerry's. The biologically female characters, by contrast, are stereotypically coded as the 'gentle sex'. The agent's secretary Nellie is a soft-hearted and gullible victim of Joe's charms, while in perfect harmony with the connotations of their names, Sugar Kane is all sweet and naive baby innocence, and the synonymously-named leader of Sugar's band, Sweet Sue, displays a maternal if slightly stern protectiveness towards her charges.

Joe's pursuit of Sugar in the guise of an oil millionaire provides the heterosexual norm against which the Daphne/Osgood romance is intended to appear both ridiculous and perverse. There must, nonetheless, be a touch of conscious irony in Curtis's adoption of an accent associated with the British actor, Cary Grant: it was an open secret in the Hollywood of the 1950s that Grant was homosexual, and Jerry's ascerbic 'Nobody really speaks like that!' underscores both the sexual ambivalence of the persona (Joe double cross-dresses between Josephine and the impotent yachting millionaire), and the centrality of performance as a theme. Indeed, all of the main characters in this film are performers *within* the diegesis, from Sugar and the girl-band (Sugar also claims to be a debutante in her attempts to impress 'the yachting millionaire'), to the Little Bonaparte-led mob who masquerade as 'Lovers of Italian Opera'. Even the bell-hop and Osgood role-play as 'worldly-wise young stud' and 'woman-chasing sugar-daddy'.

Some Like it Hot, then, plays with the exchange of identities in what might be described as a carnivalesque way. The carnivalesque is a feature of Mikhail Bakhtin's theory of allowed transgression, according to which the temporary infringement of social taboos is permitted on certain popular holidays and festivals:

> As opposed to the official feast, one might say that carnival celebrates temporary liberation from the prevailing truth of the established order; it marks the suspension of all hierarchical rank, privileges, norms and prohibitions. Carnival was the true feast of time, the feast of becoming, change and renewal. It was hostile to all that was immortalized and complete.
>
> (Bakhtin, 1984: 109)

The geographical relocation of the narrative from Chicago to Florida is itself a symbolic transition from a nightmare reality to a dream wonderland, from a space of work to a space of play.[3] The association of Florida with Disneyworld in the minds of contemporary spectators also suggests an unreality, a metonymy underlying Jean Baudrillard's acute observation that America itself resembles a 'Disney' themepark where the real and the imaginary have become indistinguishable (see Baudrillard, 1994: 12). The world is turned upside-down, identities are swapped as the poor become the rich and men become women, but this is a temporary phase of permitted transgression, at the end of which everyone must resume his or her former place in the social and sexual hierarchy. As a temporary madness, an escape valve that is designed to enable the social machine to function more efficiently, the transgression of carnival can therefore be seen as essentially serv-ing societal norms.[4] From beginning to end, the norms of hetero-sexuality and gender fixity are constantly re-emphasised and sustained, principally by the pursuit, initially by Jerry and then by Joe, of the delectable Sugar to whom they are instantly and powerfully attracted. 'It's like jello on springs!' an enraptured Jerry tells Joe as the two men gaze lustfully at Sugar's hip-swaying and bottom-wiggling move-ments for the first time, 'I tell you it's a whole different sex!'.

Tootsie (Sydney Pollack, 1982)

Tootsie marked a new departure in Dustin Hoffman's acting career, and demonstrated what a versatile performer he is. The word 'perform-ance' is particularly apt in this context, given the requirements of the part. In this well-scripted, well-acted and highly entertaining film, Hoffman plays Michael Dorsey, an out-of-work New York actor who resorts to dressing as a woman in order to secure a female role in a tele-vision soap-opera. Despite the ostensibly pragmatic reasons for Dorsey's cross-dressing, there is evidence of an underlying psychological motiv-ation which invites a serious reading of this aspect of the film.

The film's script proved remarkably enlightened from the point of view of a sexual politics that – at the time the film was made in the early 1980s – was only just beginning to have an impact. Sexism and the objectification of women are both attacked, and there is some questioning of essentialist ways of thinking about gender, if not sexu-ality. However, as with *Some Like it Hot*, the film implicitly ends up reinforcing sex/gender norms. Before weighing the validity of the criti-cisms *Tootsie* has sustained in this regard, we shall begin with a review of the film's more progressive aspects which feminist critics have tended to ignore in their determination to label the film sexist in spite of itself.[5]

There is no doubting the valiant efforts made in the film script to convey a female if not feminist point of view of the problems encoun-tered by women in the workplace. Although Dorsey owes his initial success in securing an acting part to his female persona as Dorothy Michaels, he is consistently objectified and infantilised by sexist males. The aptly named John van Horn, aka 'the tongue', who plays a senior doctor in the medical soap in which Dorothy has been cast, immedi-ately begins a lustful pursuit of the new 'actress'. But far less sympathetic is the soap's director, a vain and preening middle-aged Casanova who is dating the young female lead (played by Jessica Lange), while conducting amorous dalliances with other young actresses in the show. It is this character who voices the single word of the film title, a condescending and infantilising term for women which suggests a social hierarchy in which men objectify women as beings defined wholly in terms of their sexual value to men. 'Tootsie', an American slang word for 'darling', is always associated with the sexualisation by a man of a young, attractive and, the term implies, possibly promiscuous woman. When the director, Ron, offhandedly calls Dorothy 'tootsie', she responds by vigorously asserting her subjectivity and individuality:

RON: Tootsie, take ten.

DOROTHY: Ron! My name is Dorothy, not tootsie, or toots, or sweetie, or honey, or darlin.

RON: Oh, Christ!

DOROTHY: No, just Dorothy! Now Ellen's always Ellen, Tom's always Tom, and John's aways John. I have a name, too. It's Dorothy, (spells out letters) capital D-o-r-o-t-h-y! Dorothy!

Much to the consternation of the director, she begins to rewrite the lines of a script which portrays her own character and the females she has scenes with as negative and supine. Her portrayal of a woman as the strongest character in the soap immediately boosts the show's ratings, and this positive female role-model rockets Dorothy to fame, culminating in appearances on the cover of *Cosmopolitan* magazine (symbol of a woman's success), of *MS* (symbol of feminist approval), and in a photo opportunity with icon of pop art, Andy Warhol (emblematic perhaps of Dorothy's progressive and iconoclastic influence). As he plays the part of Dorothy, Michael is increasingly seen to be 'in touch with his feminine side' – 'there's something weird about you' his agent tells him, 'since when do you care so much about what other people feel?' – and he is comically seen to fuss about what to wear in his new female persona, suggesting a Beauvoirian view of gender as acquired rather than inborn. In contrast, the ludicrous men around him are represented as the voices of an unacceptable male chauvinism (director) or an outdated view of stereotyped sex-roles (Julie's sympathetic but old-fashioned father, Les, for example, for whom 'bulls are bulls and roosters don't try to lay eggs').

The privileged insight into women's ways of thinking, especially about men, that the cross-dressing situation affords, exemplifies and reinforces essentialist notions of gender. Most specifically the popularly held belief that women are 'a different species' whose thoughts and actions are incomprehensible to men.[6] In *Tootsie*, however, this idea is parodied to some degree through the device of dramatic irony. Julie confides in Dorothy that she would prefer a man to be honest and straightforward: 'I'm not going to spin you a line,' she would like men to say to her, 'I find you interesting and I want to make love to you.' Soon after, Michael meets Julie at a party and seizes the chance to put the insight into practice, whereupon she pours her drink over him. Both Michael Dorsey and the essentialist notion that women have fixed patterns of thought that are different from those of men are thus comically deflated.

The film also goes some way towards challenging fixed gender binarism. Sandy tells Michael early in the film that there's no point in auditioning for the part of a woman because she's 'completely wrong for it!' Michael's successful audition in drag for the same part is an ironic confirmation of this anti-essentialist idea. Indeed, *Tootsie*'s central message, implicit in the acting storyline, is that, in line with the theories of Judith Butler, gender is largely a matter of performance. This message is conveyed in a number of scenes. In the film's opening shots, Dustin Hoffman as Michael Dorsey is seen to apply make-up, paint, and a false moustache – an out-of-work actor desperate for a part, Dorsey auditions his way unsuccessfully through the opening credits. As in *Victor/Victoria*, we are immediately made aware of what will be the narrative's main themes: the constructedness of identity, being 'other' – 'We're looking for someone different, someone else!' screams one casting director at the luckless Dorsey – and performance in both its theatrical and its Butlerian sense. When, as Dorothy Michaels, he is screen-tested for a female part in the medical soap, one of the casting directors observes to the cameraman: 'I'd like to make her look a little more attractive. How far can you pull back?' 'How do you feel about Cleveland?' is the camera-operator's scathing reply. The drily cutting wit of the latter's response emphasises that Dorsey in drag is a comic rather than an erotic phenomenon, but in spite of this, the exchange does draw attention to the possibility of manufacturing sexual attractiveness, and by implication, femininity. That gender is secondary in importance to qualities of beauty, internal as well as external, is in a broader sense also the implicit message of the film's central problematic, as expressed by both Julie and Michael in the closing scene. When Julie declares that she misses Dorothy, Michael confesses 'I was a better man with you as a woman than I ever was with a woman as a man. I just gotta learn to do it without the dress.' Crossing genders, in other words, enables one to view oneself critically from the perspective of the other, and teaches all involved that bodies matter less than feelings. The triteness of this moral is far outweighed by the healthy anti-essentialism underpinning it.

Tootsie does certainly help, then, to promote gender fluidity by representing gender positively as constructed rather than innate, but this aspect of the film narrative is unfortunately undermined by elements of a conventional thinking, many of which we identified in our discussion of *Some Like it Hot*.

Margaret Waller rightly argues that the sexism the film supposedly criticises reasserts itself in the way it was shot:

> Despite the film's pious support for the notion that the world is a different place for a woman than for a man in a male dominated society, no attempt seems to have been made to signify, or even to acknowledge, that difference in the visuals, which remain thoroughly sexist ... The point of view of the male, thematically acknowledged to be partial, is powerfully reinforced as universal. Male desire, supposedly discredited as a reliable pole star for female behaviour, is nevertheless catered to in every shot ... All viewers are invited to identify with a male protagonist.
>
> (Waller, 1987: 2–3)

Waller's critique of the visual dimension of *Tootsie* derives from Laura Mulvey's (1975) work in this area. Mulvey's analysis is now staple reading for all film scholars and students, and while a Mulveyan reading of the film would certainly be fruitful, limitations of space here militate against the repetition of Waller's analysis.[7] In what follows, therefore, I shall focus upon aspects of the representation of cross-dressing which have been relatively neglected by critics hitherto: the temporariness of the crossing, the linking of gender to sexuality, notions of gender-stereotyping, and a homophobia countered by the repeated assertion of masculinity and heterosexuality. I shall illustrate each of these in turn below.

!

Dorsey's strategy is necessarily a short-term solution to his professional problems. He knows and we know that the Dorothy persona cannot be sustained on a permanent basis. The quasi-inversion of Michael Dorsey to Dorothy Michaels linguistically mirrors the gender inversion. The playfulness of the inversion has a carnivalesque quality associated in Bakhtinian theory with the exchange of identities and the assumption of roles for a given period of time. (The priapic connotations of the surname, Van Horn, and the gender ambivalence of the first name, Les, an ironic diminutive for this sexually conventional character, are further examples of playfulness in the choice of names in this film.) This linguistic ludicity suggests that the process is not irreversible. Moreover, the assumed name, shortened to 'Dotty' by Julie, has connotations of elderliness and eccentricity that are quite out of keeping with the thrusting, talented and 'with-it' persona of Dorothy Michaels. Dorothy is emphatically a role that Michael is performing, and from the audience's perspective, the fundamentally temporary and carnivalesque process of acting is foregrounded on three separate but connected levels: Dustin Hoffman plays Michael Dorsey who plays Dorothy Michaels who plays a soap character. The performability of gender is thus doubly *mise en scène*, and its theatricality and artificiality emphasised. Gender, it is implied, can be enacted, as Butler has claimed, but not assumed in any permanent or real sense, and this is the weakness of Butler's use of the 'performability' metaphor, for performance is always necessarily an illusion that is destined to vanish when the curtain comes down. Moreover, the performance of gender is not seen here to be liberating for women, since it is always men who do the performing. Male control of the 'gender act' becomes evident in the film's last lines, in which the girl asks the boy if she can borrow his dress. The boy hesitates. Adrienne Auslander Munich comments: 'Gender is an act of psychic identification with patriarchal values that women may soil; it is not biologically determined but is socially acted. And men, so the film jokes, own its costumes' (Munich, 1984: 117).

The bracketing of sexuality and gender which inheres in the emphasis on Michael Dorsey's heterosexuality is also explicit in a number of telling scenes. Ronnie's reluctance to cast Dorothy is largely based on an essentially physical reaction which is not shared by his female colleague: 'There's something not quite right about her,' he muses, raising the question of gender-stereotyping according to the presence or absence of sexual attraction and gender-specific instincts (compare King Marchan in *Victor/Victoria*). Underscoring this essentialist theme, Ronnie is delighted to have his suspicions confirmed when Dorothy finally sheds her female disguise: 'I knew there was a reason she didn't like me!' When Michael enters Sandy's flat with the intention of trying on some of her clothes, she emerges from the shower and catches him undressed. Rather than admit what he is really about, he pretends to desire his long-standing friend sexually, and they proceed to sleep together. The message of this scene is clear: sex proves gender, that is, 'I am still a man because I desire women.'

Gender is also stereotyped according to other characteristics and abilities. Michael constantly worries about his appearance as Dorothy – hair, make-up, outfits, and so on – helping to perpetuate the sexist cliché of female vanity, and reinforcing notions of women as erotic objects for the pleasure of men, although there is a measure of irony in such moments which may have the opposite effect of holding up to ridicule a male-centered society which defines women principally in terms of appearance and sexual attractiveness. Less self-consciously, Dorothy never does 'female' work (cooking, cleaning, shopping and so on), but conforms to the masculine stereotype of being focused on her profession, in which she displays a 'male' energy and aggression. When Julie asks Dorothy to babysit, Michael proves quite inadequate, implying that only 'real' women know how to look after babies properly. Sandy, too, is stereotyped as clinging and hysterical (Munich, 1984: 113–14, also points to the stereotyping of Julie and Sandy), while the film's only strong woman, Miss Walsh, the soap's producer, is hardly portrayed sympathetically: she comes across as a bullying boss who imposes her views on those around her and is finally shown to have had bad judgement when Michael/Dorothy, whom she had cast against the wishes of her team, confesses the deception. Dorothy herself is little more than a caricatural figure in the ancient tradition of burlesque, travesty and the pantomime dame: 'Rather than a modern liberated female ... Dorothy is bigger than life. Past her prime, with conical breasts, exaggerated hips, bouffant orange hair, a prissy walk and a gooey Southernish accent, she is an ancient comic type, tracing her lineage back as far as the Middle Ages' (ibid.: 115). Munich might well be describing a drag artist here, and we saw in Chapter 1 how drag can be seen psychoanalytically as an unconscious mockery and even an expression of hatred for the feminine (see also Chapter 5, sections on *Priscilla, Queen of the Desert* and *Midnight in the Garden of Good and Evil*). This notion is reinforced by the contempt with which Dorothy's alter ego, Michael, continues to treat Sandy, sleeping with her at the same time as he is courting Julie.

In contrast to these female stereotypes, Julie's father is seen to engage in the stereotypically masculine pursuits of fishing and shooting pool in his local bar, the latter activity providing Michael with the opportunity for some male-bonding when he wishes to mend fences with Les after revealing himself to be a man.

The spectre of homophobia is raised by the pursuit of Dorothy by the amorous Les, and also, more amusingly and more parodically, by Michael's teasing of his agent, George Fields, played by the director, Sidney Pollack. In the first case, the male spectator is invited to identify with Dorsey's unease at physical proximity with Les and with his increasingly frantic attempts to avoid being alone with him. In contrast, Dorsey dressed as Dorothy feels safe enough to cuddle up to his agent in a restaurant, knowing full well that his fellow heterosexual George's reactions will be no more than mild embarrassment at such behaviour in public. George's embarrassment clearly springs from a fear of being thought gay by onlookers but he knows that Dorsey is not gay. This is just teasing behaviour that poses no threat to the gender or sexuality of either. Underlying such playfulness, however, is the sense, shared with the male spectator, that George's responses would be wholly different, were Michael to be a real drag-queen.

When Sandy finds that Les has sent Michael chocolates, she immediately suspects him of being gay, while his fellow soap-actor, the lovely young Julie, thinks he (as Dorothy) is a lesbian. Although it continues to be the basis, then, of much comic misunderstanding in the film, the spectre of homophobia is not entirely exorcised by its humorous context, and has to be definitively chased away by an excessive emphasis throughout the film on Michael's rampant heterosexuality and essential masculinity. These fundamentals of Michael's character are established early on in the film. In the birthday party scene, in which he flirts unsuccessfully with one girl after another, the audience is left in no doubt as to his sexuality, while his stereotypically masculine self-assertiveness in ejecting a queue-jumper from his taxi, and even the part he plays in the hospital soap of a feisty and aggressive female remind us that Michael is no effeminate man. A Freudian reading of these characteristics might see Michael as a case of denial, but such a reading is not supported by the narrative as a whole, which emphasises the dilemma that confronts Michael of how to woo Julie in his Dorothy persona, while offering no evidence of homosexual tendencies on his part. The film's dénouement re-establishes all gender identities and heterosexual relationships, reassuringly confirming norms. Dorothy reverts to Michael, Michael can now have a sexual relationship with Julie unclouded by homophobia (Julie had repressed her attraction to Dorothy as unacceptable because apparently lesbian), and even Les, we are told, is 'seeing a lady'. As in Shakespearean comedy, the world is set to rights and all three levels of performance are brought to a close, as the curtain falls. After all, Michael only ever dressed as a woman for pragmatic reasons, and as in all cross-dressing comedies, those men who were attracted to him in his cross-dressed persona (Les, van Horn) were buffoons of a kind, whose deception was actually a comic self-deception with no overtly erotic elements. The closure demanded by Hollywood is once again unambiguously normative, and while Michael may have learnt a few lessons about himself and his relationships with women, his male gender and heterosexuality remain unquestioned.

On balance, then, we cannot call *Tootsie* a feminist film, although if we read it in the context of its times, it would seem unduly harsh to condemn it as thoroughly sexist. There was arguably less awareness in the early 1980s of the very concept of sexism, and Pollack's film does make a serious attempt to show how women are objectified in patriarchy, representing aspects of this objectification with a self-conscious irony that some feminist critics have ignored. As for the representation of transgender, however, it is hard to see beyond the burlesque comedy of Dorothy's portrayal, which projects cross-dressing as an amusing game, played for a limited period, a transgressive activity that is harmless just as long as it eventually comes to an end, and the implicit confusion between gender and sexuality, between transvestism and homosexuality, in the homophobia that surrounds Dorothy's character is less likely to arouse sympathy in the heterosexual male spectator than anxiety with regard to gender transformation, howsoever motivated.

Victor/Victoria (Blake Edwards, 1982)

Albert Williams, chief theatre critic for the *Chicago Reader* described the Broadway musical that followed the film of *Victor/Victoria* as 'a whimsical romantic comedy, with a healthy attitude of good-humored openmindedness about sexual diversity that's hugely welcome in this age of reactionary backlash' (Williams, 1995: 15). Blake Edwards's film is likewise a well-written, well-acted, and amusing entertainment, replete with the stock-in-trade of comedy: dramatic ironies, misunderstandings, deceptions, coincidences, all combined with an enjoyable repertoire of stage musical numbers and dance routines.

Victor/Victoria is exceptional, for our purposes, in offering a rare filmic example of female-to-male cross-dressing. Released in 1982, the film coincided with a growing focus both inside and outside the academy on issues of gender politics. Indeed, the sexual politics of the film are overall progressive, as we shall see – there are positive images of homosexuality, binary thinking is ridiculed and gender norms questioned.

On the negative side, the script contains repeated and self-consciously anachronistic uses of the word 'gay' in the sense of 'homosexual', implying that, in spite of the film's period setting in 1930s Paris, its meanings are in fact rooted in the historical and cultural context of the early 1980s when the film was made. Moreover, the script generates a measure of confusion between cross-dressing and homosexuality, and the latter is to some degree represented as inferior to heterosexuality, so that, as Robin Wood argues, the gay couple functions as a comic foil to the straight romantic one (Wood, 1986: 243). As in *Some Like it Hot* and *Tootsie* (which appeared in the same year), the representation of transgender appears hedged around with circumstances that function as rationalisation. The film repeats the formula of the 'progress narrative' in which transvestism is represented innocuously as a means to an end, a temporary transgression which never really threatens the status quo (see above). Nevertheless, I shall argue that while the implications of 'gender-bending' are never seriously addressed, the film partly redeems itself through the use of a self-reflexive irony that academic critics have mostly failed to recognise, and that undermines the hegemony of sexual and gender norms.

Reduced to starvation by her failure to obtain a job as a nightclub singer in 1930s Paris, the eponymous heroine, Victoria (Julie Andrews), is persuaded by a gay performer named Toddy (Carol Todd, played by Robert Preston) to adopt the persona of Count Grozinsky, a gay Polish aristocrat and a renowned female impersonator. The crossing in this case is therefore a 'double-crossing' – a term which, in its literal sense, is an apt description of the effect of Victoria's deception. Toddy cynically observes that 'people believe what they see', developing the theme of visual deception upon which the plot depends. (A sub-plot in the narrative concerns a rivalry between clubs and the gangsters who operate them; and more generally, club-owners and audiences are taken in by the deceit.) This theme of visual deception is announced in an opening scene. As Toddy and his male lover awaken, Toddy quotes Shakespeare, striking the note that will resonate throughout the film: 'To quote the immortal bard: "Love looks not with the eyes but with the mind, Therefore is winged Cupid painted blind".' This quotation is positioned in the diegesis as the moral of the story that is about to unfold. Shakespeare's line has both a positive and a negative meaning: on the one hand, people can be taken in by what they see and take to be real; on the other, our feelings for others may be dictated by a profounder intelligence than that provided by the purely visual sense. Reading backward from the end of the film, it is difficult not to interpret this quasi-epigraph as a tongue-in-cheek comment on feminist critiques of 'the gaze' (see Mulvey, 1975). *Victor/Victoria* is precisely the story of visual deception, of a visual stimulus to desire. King Marchan, the night-club owner (James Garner) does not perceive Victoria's femininity in his mind, he sees (it) through her disguise (while all others simply see the disguise itself).

As part of his strategy of persuasion, Toddy tells Victoria that there are no natural differences between men and women – an apparently enlightened view in sexual-political terms, but again one that is belied by the core event of the narrative: it is because of their 'natural differences' that Marchan and Victoria are attracted to each other, in spite of the gender performance that impedes this attraction.

Performance is at the heart of the film's diegesis and is also its central metaphor. Indeed, the narrative's self-reflexivity in this regard invites us to view the film as a postmodern parody of the entire gender debate. (The ironic name of the café where Victoria and Toddy meet, 'Chez Lui', hints at the parodic or postmodern dimensions of the movie, as do the names of the main protagonists: King and Victor are show-business monarchs, while Norma holds the most 'normatizing' views on sexuality and gender, and Squash, the name of Marchan's bodyguard, aptly suggests both his boxing past and perhaps also the repression of his homosexuality.) Performance (or play-acting) is foregrounded in all of the main scenes and touches all of the film's protagonists:

- the double performance of a woman pretending to be a man pretending to be a woman;
- the play-acting in the café when Victoria and Toddy, who cannot pay for their meal, pretend that the food contains a cockroach;
- the performances of the other acts at the nightclub which are all about men pretending to be women, especially the dance sequence involving costumes half-men, half-women – a metaphor for the in-between, or the Platonic whole;
- the closet homosexuality of Marchan's bodyguard, Squash, play-acting heterosexuality;
- the self-conscious performance of femininity by Norma Cassidy (Lesley-Ann Warren) as a Marilyn Monroe figure, all dizzy peroxide blonde, false eyelashes, passion-red lips, and girlish giggles.

Norma Cassidy is another 'woman playing a woman', more Marilyn than Marilyn, simpering in her heavy Brooklyn accent throughout the movie, a parallel and counterpoint to Victor, and ironically, considerably more 'drag'. That gender, as Butler claims, is a 'performance' is nowhere more convincingly demonstrated than in this film. Lesley-Ann Warren who plays Norma is a very sexy woman, but Norma's sexiness is heightened here to the extent of seeming to be a copy (of Monroe, of 'gangster moll' stereotypes), a performance, a simulacrum (see Chapter 7).

Victor's performance of drag displaces drag to a second level of representation, since Victoria's femininity is bound to shine through. If anything, the ironic distance created by this further layer of performativity turns her performance into a parody of drag, or since drag is itself essentially parodic, a 'drag in drag'. The spectator thus ceases to see drag and instead, is aware of the woman behind the female impersonation mask. In this way, the film avoids the anxiety associated with 'real' manifestations of transgender.

Victoria's act cannot in any sense be described as drag, since it lacks any of drag's characteristics of parody and excess (but how could a woman ever do drag, which depends largely for its effect on masculine elements in female clothes?) This does not prevent Toddy describing it as such: 'When you're dancing', he tells Victoria, 'make it broader,

with tons of shoulder. Remember, you're a drag-queen!' The lack of con-
sonance of this statement with the reality of Victoria's performance
itself underlines the theme of performativity in the Butlerian sense
that will become a dominant motif in the diegesis. (See Garber, 1993:
125–6; even when women began to play female parts in Shakespeare,
artifice was still present and the phallus still veiled: is it there or not?)

The very title of Blake Edwards's film disrupts gender binaries: the
diagonal slash fusing a man's and a woman's name, juxtaposing the
masculine and the feminine, and the six letters shared by the two
names imply a merged rather than a divided identity, challenging
conventional polarities. Seen from this perspective, the title inevitably
recalls a well-known work of French structuralism, teasingly inviting
a postmodern reading. *Victor/Victoria* thus suggests itself as an ironic
homage to Roland Barthes's commentary on Honoré de Balzac's short
story *Sarrasine* in his structuralist analysis of the narrative, *S/Z*. Barthes
breaks down *Sarrasine* into small narrative units and proceeds to
analyse them in terms of a number of codes. The Balzac story is especially relevant to our purposes in its main theme which concerns a
young man's (Sarrasine's) passion for an opera singer (La Zambinella)
he thinks to be a woman but who is in fact a castrato. The plot and
themes of Blake Edwards's film, right down, in some instances, to
inconspicuous details, seem to mirror the Balzac tale, and Barthes's commentary seems to hang ghost-like in the background. While not set in
the same location, both *Sarrasine* and *Victor/Victoria* have French contexts, both films feature a cross-dressed singer, and a man who falls in
love with him/her, both narratives focus on the unveiling of the deception created by the cross-dressing and the consequences of that unveiling. In every important sense, however, the film reads as an inversion
of *Sarrasine*. These dis-symmetries are best represented in tabular
form:

Sarrasine	*Victor/Victoria*
A castrato (male) pretends to be a woman	A woman pretends to be a man playing a woman
A man falls for a 'woman' because he is deceived by appearances	A man falls for a woman because he is not deceived by appearances
The love-affair has tragic consequences	The love-affair has happy consequences

Sarrasine	*Victor/Victoria*
Castration-anxiety is a recurrent motif, associated with gender instability, and this anxiety reinforces norms by being seen to have foreshadowed the tragic events of the dénouement	Castration-anxiety is equally a recurrent motif but is dispelled in the dénouement
Unveiling is prompted by sexual desire, as well as by the desire to know	Unveiling is prompted by the desire to know, as well as by sexual desire

The symmetry of titles, moreover, between *S/Z* and *Victor/Victoria* is a further invitation to read the Blake Edwards film against the background of the Barthes study and its textual subject. Castration-anxiety is evoked by both titles and is an important motif in the film. In the Balzac text as read by Barthes, the slash of the title evokes notions of cutting and division:

> the slash (/) confronting the S of SarraSine and the Z of Zambinella has a panic function: it is the slash of censure, the surface of the mirror, the wall of hallucination, the verge of antithesis, the abstraction of limit, the obliquity of the signifier, the index of the paradigm, hence of meaning.
>
> (Barthes, 1990: 107)

Victor and Victoria are in a similar sort of graphic inversion to that of Sarrasine and Zambinella, except that in this instance, the Vs remain the same, which perhaps signifies the lack of biological difference between the two. Whilst in the case of *S(arrasine)/Z(ambinella)*, the linguistic castration occurs at the beginning of the word, it is the suffix of *Victor/Victoria* where difference is signified. In this case, it is the masculine that is the castrated version of the feminine (as the feminine name, Victoria is shortened, cut short, elided to the masculine name, Victor). This suggests that in this film narrative, it is the feminine that is constricted into the masculine, as Victoria has to lose part of her identity in order to perform a masculine role (a man playing a woman is still a man). What she loses is her freedom as a woman to attract men, a freedom that she must regain for equilibrium to be restored. The retrieval of this freedom is the principal narrative pro-gramme of this central character in the second part of the narrative. (In the first part of the narrative, her narrative programme was the quest for money.) Victor must again become Victoria, symbolised by the reversal of her linguistic castration.

The woman has nothing to lose physically by crossing, only linguisti-cally. The film title and the inversion in the diegesis of the masculine and the feminine across the castrating bar suggests a parody of castration-anxiety and of the Lacanian 'Name of the Father'. In a general sense, moreover, each element of the film title functions ludically: Victor = the winner (success for Victor as a cross-dressed performer); Victoria = the 'Queen', but also the emblem of the asexual (performativity, androgyny, neutrality); the slash = an important icon of gender/Queer Theory.

Some have interpreted King Marchan's failure to achieve an erection with Norma after seeing Victoria's act in terms of castration-anxiety, generated by the destabilisation of genders and his own sexual attrac-tion for the ambivalent Victor. However, Marchan is convinced that Victor is a woman, and his lack of interest in Norma makes more sense on a romantic level. It is also claimed by some critics that when he and Victoria begin sleeping together after he has discovered her to be a woman as he suspected, his concerns about how others will react to his apparent homosexuality are homophobic. However, in the con-text both of the plot and the historical and cultural setting, such con-cerns are understandable. If anyone is homophobic, it is the American gangsters who provide him with financial support and who would not be best pleased to discover that King Marchan had 'turned'. But even the gangsters merely represent a generally-held prejudice. In 1930s America, as in Europe, there was little toleration of a sexuality that was still illegal and that 'dared not speak its name'. If Marchan is homo-phobic, then so is the rest of society. Steve Cohan rightly suggests that Marchan picks a fight in a workers' bar to prove that he is still a 'real man', as opposed to an effeminate 'gay', but Cohan pushes his interpretation too far, turning Marchan's homophobia into homo-eroticism. Having smashed up the bar and each other, the men then begin to sing drunkenly together, an event which Cohan describes as 'homo-erotic' (Cohan, 1998: 45). An instance of male-bonding this may be, but to call this homoeroticism is an instance of over-interpretation, which does not take account of the predominant views and values of the culture and period represented, or of cinematic tradition – male communal singing as a means of reconciliation after a bar-room brawl is a Hollywood cliché that lacks any overtly erotic components. Essentialist thinking seems to creep into the narrative in two short scenes, which at face-value appear to contradict the film's generally enlightened representation of gender issues. The first of these scenes recalls an identical moment in *Sarrasine*: like La Zambinella, Victoria jumps at the popping of a champagne-cork. Both cases illustrate Barthes's theory of the circularity of cultural codes, and in both cases, the connotation is one of femininity: 'Champagne serves to prove La Zambinella's pusillanimity. La Zambinella's pusillanimity serves to prove her femininity' (Barthes, 1990: 147). In *Victor/Victoria*, too, the cork pops, she jumps, so she must be pusillanimous and so a woman. We know she is a woman, but others present do not, so this is a classic comic moment of dramatic irony. The irony functions in part to undermine such stereotyping. Again, the self-referentiality of codes produces a circular logic:

> imperfect syllogisms ... all women are timid; La Zambinella is timid; therefore La Zambinella is a woman ... Women are adorable, women are fearful, women are beautiful – all this is 'common knowledge', an *endoxa*. Thus the snares Sarrasine sets for himself are based on the most social discourse.
>
> (Ibid.: 148)

So, social discourse, current opinion (which is culturally and temporally relative) determine definitions of the feminine.

Victoria's nervous reaction has the reverse effect to that of La Zambinella: while the latter's nervousness deceives those present as to her 'real' gender, Victoria's threatens to expose it. This ironic reversal must surely, at the same time, be a self-conscious rewriting of the Balzac text and of Barthes's commentary on it.

In the second scene, two separate events are comically juxtaposed: when King Marchan takes Victoria to a boxing-match, she vomits, while a visit to the opera bores Marchan and moves Victoria to tears. Is this juxtaposition intended to point up the silliness of gender-stereotyping, or does the comedy simply highlight differences dictated as much by social class as by gender? (King Marchan is a working-class self-made man of simple tastes, somewhat implausibly matched with the more sophisticated middle-class, operatically-trained Victoria.)

All of these scenes appear to invite a reading in terms of 1980s progressive sexual politics – castration-anxiety linked to homophobia – whereas I am arguing that the humorous context in every case raises the possibility of a second-level interpretation based on a postmodern parody. There is a self-consciousness about the inclusion of these sexual-political motifs that is irresistibly ironic. This is not to say that *Victor/ Victoria* is reactionary with regard to sexual issues – far from it – but simply that the film treats such issues with the ironic distance of comedy, and that this approach is ultimately more effective in promoting awareness than a more serious treatment would be.

The Fort!da! of comedy: unveiling as dénouement

Deception and unveiling are as central to the narrative of *Victor/Victoria* as to all other cross-dressing comedies. There is much play between concealment and disclosure in a succession of scenes involving the police, a rival nightclub-owner, the identity of the fraudsters in the restaurant, King Marchan's bodyguard's sexuality, and so on. Much of this is the stuff of knockabout comedy. In the context of a now well-established genre, all of this has the feel of self-reflexive parody.

Victor/Victoria contains no less than three revelation scenes. In the first of these, after Victor's first number at the new nightclub, when the audience applaud rapturously assuming she's a woman, (s)he takes off her/his head-dress to reveal a masculine haircut. King Marchan's face drops: he was 'deceived' (dramatic irony). 'It's a guy!' exclaims his girlfriend, Norma, delighted to discover that she has no rival for Marchan's affections after all. A look of disgust crosses Marchan's face. The gesture of removing the head-dress signifies 'I am really a man' for the nightclub audience, but for the film spectator, the meaning is 'I am pretending to be a man dressed as a woman.' Thus, the gaze is again cheated in two ways: the intradiegetic audience think she is a woman, then think she is a man. A third level of signification relates to the very act of dewigging which becomes a ritualistic finale for all Victor's numbers, to an act of striptease which is a metaphor for the very notion of unveiling as revelation of an underlying truth.[8]

The moment of revelation comes early in the film, partly because the audience already know of the deception, partly because the focus will now be on King Marchan's reactions. But this is a *faux dénouement*, the 'real' one, that is, that Victor is actually a woman, is yet to come. Revelation in *Victor/Victoria*, however, is directed at other characters and not the film's audience, which provides ample scope for further dramatic ironies, the stock-in-trade of comedy. For example, when Norma Cassidy declares the truth as she understands it, it is the voice of conventionality that we hear: 'There are some things you cannot fake!'; 'I knew he was a man!' The comic effects of this dramatic irony effectively undermine the essentialist view.

In the second revelation scene, King Marchan hides in Victor's and Toddy's hotel room to watch Victor disrobe for a bath. There is a double irony here: while we up until now knew what he didn't, he now sees what we don't (her naked female body). During the scene, Toddy comes in to offer Victoria a drink in her bath 'to warm her cockles', to which she replies 'That's the trouble, I don't have any cockles!' ... which Marchan has just verified!

The third and final revelation scene is another intimate moment, as Victoria shows herself to Norma, woman to woman. The convoluted phrasing of Norma's astonished exclamation, 'You two-timing son of a bitch! He's a woman!', while wittily exposing two truths (Marchan's infidelity and Victoria's real sex), at the same time manages to retain a degree of ambiguity in the seesawing of male pronoun and female noun, a seesawing which is ironically reflected in the term of abuse she hurls at Marchan.

A parody of closure

In the final scene, all characters resume their 'proper' gender positions, be they hetero or homo. Toddy takes over the dancing part from Victoria in a comic knockabout routine. This *is* drag – a man transparently and comically dressed as a woman. There is no gender performance here, since what drag performs is the parody of femininity. Victoria mouths the song's words sitting in the audience as a woman who has accepted becoming a woman again in order to make the relationship with King Marchan possible, but also to save him from the gangsters he does business with who do not tolerate what they think is homosexuality. The apparent closure represented by this scene is based on the manifest message that all is now as it should be, homophobic anxiety is quelled, the man gets the girl, and the practical reasons for cross-dressing give way to the desire for heterosexual conjugal bliss. All of this is symbolically enacted in Toddy's performance, in which a homosexual does drag, a man (Marchan) and a woman (Victoria) watch, and everyone else cheers, including Norma.

Cohan (1998: 51) usefully summarises the critical consensus (which includes Judith Butler) that this ending works to contain the transgressions of transvestism and homosexuality:

'This is drag as high entertainment', Butler comments, with the cross-dressing 'providing a ritualistic release for a heterosexual economy that must constantly police its own boundaries against the invasion of queerness' (1993: 126). Wood draws the same conclusion, arguing that the film follows a typical 1980s' strategy of separation, recognising heterosexuals and homosexuals but as 'two distinct species', effectively subordinating gays and women to the authority of straight men (1986: 241). Bruce Babington and Peter William Evans likewise claim that the film's closure removes 'the heterosexual female from the setting ... of sexual experiment, reversal and metamorphoses of sex and identity' by redefining that setting as a marginalized, stereotypically queer space (1989: 296–7).

The critics cited by Cohan fail to appreciate the extent to which this scene and the performances it contains are a parody both of closure and of the very notion of performance. As the scene draws to a close, the Shakespearean device of allowing the actors to step out of character and self-consciously to address the audience is hinted at, as everyone cheers in a manner that suggests a different kind of 'crossing', a crossing beyond the cinema screen to the position of the spectator. All involved in the scene exchange intimate looks, the kind that imply a shared knowledge and endeavour. The Shakespearean lines that opened the film are implicitly mocked in the strongly visual focus of this scene. Shakespeare's greater insight that 'all the world's a stage', that illusion and reality are ultimately inseparable, is the dominant theme of this ending. Toddy the drag-queen performs drag, Victoria joins in from the 'real world' of the audience, mouthing the words of the songs she knows so well, and the most intensely theatrical of all the protagonists, Norma, the voice of a comically naive prejudice throughout the film, cheers like a pantomime or music-hall spectator, both genres in which there is frequent crossing between spectators and performers.[9] Less real than any character in the film, Norma is nevertheless and paradoxically performance personified. *Victor/Victoria* has explored the age-old conundrum of whether one can discard representation and simply 'be oneself', which the narrative has shown to be an essential prerequisite for the fulfilment of love's ambitions. But by applauding representation or performance, and treating character as a mantle easily discarded, the actors of this cross-dressing farce are implicitly undermining the closure of the 'happy ending' that they have just enacted. Thus, the very notion of closure is itself rendered unstable.[10] Blake Edwards's film is an early example of postmodern scepticism with regard to the truths of all narratives and all ideologies, found either side of the imaginary line between fact and fiction, the represented and the real.

Mrs Doubtfire (Chris Columbus, 1993)

Although based on a novel by Anne Fine (*Alias Madame Doubtfire*), this last of the major cross-dressing comedies contains many of the themes and motifs we have identified in earlier films in the genre (especially, *Some Like it Hot*), and it seems inconceivable, therefore, that the scriptwriter was not influenced by them. In an article that concentrates on cross-dressing in *Some Like it Hot*, Jennifer Wicke devotes scant space to *Mrs Doubtfire*, which she describes as 'Down many levels from the cerebral, transcendent heights of Billy Wilder's film' (Wicke, 1997: 370), a dismissive characterisation of the film which nevertheless seems to acknowledge a degree of what we might nowadays be tempted to call 'trickledown influence'. On the other hand, there are significant differences which, in my view, justify the inclusion of the film in this discussion alongside its more famous ancestors.

Once again, the cross-dressing is an act of desperation *in extremis*. In this case, the central character, a voice-over artist named Danny (played with gusto by the irrepressible Robin Williams) finds access to his children following divorce unacceptably restricted and resorts to applying for the position of nanny at his ex-wife's house, necessitating a change of gender. To the strains of 'Luck Be a Lady Tonight', Danny's gay brother, who has skills as a make-up artist, transforms him into an elderly woman with the aid of a facial mask and a body suit.

Mrs Doubtfire in a number of ways reflects the social concerns that dominated the 1980s and early 1990s: the deleterious effects of smoking and the undesirability of promoting the tobacco habit in the media (at the beginning of the film narrative, Danny quits his job doing voice-overs because of the inclusion of smoking imagery in children's cartoons), child custody following divorce (compare *Kramer v. Kramer*,

Robert Benton, 1979), the difficulties of single-motherhood (finding the right nanny proves a nigh impossible task). As regards sexual matters, however, the film displays a coyness typical of Hollywood. The 1990s saw the emergence of political correctness, and following the witchhunts conducted against gays in the AIDS-obsessed 1980s, the new decade witnessed the expression of a renewed sensitivity in the cultural representations of homosexuals. On the other hand, in a movie in which cross-dressing takes centre-stage, it is curious that there is little positive representation of transvestism or gender issues generally. Unlike *Tootsie, Victor/Victoria*, and even *Some Like it Hot*, in which there is some acknowledgement that gender might not be a biological or cultural given, and that attraction might even transcend conventional gender boundaries, *Mrs Doubtfire* not only seems reluctant to address such issues, the narrative itself turns upon the very desirability of fixed gender and sexual positions. Danny's principal narrative programme is to re-establish his position as father and husband within the nuclear family. In Lacanian terms, this means the reassertion of his subjectivity in a symbolic constructed around the Father's Law. In the opening scenes of the narrative, Danny is represented as having lost his position in the family triad by failing to maintain order (as witnessed by the pandemonium of the birthday party which he has organised for one of his children), and while he has retained the love of his children, though perhaps not their respect (the eldest child, Lydia blames her father for his lack of control), he has lost both as far as his wife is concerned. It is the degeneration of the Father's Law that leads to family breakdown. Paradoxically, the father must return as a mother in order to re-establish this law, with a view to reconstructing the family and restoring the father to his rightful place. As a mother, Danny transforms himself into a gentle but firm parental figure who wins back the children's respect precisely by asserting his/her authority: television, for instance, cannot be watched until homework has been done.

This retrieval of the 'Name of the Father' through the feminine-maternal suggests a positive reappraisal of gender norms and positions. However, the subtext of the narrative sends out a wholly different message. The real mother, Danny's ex-wife Miranda, played by Sally Field, prioritises work over family (an ironic inversion of her husband's attitudes in this respect) and so is virtually absent from the home. While Miranda has thus assumed the role of the father as breadwinner and disciplinarian, Mrs Doubtfire substitutes for the absent mother. In this sense, the film is as much about the failure of the maternal as of the Father's Law. These problems, it is implied, can only be resolved by the resumption by mother and father of their proper gender roles, a moral lesson that is rammed home through the enactment of both of these stereotypical roles by Danny who is obliged by the mother's absence to play mother and father. The maternal Mrs Doubtfire is good at housework while Danny the father is not, reinforcing another gender stereotype: that is, he is good at 'female' work only as a female.

Comedy thus helps to ridicule and hence domesticate a transvestism that might otherwise prove threatening. Consequently, the film is considerably more normative than the other comedies we have been discussing. As with its predecessors, *Mrs Doubtfire* is a tale of temporary gender-crossing for practical and not erotic purposes, and like them, the film departs from and returns to a basic premise of 'natural' gender positions and heterosexual norms. In *Mrs Doubtfire*, any suggestion of cross-dressing for fetishistic reasons is regarded as 'sick' (by the neighbours' children who see Danny undressing) and as 'unmasculine' (Danny's young son won't embrace him wearing women's clothes: 'I understand,' says Danny, 'it's a guy thing'). Indeed, the physical reconstruction of the body that many transsexuals undergo is implicitly criticised in a line designed to mock any use of cosmetic surgery to change or modify appearance: 'Not a single body that exists in nature,' quips Danny in his Mrs Doubtfire disguise, as (s)he surveys the toned and tanned bathers at an expensive club pool.

Danny is throughout represented as an unambiguously heterosexual man whose sole aim is to win back his wife and children. While apparently pointing up the ironies of Danny's situation, background music reminds the audience at unconscious levels that gender positions are in the end unalterable (for example, 'Walk like a man, talk like a man, my son').

The heterosexual and nuclear family themes are reinforced by intermale sexual rivalry. Miranda is seeing Stu Dunmire, played by Pierce Brosnan, a classically good-looking and well-heeled man-about-town who threatens to take Danny's place in the family circle and the marital bed. The name 'Dunmire' has distinctly negative connotations: a 'dunny' in Australian English means 'lavatory' while 'mire' is synonymous with 'mud'. 'Doubtfire' at once duplicates the name structurally

and through alliteration and assonance, and provides a positive counterweight to it – the first syllable suggests a sympathetic confusion
while the second connotes energy and courage. This opposing linguistic symmetry reinforces the sense of male rivalry.

Like Michael Dorsey in *Tootsie*, Danny is himself at pains to dispel
castration anxieties. In Eugene Monick's Jungian perspective, 'phallos'
(or the governing symbol of masculinity) may be damaged by a sense
of failure in the symbolic, an injury which is associated with castration:

> A man requires a sense of attainment as coefficient to his phallic
> nature since attainment for a man is parallel to erection and insem-
> ination. He must, in Karen Horney's words, prove himself. Without
> the proof, there is an implication of impotency-feminization-
> castration.
>
> (Monick, 1991: 31)

As we saw above, the gender-transformation of Danny is not merely
vestimentary, although no surgery is involved, as Danny is quick to
point out to his young son, in an attempt to dispel any castration-
anxiety on his own or his son's part.

The boy catches Mrs Doubtfire urinating from a standing position,
leading to the father's unmasking by the children. This unveiling
functions in the diegesis to make the children their father's accom-
plices in his mission to increase access to them, but more profoundly,
for both son and audience, this is a shocking visual juxtaposition of
the masculine and the feminine, an image that represents a disturbing destabilisation of genders for the young onlooker. The focalisation
of this episode, viewed as it is from the child's perspective, also recalls
Freud's primal scene. For Freud, the child's observation, real or imagined,
of sexual intercourse between the parents gives rise to sexual excitation
in the child while at the same time providing the basis for castration
anxiety (Laplanche and Pontalis, 1985: 335), while others have related
the child's interest in this event to its own pre-Oedipal experiences
with the mother and the desires aroused by them (ibid.). The urination
scene is equally resonant with castration-anxiety and pre-Oedipal
desires, but produces an effect opposite to that of the primal scene.
Instead of arousing castration fear in the male spectator, the scene
unconsciously restores the lost phallus to the pre-Oedipal mother
that Mrs Doubtfire in many ways represents.[11]

This castration-anxiety is assuaged for the male spectator in a number of other comic moments which remind us that, in every sense, Mrs Doubtfire/Danny still has the phallus. The choice of public toilet is again an issue in the film, but as in *Tootsie* and *Some Like it Hot*, the default position is always the Mens. Danny loses no opportunity to symbolically castrate his adversary, thus displacing his own castration fears onto his sexual rival. When Mrs Doubtfire is invited to accompany Miranda and the children to Stu's country-club pool, he delivers a number of castrating put-downs: on the subject of Stu's Mercedes: 'They say a man who has a big car like that is trying to compensate for smaller deficiencies'; and eyeing Stu's crotch: 'By the look of you, that water's so cold!'

Like Dorsey in *Tootsie*, Danny feels the need to accentuate his male identity to compensate for the temporary change of gender (both characters, we remember, are initially portrayed as sensitive, artistic types 'in touch with their feminine side'). Thus, he reacts to a mugging attempt with an aggression that is both physical and linguistic: 'Piss off, ass-hole!' he screams at his hapless assailant. Again like Dorsey, Danny responds anxiously to the sexual attentions of men. When a bus-driver makes mild overtures towards him, Danny appears bewildered, and while the driver seems aroused rather than revolted by the sight of hairy legs beneath the woman's skirt, the spectator at least is reassured that Danny's male identity remains intact.

The film's dénouement takes place in the aptly named 'Bridges Restaurant', where, owing to an unavoidable double-booking, Danny is forced to dine at one table as Mrs Doubtfire with the family and Stu, and at another as himself with a TV boss, Mr Lundy who is interested in employing him. Danny must move from table to table, changing in the restrooms en route, to spend equal time with each party. In other words, he must bridge a number of gaps: between the two tables, between his two identities, between his need to work and his needs as a father. Ultimately, he must also build bridges with Miranda to secure shared custody of their children. The result is predictably farcical, as Danny consumes excessive amounts of alcohol, and is increasingly incapable of navigating his way across the crowded restaurant, bumping into plate-bearing waiters and finally confusing the two personas altogether. A combination of heat, clumsiness and perspiration inevitably lead to the melting of his face-mask and the 'dewigging' of Mrs Doubtfire before an astonished Miranda.

In spite of Danny's antics in the restaurant, the benign Mr Lundy gives him a TV programme for children, in which he dresses as Mrs Doubtfire. Thus, the film ends with another performance, in this case, a highly sentimental one: Mrs Doubtfire is seen to deliver a tear-jerking sermon about mummies and daddies being happier apart sometimes but always loving their children. Miranda's heart softens, as she watches this, realising that not only the children miss the fictitious Mrs D, and she finally accedes to Danny's wish to take care of the children when she is at work. Miranda has recognised the need for a father in the family, Danny reassumes his father-identity, and the cross-dresser is safely contained within the fiction of performance. The symbolic order is re-established and, as the children's television fantasy-figure, the phallic mother disappears back into the imaginary where she properly belongs.

4
Psycho–Trans

Introduction

While the cross-dressing comedies of the previous chapter focus on the playful aspects of transvestism as a temporary disguise or means to an end, *Psycho, Dressed to Kill, The Silence of the Lambs* and *Cherry Falls* feature men who dress as women for psychological reasons. Psychiatric cases, they constitute the dark underside of the progress narratives of the comedies. In *Psycho* and *Lambs*, the narrative is at pains to dissociate itself from a negative representation of transgender: in the first, a police psychiatrist explains that Bates is not a transvestite because he does not dress in women's clothes to achieve an erotic thrill: 'He was simply doing everything possible to keep alive the illusion of his mother being alive. He tried to be his mother'; and in the second, Hannibal Lecter implies that the killer is not a transsexual. However, the subject of gender cannot in either case be so easily dismissed. In all four of our films, as in the thriller genre generally, the narrative is driven centrally by the quest for knowledge of the killer's identity, and the dénouement is dominated by the dramatic and surprising revelation of this identity, but in these films the process involves two simultaneous unveilings: that of the murderer's identity and that of his gender.[1]

In all four cases, cross-dressing, and in two cases, transsexualism, are represented as perverse or hysterical symptoms of a psychotic condition. Hence, by association if not by definition, transgender is negatively coded, associated directly with castration, madness, murder and monstrosity.

The theme of body possession, a classic horror theme since *Invasion of the Body Snatchers* (1956), features in all of these films, confronting the audience with the ultimate terror of the destabilization of loss of identity, and in three of the four cases, the invading personality is a monstrous maternal one.[2] In *Psycho*, Norman Bates's identity is in the end completely replaced by the mother persona. In *Dressed*, it is the increasingly dominant female side of Dr Elliott's psyche that commits murder, so that the masculine is seen to be mentally overpowered and possessed by a monstrous feminine. In *Lambs*, the killer willingly clothes himself in the skins of his female victims – a literal invasion of other bodies. In *Cherry Falls*, the cross-dressing Marliston's personality is shown to be almost completely shaped and driven by that of his dead mother. Implicitly if not explicitly, then, transgenderism is tarred with the same dark brush, since it is the visible and outward sign of gender instability and of rejection of the symbolic order and the Father's Law. While critics have concentrated on reading these films as misogynist, they have not given sufficient weight to their demonisation of transgender which has largely been perceived as the metaphorical vehicle for the demonisation of the feminine. In fact, it is not simply a monstrous femininity per se but the dissolution of the boundaries of gender in these films that leads directly to murder. If transgender is represented as any kind of metaphor here, it is a metaphor for the psychotic erasure of the self. Just as female monsters in film, for example the deadly female predators of *Fatal Attraction*, *Jurassic Park* and the *Alien* series, trope anxiety about feminism, transgendered killers trope anxiety about gender-bending. As Marina Warner observes, 'popular films ... often refract popular concerns in metaphorical terms, and then reinforce them' (Warner, 1994: 3).

Psycho (Alfred Hitchcock, 1960): postmodern *avant la lettre*?

Alfred Hitchcock stars in a cinema trailer for *Psycho* that was made for the film's initial release and that often features in video and DVD copies. Lasting about 15 minutes, this trailer is much longer than average, a fact which, together with the presence of the director, suggests that it should be regarded as a part of the oeuvre itself, at the very least occupying a paratextual space. The trailer is strikingly inappropriate for a film of the thriller genre. Hitchcock shows the spectator around the set, pointing out the various locations, and especially, the bathroom and stairs where the murders were committed, with tongue-in-cheek distaste of the 'You couldn't possible imagine what happened here!' variety. His commentary is punctuated by jaunty, upbeat music reminiscent of Laurel and Hardy or Charlie Chaplin movies.

This self-consciously ironic frame injects an ingredient of self-referentiality into the film which extends to certain aspects of the dialogue itself. In his conversation with Marion Crane in the back parlour of the motel, Norman Bates makes two observations the meaning of which will not become clear until the end of the film: 'My mother isn't quite herself today' and 'A son is a poor substitute for a lover.' On the basis that everything in film signifies, one can only assume that the audience is expected to recall these remarks, which, in retrospect, seem not only grimly humorous but also evidence of a psychological self-awareness that the character does not possess. A film that is less fixed in genre terms than previous criticism suggests and that displays elements of a self-reflexivity more commonly associated with postmodernism invites a reading that privileges shifting perspectives, a reading that, in the strictly Derridean sense, deconstructs critical assumptions about the film's thematic contents. Dislocation, in fact, is a key word in both the thematic, character and spatial construction of *Psycho*, and in the film's potential for reception outside conventional critical norms.

Cross-dressing, the uncanny, and the phallic woman

Hitchcock's well-known film provides the original model of the mentally disturbed cross-dressed murderer. Both *Dressed to Kill* and *The Silence of the Lambs* are heavily influenced by this model of a psychotic male who dresses in women's clothes to kill his female victims. Norman Bates is a sexually inadequate young man whose obsessively close relationship with his mother is threatened by the arrival of a lover in the mother's life. Norman is driven by jealousy to kill both of them. In denial as to the murder of his mother, he stuffs her and preserves her corpse as if she were still alive, dressing more and more often in her clothes and speaking in her voice. When young women come to stay at the motel he runs, he is sexually attracted to them, whereupon the mother-side of his personality takes over and murders them, motivated by the same jealousy with which he had killed his mother and her lover.

As a psychiatric case, Norman Bates has attracted considerable attention, and Slavoj Žižek's Freudian analysis is a characteristic one: '*Psycho* presents the ultimate version of the "transference-of-guilt" motif ... Norman's maternal superego commits the murder and then transfers the guilt to his ego' (Žižek, 1992: 269 n.50). Torn between the guilt of matricide, the surviving grip of a domineering dead mother, and sexual desires for the young women who drift into the isolated Bates motel, Bates's guilt is sexual and Oedipal. For the average cinema-goer, however, unfamiliar with psychoanalytic theory, the character is, above all, the juxtaposition of transvestism with the monstrous: as in its successors, *Psycho* represents the gesture of cross-dressing in association with insanity and violent murder.

I want to look in detail at Žižek's commentary on the film, together with that of Michel Chion, to which Žižek himself refers, as both readings emphasise notions of the shifting and fragmentation of identities. Although Norman's cross-dressing is dictated by a mother obsession rather than by any erotic motive (as the police psychiatrist is at pains to emphasise), the ego-splitting that drives it and the murderous impulses that accompany it constitute the most negative of vehicles for this early filmic image of transvestism.

The principal theme of the film is dislocation and the horror associated with it. Norman himself flags up this theme early in the film in his conversation with Marion Crane when she first arrives at the Bates motel. What he in fact voices is a neurotic desire to escape the boundaries of an ego that imprisons him:

> I think that we're all in our private traps – clamped in them. And none of us can ever get out. We scratch and claw, but only at the air, only at each other. And for all of it, we never budge an inch.

Norman's words can be interpreted both as a desire for and a symptom of mental dislocation, which is evident in the split between his own voice and that of the mother persona that gradually becomes dominant. This psychical dislocation is mirrored in the principal spaces of the diegesis: Norman is constantly pulled between the verticality of the house and the horizontal lines of the motel, which symbolise respectively his psychotic split between mother and self (see Žižek,1992: 232). The theme of dislocation extends also to Marion's situation, as she makes a life-changing decision to steal the 40,000 dollars entrusted to her by her boss, and leave behind her unsatisfactory job and emotional life, moving from city to country, from one life to another.

Chion (1992: 196) identifies the disembodied voice of the mother as playing a central role in the diegesis:

> In *Psycho*, the mother is first of all a voice ... the voice ... is heard all the time, at great length, off frame.

The voice of the mother is heard on three different occasions in *Psycho*, and each time it features in a key, linking scene:

- The first occasion is when Marion, having arrived at the motel, overhears an argument between the mother and her son, Norman.
- The second occasion (the 'landing scene') is when we hear another, almost equally stormy discussion between Norman and his mother, when he is trying to persuade her to go down to the cellar. It ends with the voice of the mother apparently becoming embodied.
- The third occasion, at the end of the film, is when Norman is shown in his cell, wholly possessed by the mother.

Commenting on Chion's analysis, Žižek (1992: 234) observes:

> *Psycho* is ultimately the story of a Voice ('mother's voice') in search of its bearer, of a body to whom it could stick; the status of this Voice is what Chion calls *acousmatic* – a voice without a bearer, without an assignable place ... The film ends with the moment of 'embodiment' when we finally behold the body in which the Voice originates – yet at this precise moment things get mixed up ... The Voice has attached itself to the wrong body, so that what we get is a true zombie, a pure creature of the Superego, totally powerless in itself (Norman-mother 'wouldn't even hurt a fly'), yet for that very reason all the more uncanny.

Žižek's use of the word, 'uncanny', is well chosen. For Freud, a sense of the uncanny is related to what is frightening, 'to what arouses dread and horror' (Freud, 1985: 339). It is also prompted by a feeling that the strange (*unheimlich*) is somehow vaguely familiar (*heimlich*):

> *heimlich* is a word the meaning of which develops in the direction of ambivalence, until it finally coincides with its opposite, *unheimlich* ...

we can understand why linguistic usage has extended *das Heimliche* ['homely'] into its opposite, *das Unheimliche*; for this uncanny is in reality nothing new or alien, but something which is familiar and old-established in the mind and which has become alienated from it only through the process of repression.

(Freud, 1985: 347 and 363–4)

In his essay, 'The Uncanny', Freud relates this feeling to a number of different figures and contexts, among which waxworks, dolls, automata are listed (ibid.: 347). Freud also relates the uncanny to a primitive fear of the dead (ibid.: 365), to a fear of insanity (ibid.: 347), to effacement of the distinction between imagination and reality (ibid.: 367), and to a womb-complex (ibid.: 368), all features of our responses to the Norman-mother figure, or of Norman's mental state. Fear of insanity and of the dead are clearly dominant in the film's reception by the audience, as they are in many examples of the genre. Given Norman's mother-fixation, the womb-complex is especially relevant. Freud explains the link between a womb-complex and the ambivalence of the uncanny:

It often happens that neurotic men declare that they feel there is something uncanny about the female genital organs. This *unheimlich* place, however, is the entrance to the former *Heim* [home] of all human beings, to the place where each one of us lived once upon a time and in the beginning ... the *unheimlich* is what was once *heimisch*, familiar; the prefix *'un'* ['un-'] is the token of repression.

(ibid.: 368)

The uncanny feeling associated with 'waxwork' or 'doll' figures also seems particularly pertinent to Hitchcock's film. Norman has stuffed his dead mother, whom he proceeds to treat like a living person, although the corpse is of course more like a waxwork or doll. Freud recounts a tale by Hoffman, 'The Sand-man', which concerns a doll that appears to be alive. Filmic examples of the uncanny effect produced by the apparent animation of the inanimate abound. For instance, in the British horror film *Magic* (Richard Attenborough, 1978), a ventriloquist's dummy gradually assumes control of his master's mind. Both examples inspire terror in a most effective way.

This perception of the Norman-mother figure as a doll is reinforced by the disembodied voice. In the final scene of the film, the voice we hear from Norman's lips, the voice of the mother, is a disturbingly uncanny voice which, as Chion rightly observes, 'is the sort of tight-lipped voice characteristic of spirit possession or ventriloquism' (Chion, 1992: 204).

It is not until this final scene that we become fully aware of the dislocation within Norman's psyche, of the split between the murderous mother side of his personality and his own sexually inadequate and guilt-racked ego. Chion talks about 'the monstrous fused couple, the two-backed beast of the primal scene, the impossible couple of body and voice' and asks 'why there is something horrible about this contact' (Ibid.: 203). One possible answer to this question may lie in the bizarre incongruity between body and voice. Reading the film backwards, the spectator remembers Norman's maternal cross-dressing and the further incongruity of body with clothing and wig. Both incongruities and the horror they evoke are metonymically associated with transvestism and the phenomenon of transgender in general. The penultimate image of the film, which dissolves Norman's gaze into the camera into the mother's skull is a powerful fusion of ideas. The image reads as a gruesome visual metaphor for the shifting of gender and the breakdown of identity in the context of psychosis, murder and death.

The phallic mother

In almost every salient respect, the imaginary mother figure of *Psycho* is a 'phallic woman', as defined by Freud and others. The notion of the 'phallic woman' originates in Freud's theory of fetishism which he first presents in his essay, 'Fetishism': 'the fetish is a substitute for the woman's (the mother's) penis that the little boy once believed in and – for reasons familiar to us – does not want to give up' (Freud, 1984: 352). This phallic mother figuratively castrates her son to the extent that his own personality is eventually entirely submerged by hers. In Jungian terms, too, 'mother-castration' is Bates's condition: 'A present-day son who remains, beyond childhood, obedient to his mother effectually castrates himself. His sexual life belongs not to himself but to her … The irrationality of his fear points to the awesome power of guilt and its connection with auto-castration in the unconscious' (Monick, 1991: 87–8). Norman's sexual impotence (he is afraid of women's sexuality, and can only express himself erotically through incomplete masturbation) is sign and symptom of his castration. In a physical and material sense, 'mother' is imaged in phallic dimensions: 'she' is associated exclusively with the verticality of the house (see above), and her body is kept bolt upright in her rocking-chair. In the scenes representing the murders of Marion and the detective and the attempted murder of Marion's sister, Lila, 'she' is to all intents and purposes a woman wielding a knife. We remember that, with the exception of the 'unveiling scene' of Lila's attempted murder, the audience have no reason to doubt that this figure is a feminine one, and that the spectator is thus unconsciously invited to identify the figure as a phallic woman, and not as a man dressed in women's clothes. This is especially true of the first two scenes in which this figure corresponds closely to the unconscious image of the castrating phallic woman. In all cases, the knife, masculine symbol of violence and power and phallic in shape, stands in for the missing phallus. Moreover, the knife blows are delivered from above in repeated vertical strokes that, like the house, have the shape of the phallic, and that both literally and figuratively are signs of a superior force usually associated with the masculine.

This castration motif is also identifiable in a focus on the eyes of attack victims, and on Norman's own eyes at the end of the film, by which time he himself has become a victim – in this case, of the castrating mother within him. In the shower scene, the woman's knife appears to make multiple penetrations of Marion's body. Marion sinks to the floor, as blood runs down the plug-hole, a literal draining away of life. This shot then dissolves into a shot of her open but lifeless eye, signifier of a knowledge extinguished in death. In the staircase murder scene, although the camera focuses on Abogast's face and wildly flailing arms, as he falls backwards down the stairs, it is his eyes that rivet our attention – the intensity of expression of shock, fear and terror. In the scene in which Norman attempts to murder Lila, who has come to the motel and house to investigate her sister's disappearance, it is the empty eye-sockets of the mother's skull that draw our attention. Having retreated to the fruit cellar when Norman enters the house, Lila discovers the mother's mummified body and in fright, sends a light-bulb swinging to and fro. The knife-wielding Norman rushes in dressed as his mother, and launches himself at Lila but is disarmed by Sam Loomis, Marion's lover. The scene ends with a focus on the skull, its eye-sockets alternately in light and shadow in rhythm with the swaying bulb. In the penultimate scene of the film, in which the figure of Norman-mother sits wrapped in a blanket, it is once again the eyes that occupy the central focus, becoming decidedly demonic as they stare directly into the camera before the dissolve into the skull of the mother.

In a well-known passage in 'The Uncanny', Freud links fear of blindness, or of any assault on the eyes, with both the uncanny and castration-anxiety. This passage is worth quoting at some length:

> We know from psychoanalytic experience ... that the fear of damaging or losing one's eyes is a terrible one in children. Many adults retain their apprehensiveness in this respect, and no physical injury is so much dreaded by them as an injury to the eye ... A study of dreams, phantasies and myths has taught us that anxiety about one's eyes, the fear of going blind, is often enough a substitute for the dread of being castrated. The self-blinding of the mythical criminal, Oedipus, was simply a mitigated form of the punishment of castration – the only punishment that was adequate for him by the *lex talionis*. We may try on rationalistic grounds to deny that fears about the eye are derived from the fear of castration, and may argue that it is very natural that so precious an organ as the eye should be guarded by a proportionate dread. Indeed, we might go further and say that the fear of castration itself contains no other significance and no deeper secret than a justifiable dread of this rational kind. But this view does not account adequately for the substitutive relationship between the eye and the male organ which is seen to exist in dreams and myths and phantasies; nor can it dispel the impression that the threat of being castrated in especial excites a peculiarly violent and obscure emotion, and that this emotion is what first gives the idea of losing other organs its intense colouring. All further doubts are removed when we learn the details of their 'castration-complex' from the analysis of neurotic patients, and realize its immense importance in their mental life.
>
> (Freud, 1985: 352–3)

Freud here notes the association between fear of blinding and castration-anxiety with mother-son incest (Oedipus). In Oedipus' case, self-blinding is the only acceptable punishment (we must assume, therefore, that it is regarded in the myth as worse than, or at the very least, as a substitute for death). Freud also emphasises the metaphorical substitution of eye for male genitals, and the exceptional emotion aroused by the threat of castration, to the extent that it surpasses the fear of 'losing other organs'. Reading between the lines, castration is, therefore, for

Freud a symbolic death. Norman's excessive attachment to his mother is clearly incestuous in a metaphorical and symbolic, if not a real sense. But in his confused psyche, all sexual guilt, as we have seen, is projected onto the young women he encounters, and upon whom the 'punishment of castration' must therefore be inflicted, as scapegoats for his sexual crimes: it is they who must be castrated in his place. It is equally arguable that the 'mother' part of his psyche similarly displaces punishment from her beloved son to those objects of desire that contrast with, detract from, and so indirectly draw attention to his incest.

Freud's essay also includes a passage on 'the dread of the evil eye' as 'one of the most uncanny and widespread forms of superstition' (ibid.: 362). Hitchcock's focus on the eyes of his victims in both of the murder scenes implies a vicarious function. In both cases, this focus occurs at the precise moment of death.

In the shower scene, Marion's open but lifeless eye appears to reflect a retreating shadowy evil, while Abogast's eyes express a mixture of shock, horror, and the extinction of life. Again in both cases, the surprise in the victims' eyes may in part be attributable to a discovery which the audience do not share – the real identity of the killer. In this sense, then, their eyes are displacements of the 'evil eye' in that they reflect an evil presence. One might say, finally, that by the time he is in custody in the police cell, Norman's gaze has been completely stolen from him by his mother. Thus, the film ends with the mother's castrating 'evil eye' once again made flesh.

In summary, then, the clear linking of the knife attacks with the victims' eyes suggests that the murders operate on an unconscious level as metaphors of a castration which is strongly associated with the cross-dressed phallic woman. Such metaphors combine with the motifs of dislocation that run through the diegesis to create a powerfully negative perception of shifting gender identity. Transgender and horror are thus subtly intertwined in *Psycho* in a complex network of conscious and unconscious signifiers and signifieds.

Dressed to Kill (Brian de Palma, 1980)

Brian de Palma's homage to Hitchcock, *Dressed to Kill* exhibits strong structural and thematical similarities to *Psycho*, aspects which some critics have found derivative and unoriginal, while others, such as

Garber, have emphasised the way in which the film reflects a more topical anxiety about physical transformation:

> Both Myra (Breckinridge) and Bobbi (in *Dressed to Kill*) mark trans-sexualism as a site of cultural anxiety so profound that it manifests itself in psychosis – the psychosis of the character absorbing and displacing, if it does, the public's fears about crossing these forbidden boundaries. … By locating Bobbi/Robert specifically and medically on the borderline ('pre-op transsexual') Brian de Palma's film capitalizes on the increased anxiety that the possibility of surgical transformation permits. In this the film shows its difference from Hitchcock's cross-dressing landmark *Psycho* (1960), to which it is greatly indebted, by moving the focus of attention from the mind to the body.
>
> (Garber, 1993: 115–16)

Carol J. Clover describes the similarities with apparent objectivity, but her use of the word 'imitation' betrays a thinly-veiled contempt for de Palma's film:

> The notion of a killer propelled by psychosexual fury, more particularly a male in gender distress, has proved a durable one, and the progeny of Norman Bates stalks the genre up to the present day. Just as Norman wears his mother's clothes during his acts of violence and is thought, by the screen characters and also, for a while, by the film's spectators to *be* his mother, so the murderer in the *Psycho* imitation, *Dressed to Kill* (1980), a transvestite psychiatrist, seems until his unveiling to be a woman; like Norman, he must kill women who arouse him sexually.
>
> (Clover, 1996: 75)

Shelley Stamp Lindsey also draws attention to the *Psycho*-inspired shower attacks with which *Dressed to Kill* begins and ends, but is no more measured in her appraisal of de Palma's films generally, which she describes pointedly as 'notorious for their allusions to Hitchcock' (Lindsey, 1996: 294). We might add that, as in Hitchcock's film, it is thanks to the determination of a young woman rather than a man (which was far more typical of the genre) that the cross-dressed serial-killer of young women is eventually run to earth, although the sexism inherent in other aspects of the film tends to overshadow this otherwise positive feature from the perspective of a gender politics. That de Palma also borrows from his own earlier film, *Carrie* (1976), on the other hand, might be viewed as a piece of ludic self-irony: as in *Carrie*, the killer appears to return in a final scene to attack the victim, though this turns out to be just a bad dream.

The extent to which de Palma is an unscrupulous (self)-plagiarist, or a postmodern film-maker whose work is enlivened by ironic allusions to earlier work is, as the above examples suggest, a matter of individual perception. *Dressed to Kill*, I would argue, can be read either way, depending perhaps on your political agenda. Those critics who show contempt for his work on grounds of its voyeuristic and misogynist depiction of women are less likely to take a sympathetic view of the self-reflexivity of this work within the horror genre.[3] No critic has to date read this film in terms of its negative representation of transgender, which is nevertheless a central aspect of the film narrative and inextricably linked, as we shall see, to the representation of gender in general and of the feminine in particular.

The female victims, Kate Miller (Angie Dickinson) and Liz Blake (Nancy Allen), are both represented as 'bad girls', who, in the words of the investigating policeman, are 'asking to be murdered'. Kate is portrayed as a sexually frustrated wife who seeks satisfaction in the arms of a sinister stranger, while Liz is a call-girl. There is an implication here that women like Kate who go out looking for sex, or Liz who is a prostitute, 'deserve everything they get'. In contrast, it is technology, coded masculine, that helps to solve the crime of Kate's murder, as Kate's son, Peter, installs a hidden camera outside Dr Elliott's surgery to record the comings and goings of suspects. This implicit privileging of the masculine over the feminine is reiterated later in the narrative when Peter jokes with Liz about 'making a woman out of himself' as his next project. After she has explained to him in some detail what reassignment surgery for transsexuals involves, he is quick to change his mind, saying that he will 'stick to his computer' after all – a symbolic choice of the masculine over the feminine on the part of a young man who appears undecided about his sexuality. Like Peter, we are both horrified and fascinated by Liz's description. As Garber rightly observes, the element of physical and surgical possibility heightens the fascination, ups the stakes (Garber, 1993: 115–16).

The male gaze, moreover, is adequately rewarded in shots of Kate in the shower, and especially, in scenes in Dr Elliott's office towards the end of the film, in which the young and sexy Liz strips off to bra and panties, fetishistically enhanced by stockings and suspenders. In line with Laura Mulvey's theory of a visual pleasure reserved for the male spectator, the latter is thus invited to share Elliott's objectifying gaze (see Mulvey, 2003). Some critics have consequently condemned the film as following the male-centred tradition of representing the woman principally as a source of visual pleasure for the active male subject and his spectator counterpart. Compared with Clarice in *Lambs*, both Kate and Liz have been described as passive, eroticised objects (Liz's active role in resolving the murder of Kate is undermined both by Peter's male surveillance technology and by the heroic act of the male policeman who shoots Elliott dead as (s)he is about to deliver the oblivious Liz a fatal knife thrust).

Clearly, then, de Palma's film is vulnerable to attack on the grounds of its titillating, sexist and misogynist contents. But *Dressed to Kill* can also be read as demonising transsexuals. The title immediately draws our attention to the sartorial theme, juxtaposing dress and murder in a clichéd expression that links clothing with female sexual attraction. But the depiction of female sexual promiscuity as culpable and deserving of punishment seems incompatible with a title that makes the sexually provocative dresser into the murderer, not the victim. It is Elliott's cross-dressing persona, the would-be transsexual Bobbi who kills, not the biological women of the narrative. If *Dressed to Kill* is misogynist, it is also gender-normative.

The condition of transsexualism is itself represented in entirely negative terms. There is no attempt, as in *Psycho* or *Lambs*, to distance the narrative and its homicidal themes from transgender proper: Bobbi's 'I'm a girl inside this man's body and I gotta get out!' is typical of the discourse of real male-to-female transsexuals.[4] Moreover, the stock psychiatrist figure, Dr Levy, is there to confirm a diagnosis of transsexualism, a condition which is negatively defined in terms of a conflict between the masculine and the feminine, leading to psychosis and murder. Levy's explanation reads more like popular psychology than expert opinion:

> DR LEVY: He was a transsexual ... about to make the final step, but his male side couldn't let him do it. There was Dr Elliott and there was Bobbi. Bobbi came to me to get psychiatric approval for a sex-reassignment operation. I thought he was unstable and Elliott confirmed my diagnosis. Opposite sexes inhabiting the same body. The sex-change operation was to resolve the conflict. But as

much as Bobbi tried to get it, Elliott blocked it ... so Bobbi got even.

DETECTIVE MARINO: By killing Mrs Miller?

DR LEVY: Yes. She aroused Eliott just as you did, Miss Blake.

LIZ: You mean, when Elliott got turned on, Bobbi took over?

DR LEVY: Yes, it was like Bobbi's red alert. Elliott's penis became erect and Bobbi took control, trying to kill anyone that made Elliott masculinely sexual. When Elliott came to my office, it was the first time I saw Bobbi's masculine self. When he told me that he thought Bobbi had killed Mrs Miller, he was confessing himself.

The underlying message is that transsexuals are potentially dangerous deviants, psychotic schizophrenics (Elliott has two warring personalities, one male, one female) who cannot be trusted. The convergence in this film of transsexuality and psychiatry suggests that the former is an illness that requires treatment.

The residual masculinity (and indeed machismo nature) of transsexuals is emphasised in a scene in which Elliott watches a very masculine-looking transsexual on television, while Liz arranges to meet a client on the phone and then puts on make-up as she prepares herself for her escort date. The screen is split between Eliott and Liz throughout, with at times the added image of the TV screen making a three-way split. Both Liz and Eliott look at their reflections in mirrors (see below). At one point, Liz asks if the client has any special requests. When she is told no, her delight is evident in a telling line: 'Thank God straight fucks are still in style!' The juxtaposition of Liz's conversation with the transsexual interview implies a contrast between normality on the one hand (a 'real' woman and 'normal' heterosexuality) and perversion on the other (a 'fake' woman who has forsaken heterosexual marital relations). The TV interview, an actual clip which, according to the credits, is shown by arrangement with Phil Donahue, a well-known American talk-show host, is worth quoting because, despite its alleged authenticity, it places a misleading emphasis on the masculinity of male-to-female transsexuals, and depicts transsexualism as a struggle for dominance between the two genders:

INTERVIEWEE: I was a war-correspondent, among other things ... I did a lot of police-reporting, I dove on Spanish treasure wrecks.

INTERVIEWER: You did a lot of macho things, then?

INTERVIEWEE: This is very common among transsexuals ... an awful lot of [male-to-female transsexuals] have real macho backgrounds. I know a police-captain, a West-Pointer, a couple of fighter-pilots ... hmm, most of them tried real hard.

INTERVIEWER: You were married twice, you were also the father of three children. Hmm, so you enjoyed ... the traditional role of father ... and you have engaged in at least two heterosexual relationships.

INTERVIEWEE: Oh, more than that. I've always been a devout heterosexual!

There is, finally, a hint of fetishism, and of a link between fetishism and violence, in the final scenes of the film. Elliott-Bobbi has once again cross-dressed in the uniform (and, we assume the fetishistic underwear, comprising stockings and suspenders) of the nurse he has strangled to escape from detention in the asylum. In a scene which is both a homage to Hitchcock and an echo of the film's opening sequence, he lies in wait for Liz, as she takes a shower. A white nurse's shoe protruding around the doorway betrays his presence to the terrified Liz. Transsexualism is here bracketed with the related fetishism of stockings and shoes which is in turn bracketed with perversion and murder. Moreover, these fetishistic elements combine with the machismo aspect mentioned above to imply that male-to-female transsexuals are phallic women, with inherently masculine psyches, beset by castration-anxiety. We recall that Freud defines the fetish 'as a substitute for the woman's (the mother's) penis that the little boy once believed in and ... does not want to give up' (Freud, 1984: 352); it is also 'a triumph over the threat of castration and a protection against it' (ibid.: 353; and see section on *Psycho* above for discussion of 'phallic women').

'Bobbi' is true to this stereotype of the castration-complex as underlying the desire of many transsexuals for surgery. The procedures described in such detail by Liz to Peter have been interpreted by some psychiatrists as a yearning for self-castration. Such a yearning is clearly at odds with the phallicism mentioned above, but this conflict is at the heart of the split between Elliott and Bobbi: while the former fears the castration threatened by Bobbi, the latter sees it as an act to be committed against Elliott, as distinct from Bobbi as a separate persona. When she is denied the knife of surgery, Bobbi cuts open those women who stand in her way by arousing Elliott as a man. Gender reassignment surgery is thus implicitly bracketed with violent knife attacks. Both involve a tearing open of the body and both may endanger life, but most importantly, the projection in this film of the violence of male-to-female reassignment surgery into homicidal rage is hardly a positive model of transsexuality. Bobbi's use of Elliott's razor to cut women suggests a symbolic appropriation of the phallus: 'I'm glad I took care of that cock-teaser. And you would have done the same thing yourself' she tells Elliott, after Kate's murder, 'I guess that's why I used your razor.' Appropriating Elliott's phallic power, she symbolically castrates Elliott by removing the female objects that arouse him. Her attacks are also interpretable as a symbolic castration of the women themselves. As a witness to her murder of Kate – in retrieving the razor used to kill Kate, Liz has symbolically sided with the masculine – and as a sexually attractive young woman, Liz is doubly targeted: 'I'm going to cut those spying eyes out!' shrieks Bobbi in a phone-message to Elliott, recalling the direct link observed by Freud between blinding and castration.[5] Both castrating (Bobbi) and castrated (Kate, Liz, and all women), women are thus shown to be the damaged and dangerous creatures that the male unconscious has always known them to be.[6] The character of Bobbi implies that the same goes for transsexuals.

The shifting boundaries between the real and the imagined, between self and (m)other that we have seen to occupy an important space in the narrative of *Psycho* are also central to the themes and structures of *Dressed to Kill*, connoting mental instability and ultimately, irremedial psychosis. This slippage is foregrounded by the framing device of the first and last scenes of the film, in which apparently real events are revealed to be the products of dreams and fantasies. The film begins with a slow and dreamy sequence, in which Kate Miller fantasises about masturbating in the shower, her fantasy brutally interrupted by the sensation of being violently raped. Cut to the bedroom where she is in reality being maritally near-raped by her insensitive and inattentive husband. The final scene, as already noted, is also the product of the unconscious, this time expressing unresolved fears. Both scenes are extremely violent, both depict female victims of men, and both are deceptions, designed to convince the audience that they are real. Liz's continuing terror even after she is awakened by Peter whom she treats as an attacker underlines the fuzziness of the borders between reality and nightmare, between the conscious and the unconscious.

Unclear images in mirrors and glass contribute to this sense of a shifting and unfocused line between the real and the imaginary. Such images are recurrent motifs throughout, reflecting illusory desires and fears. Kate is unable to see properly through the steamed-up doors of her shower cubicle. During the transsexual TV interview, the audience's attention is confusingly divided between three different parts of the film-screen, depicting Liz, Elliott and the TV-screen, which may be read as representing the three genders of woman, man and transsexual, around which the story turns. The 'drag' appearance of the middle-aged transsexual interviewee compares unfavourably with the youth and beauty of the biological woman, Liz. Throughout the scene, mirrors again feature prominently: Liz is seen in reflection only as she makes up, and Elliott glances from the TV to his own reflection in the desk-top mirror. In this instance, the notion of self-image and identity takes specular shape as the transsexual provides a spoken commentary on the subject, and the splitting of the audience focus between three different images in glass renders identification of meaning in the scene intentionally problematic.

Elliott misrecognises himself as Bobbi in the mirror sitting on his desk and smiles knowingly at his (her?) reflection as he prepares to assume Bobbi's clothing and persona to kill Liz. Bobbi smiles back and Elliott begins to undress prior to donning the 'Bobbi' clothes and blond wig. Peter trusts the male technology of the time-set camera to monitor the comings and goings at Elliott's surgery, but the similarly male technology of his binoculars later fails him as he stands outside the surgery in the rain trying to keep a watch on Liz inside – all he and the audience see through the rain-soaked and steamed-up windows are blurred images. In the final dream-sequence, Liz thinks she sees Bobbi's reflection in the bathroom mirror, but once again, the mirror turns out to be merely a feint in the wider feint of her nightmare. Specular images may be delusory, threatening a sense of secure and stable selfhood. Liz, however, is able to separate reality and illusion. In contrast, the transsexual, who returns his/her own gaze in the mirror (Gumb does this too in *Lambs*) is especially dangerous because of the psychosis implied in this gesture of misrecognition. We might usefully note, in this context, the importance for Jacques Lacan of the mirror-stage, its role in the Oedipal phase, in the formation of the identity of the ego, and the ego's acquisition of an ability to separate the imaginary from the symbolic and the real. Lacan emphasises the visual character of the subject's self-identification, and the crucial role played by the mirror in helping the subject to construct an ideal, imaginary unity:

> The mirror stage is interesting in that it manifests the affective dynamism by which the subject originally identifies himself with the visual *Gestalt* of his own body ... it represents an ideal unity, a salutary *imago*.
>
> (Lacan, 1977a: 18–19)

One might conclude from Elliott/Bobbi's dependence on his/her mirror-image that (s)he is suffering a regression to the mirror-stage, where a new female self is being constructed in this specular imaginary.

The gesture of connecting with the specular gaze is at once a *mise en abyme* and a symbolic enactment of the link between transgender and psychosis underpinning the narrative of de Palma's film. When the imaginary self behind the mirror has emerged to assume total control, the would-be transsexual is once again (cross-)dressed to kill.

The Silence of the Lambs (Jonathan Demme, 1991)

At the start of this highly successful thriller, based on a novel by Thomas Harris, four women have been murdered (and a fifth has been kidnapped) by a 'would-be' transsexual who has been turned down for gender reassignment surgery. Eaten away with resentment for all women who are what he is not, Jame Gumb resorts to killing and skinning women in order to 'put on' their skins – hence his nickname in the press, Buffalo Bill.

Buffalo Bill stuffs a death's-head moth into the mouth of each of his victims. Hannibal Lecter (Anthony Hopkins), the imprisoned serial-killer who helps the young FBI agent, Clarice Starling (Jodie Foster) to solve the mystery of Buffalo Bill's identity, explains why:

LECTER: The significance of the moth is change: caterpillar into crysallis, or pupa, from thence into beauty. Our Billy wants to change too.

CLARICE: There's no corollation in the literature between transsexualism and violence. Transsexuals are very passive ...

LECTER: Clever girl! ... Billy is not a real transsexual, but he thinks he is, he tries to be. He's tried to be a lot of things, I expect.

We may explore the death's-head moth's meaning in more depth. It is a question of visual deception, the moth taking on the features of a mimicked object. The impression conveyed unconsciously here is that transsexualism is a condition dependent on the trickery of mimicry. For Slavoj Žižek, the moth's design aims also to return the subject's gaze – a disturbing mirroring of the viewer's voyeuristic desires. As we shall see below, the gaze is central to the representation of Buffalo Bill's transsexualism (Žižek, 1992: 264–5, n.11).[7] Lecter tells Clarice to investigate centres for reassignment surgery. 'Billy' will have been rejected for this, he says, on the grounds of

> severe childhood disturbances associated with violence. Our Billy wasn't born a criminal, Clarice, he was made one through years of systematic abuse. Billy hates his own identity and he thinks that makes him a transsexual, but his pathology is a thousand times more savage, more terrifying.

In spite of this politically-correct denial, embedded in the film script, that the killer is a transsexual, the question of what a transsexual is remains unanswered. In the absence of a more profound debate on this issue in the film narrative, the conventionally accepted definition of transsexuality turns upon the desire to change sex, either hormonally or via surgery. Annabelle Willox (2003: 414) observes that, under the technical definition of transsexuality, it is the desire for surgery that classifies a person as a transsexual, but she rightly points out in a note (423 n.9) that this definition is questionable since there will be cases where surgery is not necessary or not desired. Julie Tharp, on the other hand, sees Gumb as homosexual, thus critically evacuating the transsexual theme (Tharp, 2003: online version, 3; and see Chapter 1, 'Sex, gender, sexuality' and Chapter 6 for further discussion of the problem of definition in relation to transsexuals).

Tharp's interpretation notwithstanding, the notion of gender change is central to the killer's motivation and, as we saw above, to his modus operandi, even if his conception of that change is a deeply perverted one. The title itself, which refers to a recurrent nightmare of Clarice's, carries connotations of anxiety in relation to death, but also in relation to change. Clarice recounts a traumatic childhood event to Lecter. Following the murder of her policeman father, the ten-year-old Clarice was sent to stay with cousins on a ranch in Montana. During her stay, she was awoken early one morning by the screaming of spring lambs about to be slaughtered. She tried unsuccessfully to rescue these lambs, with which she clearly identifies: both she and the lambs are orphaned, lambs are coded feminine in our cultural imaginary (Mary had a little lamb, for example, metonymically linking lambs with young girls), both are represented as fearing violent death; Clarice identifying here with her murdered father, another 'sacrificial lamb'. But in addition to being a symbol of sacrifice, the lamb is also an emblem of transformation or renewal:

> Its etymology suggests ... that *agnus* is related to the Greek *agnos* and therefore symbolizes the unknown; and that it is also related to *agni* (fire) and so is a sacrificial symbol of the periodic renovation of the world.
>
> (Cirlot, 1993: 176)

We remember, too, that it is from fire that the phoenix of myth emerges, reborn, while the lamb is literally shorn or skinned, a metaphor for Buffalo Bill's flaying of his own female sacrificial victims. The association in Clarice's traumatic memory of the lamb, symbol of transformation, with violence and death thus metonymically infects the theme of gender change with highly negative connotations. This association mingles with the monstrosity of Gumb's methods of achieving transformation and with his deeply misogynistic motivations to produce a frighteningly dark portrait of transsexuality. The metaphor of the death's-head moth signifies not only a desire for change, but a desire to be beautiful, as Lecter himself explains. In a culture in which beauty is coded feminine, it is hard to see how this desire is incompatible with male-to-female transsexualism. Moreover, Gumb exhibits traits that are recognisable characteristics of transsexuals. He feminizes himself with brightly-coloured clothing, make-up and nipple-rings, adopts at times a less masculine tone of voice, and identifies himself as effeminate if not feminine in his choice of dog, a miniature poodle he preciously names 'Precious' (the poodle has become the clichéd choice of the effeminate gay man). Above all, the gruesome use of his female victims is not just a symbolic but a real substitute, providing him with the skin or body casing which he feels he has been denied by the medical profession.[8] In this sense, Gumb is both transsexual *and* transvestite: trained as a tailor, he makes himself a girl-suit out of real girls.

This is a literalization of the idea, more akin to transvestism than transsexuality, that gender is a matter of appearance alone, an image that can be visually performed, as if the essence of the feminine resided solely at the surface of the body. At the same time, Gumb is undeniably transsexual in his orientation and not simply transvestite or homosexual. However, his understanding of transsexuality is a superficial one that undermines the claims of transsexuals to be taken seriously. Judith Halberstam describes the film as a 'skinflick', drawing attention to the way in which, by representing the transsexual murderer as motivated by the desire to wear the skins of his girl-victims, it demonises the feeling, common to the transsexual, of being 'in the wrong skin' and wishing to replace it with the skin of the opposite sex (Halberstam, 1991: 43). Halberstam's argument that the killer's treatment of his victims' bodies as bags into which identity is stitched 'challenges the heterosexist and misogynist constructions of humanness, the naturalness, the interiority of gender' (ibid.: 51) is a Butlerian one that does not promote the cause of real transsexuals. Such a view of gender as a surface phenomenon (a view encouraged by Butler's theory of performativity) trivialises transsexualism, relegating it to a purely cosmetic and vestimentary level. The transformation desired by the transsexual is a profound one, touching all physical, hormonal and psychological dimensions of the individual.[9]

Indeed, Gumb is seen to focus on the surface of his body, privileging the superficiality of the visual. In other words, the man who wants to be a woman retains masculine priorities of which the gaze is paramount. 'We covet what we see' Lecter tells Clarice, a line that encapsulates the significance of the male gaze. In a shot that is revealing in more than just the physical sense, the killer admires himself semi-naked in a full-length mirror, wearing only a multi-coloured cloth draped over his shoulders like the wings of a butterfly, his penis and testicles tucked out of sight between his legs, creating the visual and for him satisfying illusion of having a female anatomy. He thus performs the feminine, to the point of effecting a painless castration. For Diane Dubois, Gumb's idea of femininity is a wholly negative one, 'expressed in excessively glamorous drag'. Moreover, as Dubois points out, he projects the pain of his self-castration onto his female victims (Dubois, 2001: 301–2). We would add that, in so doing, he is repeatedly and morbidly re-enacting the castration of all girls imagined in the male unconscious.

In contrast to the negativity of Gumb's residual masculinity in the context of the representation of transsexuality, critics have argued that Lecter and Clarice Starling do not conform to their respective genders, and that this aspect of the film's characterisation is a positive one in relation to the representation of gender generally. Dubois claims that Lecter and Clarice 'blur conventional boundaries between gender traits'. While Clarice is masculinised, she argues, Lecter displays stereotypically feminine qualities (Dubois, 2001: 302 and 308). While I would agree that Lecter does exhibit refined tastes in food, wine, music, art and intellectual pursuits generally, it seems excessive and just a little sexist to regard these qualities as 'feminine'. The tendency to read Clarice as masculine or even as lesbian (see Tharp, 1991; and Dubois, 2001: 302 and 309 n.4 – Dubois notes that Starling was widely perceived by the viewers to be unfeminine) is probably motivated, as Dubois suggests, by gay identification with Jody Foster, the actress playing the role. In fact, on any objective evaluation, Foster plays Starling as an insecure young woman in a man's world, trying hard to masculinise herself in order to compete and prove herself to her male superiors. Foster's pretty features, petite slim figure and charming Southern lisp are enhanced in many scenes by lipstick and blushing cheeks, all of which convey a femininity which the character is doing her best to suppress for the sake of her career as an FBI agent. She is shown to fail to match her male colleagues on a purely physical level. Tharp maintains that she is 'attractive in her tough, self-controlled manner' (Tharp, 1991: 4), but on the contrary, she is constantly unsure of herself, and when confronted with danger, visibly shaken and rattled. The result is that we admire her determination, yet warm to her vulnerability.

This preoccupation on the part of feminist critics with the gender of Lecter and Starling tends to detract attention from the equally important issue of Gumb's transsexuality, except where in Lecter's case, the bracketing of feminine traits with monstrosity mirrors and reinforces a similar juxtaposition in the figure of Gumb.[10]

Ultimately, then, it is difficult not to read *Silence of the Lambs* in terms of anxiety about transgender. The film represents Gumb as a case of confused gender identity and this, together with the masculinity of his gaze, conveys a generally negative impression. The implied messages are that gender dysphoria is a state of uncertainty in which the subject hovers between the masculine and the feminine, a state of confusion that might even lead to psychosis and murder.[11] Furthermore, as Dubois observes, 'the killing off of Gumb has the *appearance* of reasserting gender hegemony' (Dubois, 2001: 303).

Cherry Falls (Geoffrey Wright, 2000)[12]

According to the perverse morality of most teen horror films, it is the sexually promiscuous girls who become the victims of the psychotic killer, their murder implicitly perceived as the ultimate penalty for their sins (for example, *Halloween*). In our most recent example of the thriller genre, the teen slasher movie, *Cherry Falls*, this situation is ironically reversed, so that the killer preys on young virgins, encouraging the local teenage population to lose rather than preserve their virginity. A postmodern film in its ludic ironies and self-referentiality, this film typifies developments in the genre towards a more comic self-awareness and self-commentary, and as such bears some similarity to the recent *Scream* series (small-town high-school, teen characters, lewd adolescent humour). On the other hand, while the script often wittily shares intertextual references with an audience assumed to be familiar with well-known examples of the slasher genre, the narrative betrays clichéd and profoundly normative characteristics. Representations of gender are dictated by a conservative agenda that serves the simplistic moral code of small-town America. This code reinforces the Lacanian symbolic by promoting the Father's Law and by demonising deviations from this law in the form of transgressive manifestations of gender and sexuality. In particular, *Cherry Falls* follows the other thrillers we have been discussing in this chapter in identifying transgender with homicidal psychosis.

The transparent puns of the film's title strike a self-consciously tongue-in-cheek note: while 'Cherry Falls' is the name of the small town in which the murders take place, 'Cherry' clearly alludes to the issue of virginity that must be lost to stay safe (as in the colloquial expression, 'to lose one's cherry' which figures in the flier advertising a party organised by the teenagers: 'Pop Your Cherry Tonight!'), while 'Falls' suggests both loss and sexual release, as visually symbolised by the waterfalls that give the town its name.

The film both begins and ends significantly with images of these falls. It is here that the first victims, a young couple, are parked up in what is obviously a favourite trysting-place for young lovers. The final frame, however, directly links sex with death by showing the waters turning blood red, a clumsy metaphorical full-stop dispelling any residual doubt about this association. (Sex and death are inevitably linked in an era dominated by fear of AIDS.) Thus, the ostensibly postmodern dissolves into cliché, as the extended punning on 'cherry' and the colour red that can be traced throughout the film are seen to have stereotypical connotations that serve a normative agenda.

As the colour of blood, red is conventionally associated with passion, but also with danger: the two coincide in loss of virginity (which is often accompanied by bleeding), as well as in menstruation which signals the onset of puberty in girls and the potential for sexual activity and child-bearing. Much of the narrative is concerned with the dilemma confronting Jody (Brittany Murphy), the main character, a latter-day Little Red Riding-hood of seventeen who wears red clothes and paints her toe-nails red: should she or shouldn't she sleep with her boyfriend of one year's standing, Kenny (no pun intended!)? The violent associations of red are foregrounded in a scene in which Jody tries to persuade Kenny to have sex with her: she asks him to bite her red-painted toes harder and harder, but Kenny is visibly repulsed by this masochistic display – it is as if Jody's penchant for red brings out an unattractive violent streak which even her boyfriend finds unacceptable. Red nails are, in fact, a dominant motif in the film, since, until his eventual unmasking, the killer's presence is denoted by them. Along with a female wig, red finger-nails feature prominently in all shots of the killer, and help to deceive the audience into thinking that the killer is a woman. One such shot early in the film directly links these with potential violence, as the killer's red-varnished fingers are shown sharpening kitchen knives. There is, in fact, a vampiric quality about this particular murderer: in the opening scene, he licks the blood from the face of the girl he has nailed to a tree and is about to torture and kill, and according to the police, 'a lot of blood was pumped out of her (numerous) wounds ... while she was still alive!'; in the final scenes in which he pursues Jody brandishing a large knife, facial close-ups show blood dripping from his mouth; and finally, he is staked through the heart, having been hurled through an upstairs window by Jody to land on the spikes of a garden fence below. The cross-dresser in this film is not just a homicidal maniac, he is also a metaphorical blood-sucking vampire! Red – and in particular, the red of the cross-dresser's finger-nails – is, therefore, connotive throughout *Cherry Falls* of the mortal dangers that are associated with taboo forms of gender and sexual behaviour, whether transvestism or teenage sex before marriage.[13] The bracketing of transvestism with taboo sex thus reinforces normative ways of thinking with regard to both. In addition to pre-marital sex, both rape and incest represent undesirable expressions of sexual desire that can have lethal consequences, and which must be defended against and punished by the Father's Law.

The killer is eventually revealed to be Leonard Marliston (Jay Mohr), a teacher of English literature at the George Washington High School (named after the founding father of the American republic, and so symbolically associated with the Father's Law). But he is also the son of a woman named Loralee Sherman, raped twenty-seven years earlier by four young seniors at the same high-school, two of whom have since become leading citizens and representatives of the law: Tom Sisler is principal of the school (and so father of the educational community), while another is sheriff of the town and Jody's father – literally both a father and enforcer of the Father's Law. Because the rapists were from good families, we are told, no one was charged with the offence, and consequently, Loralee was left to nurture her anger which she projected onto the child born of the rape, inflicting regular beatings on the boy which warped his psyche and instilled in him a hatred that only murder could assuage. Marliston is therefore impelled to commit murder by a combination of desire for revenge and mental imbalance, both stereotypical motivations in the slasher genre. (In the kind of twist which has also become something of a cliché in the genre, the killer turns out to be the son of the sheriff, who is destined to become one of his victims: in a variation on the Oedipal theme, the mother-identified Marliston therefore kills his own father.)

Marliston's killing the town's virgins is thus an impersonal symbolic gesture: 'It's a stinking hypocritical world, he exclaims, where rapists become the pillars of the community ... so what better than to deprive them of the one innocence they have left? – their precious, virginal children!' He steals away the community's innocence, as symbolised by their virginal children, as punishment for their crime of stealing his mother's innocence. As he murders each victim, he carves the word 'virgin' into the thigh – defining the victim's innocence in the very act of removing it.[14]

In addition to the children, the two main representatives of authority in the town, Principal Sisler (education) and Sheriff Marken (the law and justice), are also killed, showing that, while virginity is the metaphor he chooses for innocence, Marliston's real target is this 'hypocritical world'. Given the period in which the film was made, a time of grow-ing discontent among liberal intellectuals with the Bush administra-tion, culminating in late 2000 in what was widely perceived as its 'theft' of the presidential election, it is tempting to read a commentary on the contemporary political situation into Marliston's motivation. When the sheriff refuses to divulge information regarding the first murders, the irony of the adage Marliston quotes from Plato could hardly have been lost on viewers in 2001 when the film appeared on video and DVD: 'The polis can only remain healthy if truth is available to all cit-izens.' Driven by a righteous anger and a thirst for justice, Marliston thus carries out a massacre of the innocents of biblical character: the sins of the fathers are, literally, visited upon the children, whom he sees as sharing in the community's collective guilt.

Loralee Sherman possesses many of the characteristics of the scape-goat victim, as identified by René Girard. In *Violence and the Sacred*, Girard develops the hypothesis, based on a close study of myth, espe-cially the Oedipus myth, and religious ritual, that when difference is threatened, and the symbolic order founded upon it, a collective vio-lence ensues, which is neutralised only by the sacrifice of a surrogate or scapegoat victim (see Girard, 1988: chs 1, 2 and 3). If the tight-knit community of Cherry Falls is seen as an extended family or clan, then the multiple rape may be viewed as an instance of metaphorical incest which threatens the symbolic order by breaking the incest taboo that ensures its continuation. The rape thus gives rise to a potential for violence which endangers the entire community, a potential which can only be diffused by being displaced outside the 'Cherry Falls' family towards a scapegoat, Loralee herself, who in Girard's terms, is a perfect victim, in that she belongs both inside and outside the community: though a member of the clan by residence, her mon-strosity as connoted by the grey streak in her hair, suggests and reflects her hybrid nature as strange (the mark of the devil, but also, the opposite of the 'virgin' branded on the murder victims, a signifier of age and lost innocence) as well as familiar (she is described by the sheriff as 'a weird kid' and 'a loner that nobody cared for').[15] The threat to social stability and collective harmony can only be averted by being displaced outside the clan onto the 'outsider', Loralee. After the rape, she 'disappears', exiled from a community that preferred to project its own guilt onto her: Loralee Sherman was thus doubly victimised. Her son Leonard inherits her status as scapegoat: incestuously close to the mother, his cross-dressing is more than just a mark of strangeness, it also poses a visible threat to difference and the symbolic order.[16]

These biblical resonances suggest that we are watching a morality tale, in which disobedience to the Father's Law is ultimately punished. This law and the symbolic order which it defends promote fixity and restraint, and abhor lack of control and instability in all things, especially in sexual relations and gender positions. Those who infringe the law include those hypocritical 'pillars of the community' whose children are slain, either because they took part in the crime of rape, or because they colluded in suppressing it, but the victims also tellingly include Timmy, a gay reporter for the school magazine. Homosexuality may be as much a threat to the symbolic order as strangeness or transgender. Jody herself is not completely innocent. She is pursued by Marliston as the daughter of the rapist-sheriff, but on a number of occasions throughout the film, there are strong hints of an incestuous eroticism between father and daughter that make both doubly criminal. 'Oh, daddy!' she sighs as she watches her father leave the house from her bedroom window after the first murders, and again, as she spies on the parents' meeting at the high-school called by him. Both exclamations are accompanied by lingering and sensuous looks.[17] As he teaches her moves in self-defence, they both end up on the floor, with her father lying on top of her. They exchange guilty looks, like two shy would-be lovers. Most significantly of all, the sheriff is 'very, very proud' to learn that his daughter is still a virgin: 'You're still my little girl', he murmurs, caressing her sensually; 'I love you!' she whispers in reply. The underlying eroticism of this exchange is accentuated by its location: Jody lies in bed, her father's arms around her.

In addition to their 'shared' guilt for the rape, Jody's and her father's deviant incestuous longings thus mark both of them out as potential victims. The sheriff is killed, but Jody survives, partly because she resumes her normative relationship with her boyfriend, Kenny, and so symbolically passes through the Oedipal phase (which is also expressed in her reverence for Marliston as a father-figure, and for the literary fathers – Plato, Eliot – he promotes). Her survival must also be ascribed to the fact that she remains a virgin, and so as the classic 'good girl', obeys the moral code of the genre, according to which promiscuity leads to murder. As scapegoats for their fathers' crimes, the virgins who have died, we remember, were exceptional cases in this film. In a sense, Jody takes her father's place as upholder of the law, following his death. It is Jody who, in the long tradition of slasher heroines whose virtue has remained intact, deals the killer the knockout blow, in a judo move taught her by her father. The deputy-sheriff, another woman, finishes him off with her gun/phallus. Following the killer's death, Jody is seen to rebond with her mother, who now re-emerges from the background of the narrative to accompany her daughter to the police bureau and make the official reports required by the justice system. With her father gone, Jody can resume a healthy relationship with the mother which does not threaten normal sexual relations with boys. In the father's absence (father as sheriff and biological father), women, then, are seen to uphold and enforce the Father's Law.

Unlike the other thrillers considered in this chapter, the narrative of *Cherry Falls* never offers a psychological explanation for Marliston's cross-dressing, but there is a strong implication that, like Norman Bates, he has assumed his mother's persona. After an attack on Jody at the high-school, a sketch is drawn from her description of the attacker that the sheriff and Sisler immediately recognise as Loralee Sherman, the rape victim, right down to a grey streak in her hair, signifier of difference and strangeness. Unlike Bates, however, Marliston's personality has not been completely taken over by the mother (who may or may not still be alive) – he is sufficiently lucid to explain his revenge motives to Jody and her father – but like Bates, he is certainly identified with a phallic, knife-wielding mother figure.[18] There is even a suggestion of effeminacy in his teacher persona (an impression which may gain ground among the less sophisticated of spectators on account of his literary background). His attitudes towards women are strongly ambivalent: an excessively close relationship with his mother, would have made him, like Bates, frightened of the sexual power of young women, and so led him to repress any sexual attraction towards them.

Marliston's shyness in the company of young women, and his repressed sexuality are pointed up in an interesting scene at the school, when he is visited by Jody, whose ostensible intention is to deliver a paper on T.S. Eliot. Jody announces her love of the poet's work and proceeds to quote from his poem, 'The Hollow Men'. Jody's quotation omits the poem's first four lines, but I include them below, because they seem particularly relevant to Marliston's motives for murder, discussed above, and to their political resonance:

> We are the hollow men.
> We are the stuffed men.
> Leaning together
> Headpiece filled with straw. Alas!
> Our dried voices, when
> We whisper together
> Are quiet and meaningless
> As wind in dry glass
> Or rats' feet over broken glass
> In our dry cellar.

Marliston joins Jody to quote the last two lines, which demonstrates his close familiarity with the piece, and perhaps can be seen retrospectively to prefigure the scene in his basement, in which he tortures Jody and her father: rats and broken glass have connotations of aggression, cutting, and therefore, castration. The cross-dressing killer is once again, therefore, symbolically portrayed as a potential castrator.

'Do you think that's how it is between people, Mr Marliston? Everything dry and meaningless and empty?' asks Jody when they have finished reciting. That Marliston instantly interprets this question as concerning relations between men and women is clear from his comment: 'I've heard you broke up with Kenny.' Dryness in a Freudian perspective is opposed to the fluidity associated with the sexual. Dryness, which Jody implicitly rejects in her question, describes Marliston's world and the repression of sexuality that has warped his psyche.

When, at the end of this scene, Jody expresses her pleasure in talking with him, and asks if they can spend time together again, he reacts with a revealing gaucheness and reticence. His lack of sexual desire for women would also have been the effect of the only model of male-female relations presented to him in his formative years: the rape of his mother. On the other hand, it is Leonard and not the mother who exacts revenge on them, but also on male virgins. Leonard's sexual energies have been displaced into a sadism which is principally directed against sexual absence, a virginity which he may also share, and which he may symbolically wish to obliterate. This sadism is also the consequence of his frequent beatings by his mother as the fruit of her rape and constant memory of that awful event. Torn between sexual innocence and its violent destruction, Leonard takes refuge in the safety of his mother's desire for revenge. As a product of the community that has thrust him outside its boundaries and which he returns to terrorise, he is a classic slasher villain.

Marliston's outsider status condemns him to death, just as his mother's condemned her to exile outside the community in West Virginia (as a state named after the 'virgin queen' Elizabeth I, Virginia is an ironic choice of retreat for the virginal rape victim and the son whose own innocence is robbed of him). He is more of a threat to the law than Sisler or the sheriff, not simply because he is a homicidal maniac, but because his mother-identified killing persona is represented in transgender terms. Each is a metaphor for the other, and both destabilize the law.

5
Drama Queens and Macho Men

Introduction

In contrast and counterpoint to the Hollywood comedies we looked at in Chapter 3, the four films discussed in this chapter reflect a growing tendency in the 1990s to treat transgender seriously, and to portray it in sympathetic colours. Unsurprisingly, two of these were made outside the USA, while the other two are far from being typical Hollywood products.

The Crying Game was a British production, directed by an Irish filmmaker, Neil Jordan; *The Adventures of Priscilla, Queen of the Desert* was made in Australia; *Boys Don't Cry* was a long-term low-budget project, directed by a relative newcomer, Kimberly Peirce; and *Midnight in the Garden of Good and Evil*, while echoing the cross-dressing comedies in certain respects, features a transsexual rather than a cross-dresser, and consequently there is a complexity in the representation of this character of the kind we have come to expect from a Malpaso production (Clint Eastwood's innovative and highly-regarded film company).

Both *Midnight in the Garden of Good and Evil* and *The Adventures of Priscilla, Queen of the Desert* are entertaining and well-made examples of 'off-piste' cinema, in which transgender is treated with sympathetic irony. However, less space is given to discussion of these two films, partly because they are less well-known and therefore less influential,[1] but above all, because *The Crying Game* and *Boys Don't Cry* are the only films of my corpus to explore sexual desire for transgendered characters in any real depth, and this extra dimension merits closer critical attention. In spite of their sympathetic approach to the subject, on the other hand, all four films are guilty either of perpetuating stereo-typical thinking to some degree, or of pandering to the spectator's voyeuristic pleasure, and in this sense, all bear witness to the survival of a fundamental ambivalence towards the transgendered that can be traced in artistic representations of the subject since ancient times (see Chapter 2). The four films have been grouped together in this sep-arate chapter for the reasons outlined above, but also because they belong to a different genre from the films of chapters 3 and 4, their over-riding dramatic content suggesting 'drama' or 'comedy-drama' to be the most appropriate description. *The Crying Game* and *Boys Don't Cry* have some characteristics of the thriller (violence, death, mystery), although neither sits easily in this category; similarly, neither *Priscilla* nor *Midnight* qualifies as pure comedy, the former strictly speaking being a comedy-drama and the latter a drama with comic elements. Moreover, while neither *Boys Don't Cry* nor *Priscilla* can be described as a musical, they both contain elements of the musical genre.

The Crying Game (Neil Jordan, 1993)

Neil Jordan's remarkable exploration of difference of gender, sexual-ity, ethnicity and politics in *The Crying Game* is relatively sophisti-cated in its approach to the issue of transgender. This extraordinary film demonstrates an intelligent and sympathetic awareness of the issue's complexities, situating them at the very centre of the diegesis. Unusually in a political thriller, Jordan's film shows how the political may also be sexual. Yet, in spite of the film's exceptionally sensitive treatment of the issue, there is, even here, an underlying ambivalence towards the transgression of boundaries generally.

The film begins with the kidnapping of a British soldier in Northern Ireland by an IRA cell. The soldier, a black man from Tottenham named Jody (Forest Whitaker), is enticed away from the crowds at a funfair into a deserted field by the siren charms of Jude (Miranda Richardson) who, like the biblical Judas her name suggests, delivers him into the hands of his enemies. The cell threaten to kill Jody unless certain prisoners are released. As the moment of Jody's execu-tion approaches, he and his minder, Fergus (Stephen Rea), gradually forge bonds of a kind of friendship, to the disapproval of Maguire (Adrian Dunbar), the leader of the gang, and of Jude who has been Fergus's lover. The motif of looking is an important one in the film, beginning with the temporary blinding of Jody whose face is covered with a sack when he is taken captive. The ability to see is underlined as a human need, as Jody begs for the sack to be removed. That Fergus relents and does this is an indication of a growing personal relationship between the two. But the gaze is subsequently shown to be a source of deception. Jody gives Fergus a snapshot of his mixed-race lover, Dil (Jaye Davidson), asking him to take care of her should the worst happen. Jody does in fact die, ironically killed by his fellow-soldiers, crushed beneath the wheel of a British tank as he tries to flee from Fergus who has been instructed to execute him but proves incapable of shooting in the back a man he has befriended. A fierce gun-battle ensues between Maguire and Jude and the British troops, but miraculously, all three terrorists manage to escape untouched.

The narrative then switches to a bar in London where Fergus seeks out Jody's lover, Dil. This bar is aptly named *The Metro*, which suggests the modern metropolis, a place of complexity, and glam/sham, a contrast and counterweight to the rural simplicities and political polarities of Northern Ireland. Fergus is immediately attracted to Dil, hairdresser by day and singer in *The Metro* bar by night. In *The Metro*, as Col the barman implies in conversation with Fergus, all is not what it seems. In both of the locations where Fergus first sees Dil (hair-salon, *Metro* bar), the two view each other in mirrors; as Col intimates, both see an image that does not correspond to reality, continuing a theme initiated during the captivity scenes, when Jody gives Fergus the snapshot, purporting to show Dil as a beautiful young woman.[2] Following a confrontation with Dave (Ralph Brown), Dil's abusive boyfriend, Fergus's and Dil's relationship becomes progressively sexual, leading to the dramatic revelation of Dil's true sex. The film is in fact structured around this pivotal moment of Dil's undressing in front of Fergus, which occurs roughly halfway through the narrative, a moment of revelation that is designed to shock both the male character involved and the audience watching. Thanks to Jaye Davidson's 'passability' as a woman and the director's insistence that the character's real sex be kept secret, heterosexual spectators in particular were deceived along with Fergus. The scene is one of unveiling of truth, common to all transgender narratives. The truth that is unveiled concerns Dil's biological sex: to all appearances a beautiful and sexy young woman, Dil is here revealed to be a man. Three marks of masculinity are revealed in this scene that contribute to the shock-effect: the penis, the tattoo clearly visible on Dil's right arm, and the absence of breasts, emphasised by a side-angle shot of Dil's naked body. The moment is pivotal in thematic terms, as we shall see, but also structurally since everything that precedes it has to be reviewed and understood in the light of it.

With Fergus, the spectator discovers, not only that Dil is biologically male, but in the light of this discovery is obliged to reread and revise many of the assumptions (s)he has made hitherto. The heterosexual male spectator may find this process especially problematic, if he has been attracted to Dil prior to the unveiling scene.[3] In this pivotal scene, it is not only Dil's male body that is revealed but more crucially, the duping of both Fergus's and the male spectator's objectifying gaze. Thus, the eroticising effects of this gaze are instantly dispelled. The effect on Fergus is equally dramatic: overcome by repulsion and disgust (probably recalling the blowjob Dil had given him the day before), he is violently sick and leaves. The relationship, however, continues, fed by an affection that persists between them in spite of Fergus's resistance to Dil's physical overtures towards him.

The dénouement of the narrative, in which the ethnic, sexual and political conflicts addressed in the film find a kind of resolution, is precipitated by the arrival in London of Maguire and Jude, who pressure Fergus into involvement in a plot to assassinate a British high-court judge. Motivated in part by sexual jealousy, Jude threatens to harm Dil if Fergus does not cooperate. The parody of femininity that is the stereotyped transvestite is undermined when Dil takes control of the situation. On the day of the planned hit, Dil, to whom Fergus has confessed his role in Jody's death, ties Fergus to her bed with the intention of shooting him with his own gun. Like Fergus in relation to Jody, however, Dil's feelings of affection for her new friend prevent her from killing him, and she collapses in his arms, at which point Jude arrives in search of her comrade who has failed to carry out his mission (Maguire, who was forced to take his place has been shot dead by security men). Bent on revenge, Jude is about to fire at Fergus, when Dil shoots her dead. Fergus sacrifices his liberty for Dil by assuming responsibility for Jude's murder. The film ends with Dil visiting Fergus in prison. Like any loyal sweetheart, Dil will wait for the man she loves through the long years of his life sentence.

This film has been much critiqued since its appearance in 1993, arousing considerable interest among feminists, Queer Theorists and post-colonial critics alike. This interest has typically focused on the film's transgression of political, ethnic, and gender/sexual boundaries, and, to a lesser extent, on the film's treatment of the Irish question, and the conflict between the IRA and the British forces in Northern Ireland (see Jennifer Wicke's brief discussion of this aspect of the film, 1997: 375–6). In my view, the political dimensions of *The Crying Game* are overshadowed by the personal relationships represented in the narrative, and therefore, my reading is not politically focused. Critics have very effectively brought out the film's problematising of essentialist ways of thinking in relation to sex, gender and racial and political groupings (see especially, Hanson, 1999).

This film does indeed go a long way towards undermining the notion of an absolute difference between binary pairs, such as 'same/other', 'masculine/feminine' (see Hill, 1998: 89–91). In a Derridean perspective, each term of these binaries is affected by the trace of difference, and slippage occurs along an unbounded continuum, so that in between the masculine and the feminine are a theoretically limitless potentiality of positions.

The androgyny of the protagonists' names suggests the film's desire to avoid sex/gender polarisation. Dil, Jody, Jude are all gender-neutral. Dil is Irish for 'dear' or 'beloved', and may be given to a boy or girl, while Jude may be a diminutive for either the feminine Judy or a masculine name in its own right (the eponymous hero of Thomas Hardy's *Jude the Obscure*, the Beatles song, 'Hey Jude', or the contemporary actor, Jude Law are examples of male usage). Fergus is the only name lacking gender ambiguity. The name signifies an individual of superior sexual ability. As Fergus never demonstrates any such ability in the film and, indeed, appears to lose sexual though not emotional interest in Dil when he discovers that she is not a biological woman, the choice of name may be read as somewhat ironic (for discussion of the names, Fergus and Dil, see Backus and Doan, 2001: 179).

Sex/gender stereotypes are effectively challenged, too, either by self-conscious parody or by ironic reversal. Col, the bartender (Jim Broadbent), is a comic parody of the filmic cliché, the barman as source of advice and solace for lovelorn drunks. In fact, Col tries but fails to warn Fergus of Dil's sex. Both Maguire, the fanatical and intransigent terrorist leader, and Jude the femme fatale (see later) are, in many ways, comic-book caricatures of villains (Jude in particular, in her dress, make-up, if not her behaviour, seems to prefigure the character played by Uma Thurman in *Pulp Fiction*). Dil is far from being the stereotype of the male transvestite (that is, a heterosexual man who is sexually aroused by dressing in women's clothes which have a fetishistic value for him, but who has no desire to become a woman), corresponding, in all respects except the anatomical, much more closely to the pre-op transsexual. She is extremely feminine in both appearance and behaviour, and unlike the typical transvestite, never dresses as a man. We note her violent reaction to Fergus's cutting her hair, which she declares she would not permit any man to do (having just promised Fergus to do anything he asked). On the other hand, she does not manifest any of the anatomical characteristics of a male-to-female transsexual, either (that is, a man who wishes to be a woman, and who may or may not be attracted to men). Transsexuals were already taking hormones at the time the film was made and gender-reassignment surgery pre-dates the film by several decades, so the unavailability of the means cannot explain this omission in the film. The character is thus an illustration of the continuum of gender/sex identity, and as a transvestite attracted to men, Dil explodes received notions of deviation from norms, as well as norms themselves. Not merely 'passable', she is the object of beauty in the film, her only competition, Jude, being too masculine and aggressive to be an erotic object. Dil's status as the object of the male gaze, at least before the revelation scene, tends to destabilise the Mulvey hypothesis that male characters and spectators occupying the subject position always objectify female characters who act passively and submissively towards the men around them. Dil is neither a woman nor, as it turns out, a passive or submissive figure. A strong character from the outset, (s)he takes the sexual initiative with Fergus. Her tying Fergus to her bed with her stockings has strong sado-masochistic overtones, metaphorically and literally reversing captor/victim, white/black and masculine/feminine hierarchies, where Dil is viewable as victim (abused by Dave), a member of a discriminated-against ethnic minority, and (would-be) female. She refuses objectification by Dave, physically throwing him out. Dil drives the plot more than any of the men, preventing Fergus from carrying out the assassination, avenging Jody by killing Jude. (S)he is the pivotal centre of the film's diegesis and thematics, literally embodying the main theme of identity. Her singing the title song in *The Metro* bar is a musical sign of her central role. In contrast, Dave, Dil's abusive ex-boyfriend, bears the mark of machismo (tattoos on his arm), but keeps a goldfish in a bowl, suggesting a childlike quality that comically undermines the macho stereotype. While on the one hand undermining stereotype, *The Crying Game* draws attention to the absence of terms for the new types of sexual attraction spawned by the increasing presence among us of transgendered individuals. 'Heterosexual' and 'homosexual' appear woefully inadequate to convey the nature of the relationship between Dil and Fergus. Fergus's attraction for Dil is not homosexual or even homoerotic, as suggested by Kirstin Handler (Handler, 1994: 33–4). As we have seen, his reactions to the discovery of Dil's gender are violent and unambiguously negative, and there is no clear evidence of homoeroticism on Fergus's part, rather he is duped into desiring a transvestite, just as many heterosexual men in the audience presumably are. Dil's passability as a woman and her arousal of 'heterosexual' male desire in Fergus demonstrates the fragility of object boundaries and raises important questions about the nature of desire generally, but it does not imply a repressed homosexuality. While in one breath conceding that 'Fergus does not explicitly experience homosexual desire', Handler argues elsewhere in her study of the film that Fergus forms a 'markedly homoerotic bond' with his prisoner, Jody, that his 'obsession with Jody drives his pursuit of Dil', and that he 'eventually turns Dil *into* Jody, by cutting her hair, dressing her in the very cricket outfit of his dreams, and then taking her to a hotel for a "honeymoon". So that he won't have to tell her the truth, Fergus leads Dil to believe it's all because he really prefers her as a man' (ibid.: 34). Handler here forces a reading to serve her overall argument that the film does not escape binary polarities, ignoring alternative interpretations of these events. Fergus does these things to protect Dil against his comrades, constructing an imaginary identity for her, as suggested by the mirror reflections of the act of cutting her hair (see my discussion of the mirror motif in *Dressed to Kill* in Chapter 4). Handler's reading ignores the complexity of a sexual desire (Fergus's) for a fantasy object which is not satisfactorily resolved in the film's diegesis. In the final scene, in which Dil visits Fergus in prison, Fergus's resistance to Dil's attempts to construct them as a romantic couple is less plausibly an indication of denial of homosexual feelings, than of his difficulty in reconciling his desire for the woman he thought Dil was and his continuing affection for her with his repulsion for the anatomical male Dil has turned out to be. Fergus is a heterosexual man trying to make sense of a deception that aroused his desire. Their relationship suspended in time by Fergus's prison sentence, this desire, too, is left hanging in the air, demanding definition and therefore, resolution. The difficulty of naming it – not homosexual or homoerotic – is underlined by Fergus's repeated injunction to Dil not to call him 'hon'. To borrow a phrase that once summed up the social and moral inacceptability of homosexuality, this really is the desire that has no name, at least not in the context of the intensely normatising culture in which we live.

We might, then, want to use the notion of a fourth term to describe the attraction between Fergus and Dil. This fourth term lies outside or beyond the heterosexual, homosexual or bisexual positions conventionally identifiable, corresponding to the hybridity which Hill (1998: 91–2) attributes to Dil (mixed gender and mixed race, Dil's hybridity is itself emblematic of the explosion of racial binaries, while Jody is a black British soldier from Tottenham who plays cricket), but more generally to the Queer position identified by Butler. *The Crying Game*'s willingness to take us beyond stereotypes, beyond sexual as/well as gender norms is politically and intellectually pleasing for the liberal male spectator. Unconsciously, however, this spectator may feel threatened by the instability that this process implies. This may give rise to three main types of anxiety which I shall now consider.

Scorpions

The film's moral message is condensed in the fable of the scorpion and the frog told by Jody to Fergus and then repeated by Fergus to Dil at the end of the film. A scorpion wishes to cross a river but can't swim and asks a frog to take him over to the other side on his back. The frog objects that if he agrees, the scorpion might sting him, to which the scorpion replies that this would be foolish, as then they would both drown. Acknowledging the scorpion's logic, the frog relents. Half way across the river, the scorpion stings the frog. As they both sink beneath the waters, the frog asks why the scorpion has doomed them both in this way, to which the latter replies that he couldn't help it, it is simply in his nature. This dramatisation of essentialist thinking – the scorpion is innately destructive, the frog innately trusting and generous – seems highly relevant to the question(ing) of identities, sexual, gender, racial, political, raised in the film, which demonstrates that the contrary may be true, that is, that frogs can behave like scorpions, and scorpions like frogs. Handler misses the irony implicit in the foregrounding of this fable in Jordan's narrative. She recognises that Fergus, the potentially violent terrorist is progressively femininised in the film. Thus a scorpion becomes a frog. However, she remains blind to the reverse process undergone by Dil, claiming that 'the sole woman in the film [Jude] becomes the representative scorpion and ... the untroublesome kind of woman turns out not to be one after all' (Handler, 1994: 37, see also 32). Handler's desire to read *The Crying Game* as reinforcing rather than challenging sex/gender roles leads her to ignore the possibility of another, more troubling reading buried in the film's unconscious, according to which there are several potential scorpions, not least Dil, who is initially constructed as a passive victim of sexual abuse and violence on the part of Dave.

Maguire, the IRA activist who runs the kidnap operation is a stereotypical terrorist for whom the ends justify any means. Quite apart from his readiness to kill in cold blood (Jody, the judge targeted by the IRA in London), Maguire is not above abusing his own comrades: in one scene, he presses a lighted cigarette into Fergus's hand. Dave, Dil's macho lover, is another stereotype who abuses weaker individuals (he beats up Dil in a fit of jealous rage) while proving a coward when confronted by a stronger male. This is Fergus, whose mild manners do not prevent him from almost breaking Dave's neck in an alley in defence of Dil. We should not forget, either, that Fergus was prepared to execute Jody and presumably would have carried out the execution, had Jody not fled through the woods to end up beneath the wheels of a British army tank. Jude, Fergus's ex-lover, has been described as a femme fatale, as a female with masculine characteristics (Hill, 1998: 93), and in fact does read as a parody of the 'spiderwoman', the castrating dark lady of the film noir tradition who lures men to their doom. Her function as bait in the kidnapping of Jody is in part an ironic and self-conscious *mise en scène* of this dimension of her character. Her gradual change in physical appearance from tarty blond seductress to gun-toting brunette, her womanly curves concealed under an androgynous raincoat, transforms Jude into a parody of the 'phallic woman' (see Chapter 4, *Psycho*, and n.5). There is a hint of caricature about her portrayal by Miranda Richardson, a sense that she is playing at being the ruthless terrorist. Nevertheless, we have to believe that her potential for violence is real. Indeed, this is foregrounded early on when she pistol-whips Jody. Jude's mission to assassinate the British judge, and then to kill Fergus for derogation of his duty as a soldier of the IRA clearly demonstrate this potential. Finally, Dil proves just as capable of scorpion-like behaviour as either Dave or Jude, and indeed, is the only character in the narrative who actually commits murder, shooting Jude dead when the latter comes to her flat in search of her missing comrade. Dil's violent propensities, which were flagged earlier in the narrative when she threw Dave's belongings out of her flat window, are accentuated in this dénouement by the firing of no fewer than three shots into Jude's inert body.

In spite of the film's underlying moral message about the relaxation of borders and especially, the dangers of essentialist thinking in relation to ethnicity and gender, then, those figures that display a sexual or gender ambiguity in *The Crying Game*, Fergus, Jude and above all, Dil, are all problematised as posing a threat of extreme physical violence. As critics have shown, both Fergus and Jude cross boundaries of sex or gender – the former is gradually feminized by his personal encounters, first with Jody and then with Dil, while the latter shifts from a stereotype of feminity (which turns out to be a deceptive lure) to a stereotype of butchness, as she reveals her 'real' nature, that of the macho male in all but biology. The most striking example of this mobility outside sexual and gender norms, Dil is at once the focus of erotic interest on the part of Dave, Fergus and potentially the heterosexual male spectator, the perpetrator of the most extreme act of violence in the film, and the cause of Fergus's sentence of life imprisonment. There is an inescapable implication here that the transgression of borders (sexual, gender, but also ethnic and racial, as well as political) can have sorry consequences.

Castration complex

The film contains a number of castration motifs. First, Jody is blindfolded by the sack placed over his head. For Freud, blinding in art and literature is frequently a metaphor for castration. In his analysis of the Oedipus myth, he demonstrates a clear link between Oedipus' self-blinding and the guilt he feels for the crime of incestuous sex with his mother. In dreams, fantasies and myths, moreover, the eye often symbolises the sex-organ (see Freud, 1985: 352–3, and my reference to this passage in relation to the motif of blinding in Chapter 4; see also Milner, 1980: 259). Castration is also symbolised in Dil's and Fergus's first meeting, as Dil cuts Fergus's hair. (The cutting of a man's hair is associated with the sapping of his strength in the famous story of Samson and Delilah in the Bible.) The revelation scene is disturbing for the male spectator for a number of reasons, but as we have seen, the shock-value arises from a mixture of repulsion and fascination. In the case of the 'money-shot' (male ejaculation) in porn films, the male spectator may nevertheless be unconsciously reassured by the visual evidence of the phallic woman's existence that the scene provides. Relieved to discover that the lost phallus has been restored to the woman/mother, this spectator is simultaneously returned to a pre-Oedipal union with the mother before the father's threat of castration tore them apart (see Chapter 6 for further discussion of this notion). In retrospect, following the revelation scene, it is tempting to conjecture that, as Dil has the phallus, Fergus must lose his, a loss that is further imaged in the 'bondage' scene. In this scene, Fergus clearly *is* the phallus in Lacanian terms, a potential violence that must be restrained and defused.[4] Fergus retrieves the phallus from Dil when he cuts her hair in turn. This act therefore has less to do with masculinising Dil, than with symbolically removing from her the gun/phallus that she had taken from both him and the other 'phallic woman', Jude.

Deception

Play between concealment and revelation, between ignorance and knowledge, crystallised in the figure of Dil, is both a metaphor for all major aspects of the film's diegesis, and the site of the erotic.[5] This ludic dimension can also be found in the theme of game-playing underlying much of the diegesis and imaged in the cricketing whites worn by Jody, and then by Dil when Fergus is attempting to hide her from his comrades. (S)he thus becomes Jody/a man/a game-player, as much as Jude who plays the part of the femme fatale. The understated humour of the final prison visit scene confirms the impression that 'it's all just a game'. These ludic aspects function to reduce the spectator's anxiety regarding the transgression of boundaries.

The heterosexual male spectator who is taken in by Dil's (or Jaye Davidson's) performance of femininity (a performativity in the sense defined by Judith Butler) may feel as repulsed as Fergus does initially when he discovers Dil's true biological sex. While this spectator may be intellectually reassured by the rather trite moral message that love knows no gender boundaries, he may equally feel cheated by the trick the film has played on him,[6] and at a more unconscious level, experience some anxiety at the juxtaposition of gender-switching and the demonstration of castrating violence.

With the exception of *Victor/Victoria*, *The Crying Game* goes further than any other film in my corpus in challenging binary norms of gender and sexuality. This is largely due to the eroticism surrounding the transgendered figure of Dil, an eroticism evident within the diegesis but one that also reaches out to the film's spectators in ways not quite matched by any other film we are considering.[7] The erotic charge that runs through the film is itself a symptom and a product of an ambivalence that the film narrative never resolves and that betrays an underlying anxiety, a sense of the uncanny, in relation to the transgression of sexual and gender taboos in particular. This eroticism is both disturbing and fascinating because of its implications for the nature of desire (see chapters 6 and 7).

There are, as we have seen, however, a number of anxieties surrounding Dil, and associated more generally with the transgression of sexual and gender boundaries. Even in films that – with some success – set out to explore new ways of thinking about these aspects of the human condition (all of the comedies and the films of this chapter), the shadow of fears as ancient as narrative itself darken the inner screen of our imagination more often, perhaps, than we may care to admit. In the end, we may have to accept that the thrill of transgression will always be accompanied by fear and guilt, at least as long as we remain within a post-Oedipal symbolic structure. The possibilities of escaping this structure will be considered in my concluding chapter.

The Adventures of Priscilla, Queen of the Desert (Stephan Elliott, 1994)

The Adventures of Priscilla, Queen of the Desert is an Australian 'road movie' which follows three female impersonators, Mitzi, Bernadette and Felicia, from Sydney across the outback. They play gigs in towns along the way, but the real purpose of the trip is for Mitzi to find and re-establish a relationship with his son Benji, who has been living with his ex-wife, Marion, Benji's bisexual mother. The theme of father–son relations dominates the narrative, a feature that is explainable in terms of the historical period in which the film was produced, which was one in which the conventional nuclear family was beginning to break down in western societies to be replaced by extended or reconstituted families following separation, divorce and/or the start of new, 'live-in' relationships, a time when, as Lynne Segal observes, 'Men's hold on their status as fathers is less firm and secure than ever before' (Segal, 1997: 26–7). The film may certainly be read on one level as reflecting contemporary concerns about definitions of masculinity, but as we shall see, this is by no means the only possible reading.

They travel in a pink bus named Priscilla, the eponymous 'heroine' of the story. The title of this bold and highly entertaining film resonates with ironic allusions. The name Priscilla means 'ancient, old-fashioned, antique, in a strict way' and was thus much loved by the seventeenth-century puritans; hence, it is hardly surprising that the shortened form, 'prissy', regardless of derivation, has similar connotations in our popular language. Priscilla is the name of the bus, a neat piece of irony since the connotations of this name are hardly applicable to the bus passengers who, as we shall see, are quite the opposite of 'prissy'. Two, Felicia and Mitzi, are gay drag-queens, and the third, Bernadette, is a pre-op transsexual on hormones. All three, however, are 'queens' by virtue of their stage personae which, in at least one case, continues off-stage as well. Their caricatural costumes and outrageous dance numbers are self-conscious, accurate and sympathetic representations of drag-shows, although from the perspective of the representation of women, drag might be thought to have negative connotations – more of this presently.

Questions of masculinity and fatherhood are inseparable from the wider issues of gender roles and definitions, and Butler's perspective is an essential one here, particularly in view of the narrative's performance frame in which gender and sexuality are literally staged. We shall examine the main features of this staging and of the off-stage relationships with which it is juxtaposed. While there are some criticisable aspects, the overall effect of these representations is less negative, more complex than critics have suggested.

The film tries hard to portray drag-queens in a positive light, but the devices employed to achieve this effect tend to be drawn from cinema and narrative clichés. Those who exhibit bigoted and violent responses to the appearance of these outrageous figures are unsympathetic and even downright unsavoury characters from the bars of the Australian outback (shades here of the reactionary attitudes found in small-town midwest America, as depicted in countless modern movies), while other marginals (the gay community of Sydney, Bob, the unhappy husband of Cynthia, a nymphomaniac Thai mail-order bride, and most strikingly, a tribe of Aborigines they encounter in the desert) are seen as kindred spirits. Whereas an elderly white farming couple drive off in horror when confronted with cross-dressed men, reacting to an evident clash of cultures, those whose cultural difference would be expected to produce the most extreme and most hostile rejection warmly share food and drink with the three travellers, and enthusiastically join in their song-and-dance routines. The spectacle of Aborigines and drag-queens dancing to Abba records in the Australian desert is a curious and amusing scenario. However, it is not the Aborigines who are ridiculed but stereotypical expectations about them: far from being uneducated savages, they are seen to speak excellent (Australian) English and to love Abba!

The songs of the 1970s and 1980s Swedish pop-group, a well-known gay icon, dominate the drag repertoire, and together with drag itself, function to underline the role of performance. Judith Butler sees drag as a subversive political act, because it shows gender to be fundamentally performative (Butler, 1999: 25). Garber follows Butler in viewing drag as positively operating to reveal the constructed and performative nature of gender: 'In imitating gender, drag implicitly reveals the imitative structure of gender itself – and its contingency' (Garber, 1993: 151). Garber applies Butler's view of drag as subversive to art, arguing that drag tests the limits of representation (ibid.: 149). Garber also finds drag-queens interesting precisely because they are imperfect and unconvincing as women: 'drag can also be an important destabilizing element that, in performance, "questions the limits of representation ... The imperfection of her imitation is what makes her appealing, what makes her eminently readable. Foolproof imitations of women by men, or men by women, are curious, but not interesting" ' (ibid.: 149, quoting Montero, 1988: 41). Camille Paglia also views the drag-queen in positive terms: for Paglia, 'the drag-queen defies victim-centred feminism by asserting the dominance of women in the universe' (Paglia, 1992: 99). I find such celebrations of drag ultimately unconvincing. Butler is right that drag is a performance, but as I have already argued in this book, drag is equally a parody of femininity, a male joke for other men, that far from subverting masculinity, reinforces gender polarity through caricature and excess (see Chapter 3). If the drag artist is a caricatural performance of the feminine, we are never allowed to forget that beneath the carnivalesque mask of woman is a man. Indeed, much of the humour associated with drag depends on the audience's awareness of this duality, from the assumption by a deep-throated, muscular and hirsute male of the stereotyped trappings of femininity. The explicit campness of drag invites an ironic rather than a sympathetic reading of femininity, which is donned as a jester dons his fool's cap and bells. Tincknell and Chambers (2002: 7) also view the operation of drag in the film as caricaturing the feminine: 'Throughout the film [Mitzi and Felicia] foreground this performative relationship to femininity by their parodic stylisation of it as grotesque: They repeatedly stage it as a series of comic turns, from the "slags" of the Outback through primadonna musical comedy stars to the American black southern "mammy".'

Inspired by the psychoanalytically-informed work of Gaylyn Studlar and Mary Anne Doane, who view films about drag as playing out the perversity of the fetish, Robbins and Myrick (2000: 271) see drag as, at the very least, a manifestation of ambivalence towards the feminine: 'at once the female impersonator submits to the cinematic representation of woman by donning her image; however, given the ultimate power held by the male performer, he is also able to take control of women's image through the drag performance.' For them, drag is a fetishistic display which 'allays and potentially eroticises male anxiety about female space, and it relies on sadistic and masochistic impulses', satisfying the fantasy of 'reconstituting, parading, and parodying "the phallic mother"', and thus reinforcing 'phallic driven heterosexuality' (ibid.: 272–3).

Moreover, unlike transsexuality and some forms of cross-dressing, drag is never intended to be a fundamental and permanent change, arising from a genuine desire to be a woman, and so does not really threaten the established order. By juxtaposing the masculine with the feminine, by constantly reminding us that behind the mask of femininity, a man is always in control, it reinforces norms, serves the interests of the norm, rather than putting it into question as Butler maintains.

Using an analogy from stylistics, one might say that drag and transvestism both function essentially like the simile which links two

separate things through comparison but does not effect any fundamental change of meaning. The simile says that A is like B. Unlike the
metaphor, the simile, Paul Ricoeur insists, preserves a distance between
the two things compared: 'no transferral of meaning takes place; all
the words keep their meaning and the representations themselves
remain distinct and coexist with an almost equal degree of intensity'
(Ricoeur, 1975: 236; my translation). In the same way, drag and transvestism express a 'simile-type' relationship between the signifier, A
(the act of cross-dressing) and signified, B (femininity): A is like B, but
A does not become B. In the case of transsexualism, a more fundamental change occurs, a change brought about by hormones and
sometimes, surgery, and a change that is reflected in the metaphorical process, according to which the signifier A (the transsexual body)
to a greater or lesser extent becomes the signified B (the female body):

> Whereas the simile can only exist between two express terms, the
> intellectual operation of comparison necessarily bearing on two
> objects – one thing is compared always with another – the
> metaphor, figure of language and not of thought, can only express
> the signifying object, even though it identifies two objects, signi-
> fier and signified.
>   (Moreau, 1982: 43; my translation)

The representation of cross-dressing in popular film is, therefore, ultimately analogous to the figure of the simile rather than that of the
metaphor in being a likeness that retains its original identity ('my love
is *like* a red, red rose'), not a transformation that replaces its original
identity with another ('my love *is* a red, red rose').

Bernadette, admittedly, is more than a drag-queen. A transsexual
who yearns to undergo surgical transformation into an anatomical
woman, her relationship with the feminine is more complex, less
straightforwardly caricatural, but ironically she is the least 'passable'
of the three, a constant visual reminder of her insistent masculinity.
There is at least one other reminder of this in the male force she displays when confronted by a homophobic mob. Bernadette, the only
man who wants to become a woman in the film, demonstrates that
she is still capable of male strength and aggression when she delivers
a castrating blow into the groin of a thug who is threatening a similar violence against Felicia. In contrast, Bob's imported Thai wife,

Cynthia, shoots ping-pong balls from her vagina in comic enactment of the phallic power that she accuses Bob of lacking: 'you have a little dingaling!' is Cynthia's parting castratory shot at the luckless Bob. Bob's subsequent growing affection for Bernadette suggests another ironic role reversal, as the castrated/phallus-less Bob and the phallic-woman that Bernadette has proved herself to be decide to become a couple, and a model of sex and gender role flexibility. The familiar motif of castration anxiety is thus treated here with a self-reflexive irony that amusingly reverses the usual pattern. Instead of the arousal of this fear by a cross-dressed man, or in the cross-dressed man himself, it is associated in *Priscilla* with the inadequacy of heterosexual males.

Apart from the growing fondness between Bob and Bernadette, the narrative is dominated by the relations between Mitzi, Bernadette and Felicia, and between Mitzi and his son, while women in the diegesis are either marginalized or completely absent (see Tincknell and Chambers, 2002: 4). Of the two biological women in the narrative, Tick's (Mitzi's) ex-wife Marion plays a tiny role, appearing in two short scenes only, while Cynthia, Bob's Filipina bride is portrayed as a sex-obsessed exhibitionist and a screeching harridan in sharp contrast to her mild-mannered and long-suffering husband. This foregrounding of male–male relations at the expense of a feminine presence has understandably drawn the ire of some critics. Tincknell and Chambers rightly argue that this relative absence of the feminine is replaced by a more feminised masculinity which comes across as a parody of women: 'female characters are largely displaced by men who express "feminine" anxieties about the body, emotions, and relationships, but this is mediated by the use of a camp register that ironises both femininity itself and the feminisation of masculinity' (ibid.: 4–5). On the other hand, when the same critics protest that 'it is male bodies that are the site of spectacle' and yet, that 'the possibility of a desiring female gaze is disavowed by the way in which the male bodies are presented' (ibid.: 5–6), one cannot help wondering whether these critics would be similarly dismayed if 'male' were replaced by 'female' and vice versa.

In addition to the elision of the feminine, the film has been criticised for covertly reinforcing fixed, traditional notions of gender by valorising couple relationships. Robbins and Myrick see the entire film as 'centered around either the mourning over the loss of – or a drive to assimilate – male/female couples', pointing to the Mitzi/wife reunion for the purpose of child-care, Bernadette's mourning the loss of a younger husband, and her decision to stay with Bob. Such relationships, Robbins and Myrick maintain, may not be typical, but they are 'ultimately conventional' (Robbins and Myrick, 2000: 277; Tincknell and Chambers, 2002: 8, express similar views). However, it is difficult to see how Mitzi's assumption of paternal responsibilities is regrettable in the context of harmonious gender relations, and particularly from a feminist point of view. Nor is it immediately evident in what ways a relationship between a male-to-female 'pre-op' transsexual and a hitherto 'straight' man is conventional, unless this is the case with any form of coupling, whatever its complexion. Surely, it is not the couple structure per se that perpetuates gender and sexual norms, but the social and religious pressures that make this structure 'compulsorily heterosexual'.

Rather than being regressive from a sexual politics perspective, it is arguable, then, that new relationship models are promoted in *Priscilla*. These models are positively represented in metaphors of space and distance: oppositions between city and outback metaphorically connote tensions between the progressive and the traditional, but not simplistically so. As we have seen, the Aborigines the three queens encounter welcome their strangeness, with which, as a subaltern group within a dominant white culture, they undoubtedly identify. The Aborigines, however, represent the marriage of both spaces in a literal and a symbolic sense. Wearing city clothing and drinking city beer, they cling to their native territories and their historical and cultural roots in the Australian desert, a fusion of past and present, blending Aboriginal traditions with white anglophone education and technology. In relationships, too, this is the film's positive message: that non-normative identities and couplings can work alongside more traditional familial roles.

In its representation of gays and gay transvestites, the film avoids stereotyping, representing the complexity of types and attitudes within the gay community, so that, while the three protagonists certainly encounter their fair share of hostility – in addition to the attack on Felicia, they awake one morning to find 'AIDS FUCKERS GO HOME' painted on the coach – the aggressively homosexual Felicia is seen to be equally bigoted, in her case, against women. Felicia's misogyny reveals itself in particular in her attitudes towards Marion, crystallised in the following conversation between Felicia and Benji on an occasion alone together. The distaste with which Felicia pronounces the word 'girls' is telling. However, Benji's matter-of-fact acknowledge-ment of his father's occupation and his mother's bisexuality under-cuts Felicia's malicious attempts to dispel any illusions the boy may have of a heterosexual 'happy ending' for his parents:

FEL: You know what your father does for a living?

BENJI: Yes.

FEL: So I suppose you know he doesn't like girls?

BENJI: Yes, does he have a boyfriend at the moment?

FEL: No.

BENJI: Neither does mum. She used to have a girlfriend but she got over her.

Later, Benji asks his father whether he will have a boyfriend when they get back to Sydney. 'Maybe', says Mitzi, to which Benji unhesi-tatingly replies 'That's good!' In these exchanges, taken together, Felicia is ironically positioned as the voice of prejudice, whilst Benji illustrates the tolerance that can come from growing up in a sexually unconventional, non-nuclear family.

The last scene of the film, in which Mitzi and Felicia perform once again before their cheering home crowd in the local gay club in Sydney, labours this progressive message of tolerance somewhat, with insistent close-ups on Benji's happy smiling face in the bosom of the Sydney gay community, but in the post-AIDS homophobic 1990s, it is a message that bears emphasising. In ironic homage to the cross-dressing genre, Mitzi removes her wig with theatrical brio before her rapturous audience – a gesture that reminds everyone of his 'real' sex as the man, Tick, and underlines the fundamentally temporary nature of gender transformation in the drag act. At the same time, it is a gesture of complicity with an audience who were never really deceived by the transparent disguise of drag.

Priscilla is an interesting example of emergent Australian cinema – a well-acted and directed musical tragic-comedy, wittily but sensi-tively scripted, the narrative addresses issues of homophobia among poor whites in the Australian outback, the rights of gays to parent-hood, the relationships of transsexuals with straight men, misogyny within the gay community, and the plight of marginal groups in gen-eral. In contrast to the treatment of transgender in mainstream

Hollywood comedy, the humour in *Priscilla* is not centred so much on the cross-dressed figure (except in the ironic sense of 'drag-queen' excess) as on the succession of bizarre situations in which the three protagonists find themselves and the reactions of others to the unlikely juxtaposition of 'drag-queen in desert'. *Priscilla* is a morality tale which is only partly successful in promoting new perspectives, largely because of a residual misogyny which undermines the film's gender politics. *Priscilla's* enormous popularity, especially among female spectators (see Tincknell and Chambers, 2002: 9 n.10), may nevertheless be attributable to its self-ironising representation of drag and to a self-conscious but never self-congratulatory humour generated by the incongruous juxtapositions that structure the narrative: Abba/Aborigine, city/outback, drag-queen/homophobic male – not to mention those implicit in the drag act itself. Such juxtapositions and their humorous impact also help to make *Priscilla* a work that is, on balance, both hugely watchable and intensely thought-provoking, by presenting its audience with images of a healthy *rapprochement*. The film's final shot exemplifies this feature well. A blow-up girl-doll filled with helium that has escaped from Priscilla's roof comes gently to rest in a Thai temple, much to the surprise of a passing monk – a startling, over-determined image that wittily juxtaposes the ancient and the modern, the sexual and the spiritual, vice and virtue, the deviant and the normal. Like the drag-queen and the desert of the film's title, this 'afterword' closes the film as it began – with an insistence on the bringing together of the centre and the margins.

Midnight in the Garden of Good and Evil (Clint Eastwood, 1997)[8]

This esoteric tale, set in the present day, in the old colonial town of Savannah in the American deep south, focuses on a murder and the subsequent trial of Jim Williams (Kevin Spacey), self-made man, wealthy antiques dealer, bon vivant and covert homosexual. John Kelso (John Cusack) is a magazine reporter who has been sent to Savannah to write a feature on one of Williams's famous Christmas parties. He is intrigued both by Williams and by his violent young lover, Billy. Billy is blackmailing Williams, threatening to expose their homosexual relationship unless Williams continues to subsidise his feckless lifestyle and indulgence in fast cars. Later that night, Billy is found dead, shot several times through the heart. Williams maintains that he shot Billy in self-defence, although in fact, he exploited the circumstances of Billy's violent appearance at his home, as witnessed by Kelso, to rid himself permanently of his blackmailing lover. Kelso stays on to cover the murder trial. During his extended stay in Savannah, he encounters the irrepressible Chablis Deveau (Lady Chablis), a drag-queen comedienne, and a beautiful young woman named Minerva (Irma P. Hall). Interestingly, Kelso is attracted to both in different ways, and his resulting confusion largely defines his character on a personal level, a confusion which is also mirrored in his professional involvement in the trial and his judgement as to Williams's guilt or innocence.

Kelso's vacillation on both a personal and a professional level, his hesitation between a number of opposites, and Williams's dilemma of choice between truth and lies are both reflected in the dialectic of the film's title. Once again, the importance of titles in flagging up the central meanings of a narrative invites us to dwell for a while on this one, whose opaqueness is all the more suggestive. The title is derived from the voodoo theme: at night, an old black woman practises voodoo at the grave of a murdered man to chase away the evil consequences of the act. The graveyard is a garden of good *before* midnight, evil *after*. Midnight is therefore the cusp between good and evil, a moment suspended between both; midnight as opposed to 'before midnight' or 'after midnight', the fugitive present instant that holds the balance between good and evil. Thus, the graveyard scenes are a metaphor for and symbolic reflection of the dilemma facing Williams who might choose good or evil, depending on whether he confesses to Billy's murder or goes along with a technical defence that his lawyer is able to exploit to get him exonerated. Voodoo functions in the narrative as a device to restore justice when a jury is misled into freeing a guilty man: shortly after the trial, he is struck down – we are led to believe through voodoo – and dies of a heart attack. This, then, is the manifest level of meaning, circulating between the title and the narrative it announces and defines.

In Barthesian terms, voodoo serves both the proairetic code and the symbolic code. The proairetic code is associated with the narrative and advancement of it, while the symbolic code is concerned with sexual and unconscious relations in the text (see Barthes, 1990: 18 ff.). The 'garden of good and evil' is reminiscent of the Garden of Eden in which nudity and sex become sinful and woman is demonised as the first sinner. Good and evil might also be taken to refer to the film's sexual politics, since, unfortunately, all three of the film's gay characters, Billy, Williams and Deveau are negatively portrayed in varying degrees, while the only heterosexual relationship (John Kelso and Minerva) is represented as playful, tender and reciprocal, a healthy counterpoint to the other couple paradigms (Billy–Williams, Kelso–Deveau) which appeal to *schadenfreude* instincts in the male spectator. The title therefore announces the plot focus and symbolic theme of 'inbetweenness', of neither one thing or another, extending to the sexual relations depicted in the narrative. Even John Kelso and Minerva seem to teeter on the edge, in their case between friendship and romance, a single, innocent kiss which Minerva would visibly like Kelso to prolong into a lover's embrace but which, to the puzzlement of both Minerva and audience, he refrains from doing, being the symbolic instant of this inbetweenness. We are left to guess at Kelso's motives for not taking advantage of Minerva's obvious readiness for more. Is he disturbed/confused by Deveau's overtures? He was, after all, initially oblivious of her anatomical sex. Or is he simply wary of an emotional commitment with a woman living in a strange town, hundreds of miles from home? A banal and dramatically uninteresting explanation.

Williams's relationship with Billy is clearly homosexual, but it is plagued by blackmail and violence by Billy who seems motivated wholly by financial gain. In part as a consequence of these pressures, Williams's feelings towards Billy are highly ambivalent. This ambivalence may, however, have deeper roots: is Williams's attraction to Billy just a sexual one? Does the intensity of Billy's aggression suggest that more than money is at stake? And of course, in the ultra-conservative deep south, the homosexual relationship itself is 'on the edge', in that it transgresses social, moral, religious and political norms.

Finally, Deveau's flirtation with Kelso is left hanging in the air, an incomplete narrative programme. Kelso's initial deception, followed by his evident unease, and his inability to treat Deveau's caresses and innuendos lightly, is an enigma that is not entirely resolved in the 'epilogue' scenes by the developing affection between Kelso and Minerva. As the two set out on a date together, Deveau appears and interposes herself physically between them, as if competing with Minerva for Kelso's favours.

In terms of the symbolic meanings of this film, then, Deveau is a central figure, although at the level of the plot she is a peripheral character, in part the comic relief to a murder plot in the context of repressed homosexuality and hypocrisy in upper-class white society in the southern United States. On both counts, she is one of a gallery of eccentric figures which also includes a man who walks a non-existent dog daily and another who carries a bottle of poison and is constantly surrounded by flies. The implicit bracketing of Deveau with other 'abnormal' people tends to reinforce the impression that transgender, too, is an eccentric condition that is potentially dangerous to others. One of two black characters, there is an unconscious bracketing, too, of Deveau with the black 'voodoo mama' and therefore with the threat of magic. Deveau does indeed seem to cast her own spells on all the men she meets. Drag is inevitably perceived here against a backcloth of strangeness and danger, of the 'uncanny' sensation associated by Freud with the recognition of something familiar as well as strange. In this sense, Deveau might represent the threat of a repressed homosexuality.

In other ways, too, Deveau might be said to be a negative role-model for transgendered people. Her excessive flirtatiousness with apparently straight men (Kelso and young middle-class black men at a 'coming-out' dance) arouses homophobic anxiety. The impression is that all transsexuals and transvestites (represented here by a drag-queen) are sexually voracious and promiscuous. Drag-queens are represented in the figure of Deveau as effeminate gay men who dress outrageously as women while retaining the anatomy and sexual predatoriness of men. Indeed, transgender is thus subsumed into homosexuality, of which it is seen as the wild frontier. As always with drag, we cannot help feeling, too, that we are dealing with a comic parody of the feminine. Finally, the choice of a black drag-queen brackets 'trans' with another subaltern minority in a part of the US (Savannah, Georgia) where white/black segregation still applies in many areas of society. This notion is illustrated in one particular scene, the 'coming-out' dance for black girls from well-to-do families. Deveau gatecrashes the party, and her unconventional behaviour contrasts painfully with the prissy etiquette of the dance, exposing it as a mere aping of white ruling-class manners.

A transgendered character familiar from the comedies, then, on the surface Deveau appears playful and sympathetic. In the diegesis, she functions mainly as a comic foil to John Kelso – a secondary role also implicitly accorded to homosexuality and transgender in an essentially heterosexual world. Her character, gender and sexuality remain wholly unexplored, with no attempt to look at what drag is. Her real significance, however, is symbolic, and on this level, she occupies a decidedly ambivalent status, hovering disturbingly between a number of polarities: positioned between male and female, she is also suspended socially and sexually between black and white, while her relatively harmless streak of mischievousness places her somewhere between good and evil. It is this 'inbetweenness' that, in the end, makes Deveau appear threatening, both to Kelso and the black men at the dance, and to the heterosexual male spectator.

Boys Don't Cry (Kimberly Peirce, 1999)

The highly acclaimed *Boys Don't Cry* is one of only two films in our corpus which feature a female-to-male cross-dresser. The relative rarity of the fictional or filmic exploration of this phenomenon is no doubt partly due to the erroneous notion, common in our society, that female-to-male cross-dressing and transsexuality is rare or even non-existent. Garber argues that the idea that there are more male-to-female transsexuals than the reverse is a perception created by the fact that female transsexual surgery was not possible until fairly recently, and that most transsexual researchers are male and may have exhibited a bias towards male patients (Garber, 1993: 101). As for female-to-male transvestites, 'psychologists and psychiatrists still deny (their) existence ... alleging that any woman who consistently cross-dresses as a man is actually a transsexual – that is, a woman who wishes that she were a man' (ibid.: 44–5). Garber quotes Robert Stoller (1968: 195; in ibid.: 45) on this point:

> there are an extremely rare number of females who dress all the time as men, live as men, work as men – in fact, pass unrecognized in society as men. Are they not transvestites? No – and again one must be careful that one is not merely quibbling with words. These women are transsexuals, quite comparable to male transsexuals. They wish to be males, that is to have a body in every way male, and to live in all ways as a man does. They cannot stomach sexual relations with men; they are aroused only by women. Men's clothes have no erotic value whatsoever; these people have no clothing fetish.

Garber comments acerbically that women are regarded as having not sexual but cultural desires. However, she does refer to Nancy Friday and other writers on the subject as maintaining that there are women who become aroused by wearing men's underwear or other items of male clothing (ibid.: 45; see also Friday, *My Secret Garden*).

The title of Kimberly Peirce's acutely observed film draws attention both to the kind of sexism and gender stereotyping that gives rise to such erroneous ideas about women, and to the dominance in this society of a machismo culture that represses any manifestation of a more 'feminine' sensitivity in men. It is part of the project of Peirce's narrative to explore gender differences in general as they are perceived in working-class American white milieux, and to recuperate a masculinity that, in Jungian terms, is balanced by a recognised and accepted anima or feminine side. The film's principal narrative programme, however, turns around the fear and ignorance informing hostile attitudes to unconventional forms of sexuality and gender.

Boys Don't Cry is based on actual events, and the names of all places and characters remain unchanged. In Falls City, Nebraska, Brandon Teena (Hilary Swank), newcomer in a town where he has no past, charms the small rural community. Women adore him and men treat him with a laddish camaraderie that borders on the homoerotic. In Falls City, Brandon meets Lana Tisdel (Chloë Sevigny) in a karaoke bar, an ironically appropriate location for those like Brandon who fulfil their dreams pretending to be someone else. That Brandon's identity is at the core of the film's thematics is underscored in the line that Lana throws at Brandon as they catch each other's eye: 'Who are you?' Brandon is sexually and emotionally attracted to Lana who reciprocates his feelings. In fact, Brandon Teena is actually a reversal of his real name, Teena Brandon, a linguistic mirroring of the gender inversion he is performing, for Brandon is a female-to-male transsexual – he admits to living through a 'gender identity crisis', and his cousin Lonny refers to his plans for a sex-change operation. Brandon is attracted to girls, but conceals his biological sex from the young women concerned and their male kinfolk who befriend him. Inasmuch as he would like to be physically male, and is sexually interested in women, he is a heterosexual transsexual. From the point of view of the 'redneck' macho male society in which he lives, however, Brandon is a lesbian pervert who 'pretends' to be a man in order to abuse young women. It would seem that lesbianism is easier to confront than transsexuality.[9] Hence, in the opening scenes, he is chased back to his cousin's place by a mob of angry young men, howling 'faggot!', 'you fucking dyke!', 'freak!', and 'you fucked my sister!' This 'pretence' is indeed foregrounded in scenes in which Brandon inserts a phallic substitute into his pants to create a 'manly' bulge and thus puts what Freud would call 'penis-envy' into literal effect, creating the illusion of possessing one. A Butlerian perspective would view this gesture as an act of complicity with hegemonic norms, since in Butler's view, transsexuality is constrained by heterosexuality: in this view, Brandon is fooled by heterosexual ideology into believing that a penis will make him a man. (See Prosser, 1998: 48; see also Chapter 1; and see Willox, 2003, whose central argument is that the film reinforces male/female gender binaries.)

When eventually his female biological sex is exposed, the homophobia that lurks just below the surface in small-town America explodes into an extreme violence that has tragic consequences. John and Tom, a couple of violent young men who have insinuated themselves into Lana's family and who have taken Brandon under their wing, discover a penis-shaped dildo and a pamphlet on sex-change operations in Brandon's belongings, and proceed to beat up and brutally rape Brandon. In a final crescendo of violence, Brandon and Candace, Lana's friend, are shot dead by them. (John is from the first portrayed as an unstable, drugged-up, irrational and highly dangerous individual, while the equally disturbed and violent Tom is both a self-harmer and a fire-raiser who set his own family's house on fire, burning his parents to death.)

This film brings to the surface a level of hostility to difference that we have seen operating largely at unconscious levels in the thrillers and comedies of our corpus, and as such has clear socio-political aims. At the same time, the film narrative dwells upon the permeable boundary between the real and the imaginary, valorising the latter as a privileged space of play in which everything is possible.[10] The film can be read on either level, and we shall examine each in turn. The entire narrative is, in fact, structured around a number of related tensions: in addition to the opposition between the imaginary and the real, which Brandon is eventually obliged to confront, the film's violence may be seen as a product of the tension between individual desires and collective constraints, while the film as a creative work hesitates between being a 'True Crimes' murder story with mainstream erotic appeal (no doubt as the result of financial pressures on the director), and a parable with socio-political aims.

Sexual politics

Based on real events and real people, *Boys Don't Cry* has a docudrama flavour. The underlining of the narrative's rootedness in actuality enhances the film's social and moral didacticism. The film illustrates well the extreme social prejudices against sexual/gender preferences that lie outside the norm, persisting especially in ultra-conservative and homophobic small-town America. The focus here is therefore on the treatment of transgender in a corner of 'real' society. Unfortunately, Tom's and John's misreading of Brandon's transsexuality as lesbianism, based on a confusion of gender and sexuality, is not sufficiently highlighted in the narrative. Indeed, if we consider the love scenes as providing the key to a proper reading of the film, Brandon's transsexuality is in part repressed by the narrative itself. (This repression can be interpreted psychoanalytically as a disavowal of female lack: see White, 2001: 218.) When Brandon and Lana first make love, Brandon penetrates Lana with a prosthesis without her knowing, but she does glimpse his feminine cleavage, and subsequently appears to deny this knowledge to herself and others. Moreover, once Brandon confesses his true sex to Lana, both immediately begin to view their sexual attraction in lesbian terms. In a final loving encounter between them, Lana feminises Brandon in her use of language, telling him 'You're so pretty!', and asking, 'What were you like before all this? Were you like me, a girl-girl?', to which Brandon replies: 'Yeah, a long time ago. Then I guess I was just like a boy-girl.' Willox (2003: 419) argues with some justification that the use of the term 'boy' in this exchange, as in the film title itself, tends to reinforce gender binaries, but the important term in the dialogue of this scene is not 'boy' but 'girl', the use of which helps to transform their previous love-making into a linguistically-avowed lesbianism. The dialogue continues to invite a lesbian reading as they prepare to have sex:

LANA: I don't know if I'm gonna know how to do it.

BRANDON: I'm sure you'll figure it out.

Lana's apprehension is clearly related to her concerns about how to have sex with a woman, rather than with a female-to-male transsexual.[11] As

Willox demonstrates, media reportage helped perpetuate this confusion regarding Brandon's sexual and gender status, thus contributing to the denial by the film of transgendered subjectivity:

> The mainstream readings of Brandon's life include: a cross-dresser who is 'found out' ... a butch lesbian who could not come to terms with her sexuality; a transsexual man who had not yet undergone surgery or hormone therapy. The issue at stake in these readings seems to be the validity of Brandon's male gender identity in the light of his biology that, under the traditional binary understandings of gender, sex and the body, seemed to contradict his gender identity.
>
> (Willox, 2003: 413)

Homophobia and the castration complex

As already mentioned, the depiction of the killings as generated by homophobia is a further invitation to read the film as about lesbianism rather than transgender. This homophobia is seen to have its roots in castration anxiety and the absence of positive male role models.

Like many poor uneducated white communities in small-town USA, both Lincoln where Brandon lives with his cousin at the beginning of the film and Falls City exhibit deeply-rooted discriminatory attitudes to sexual difference. Such attitudes are apparent not only in the reactions of John and Tom to the revelation of Brandon's sex, but in the crude, callous and insensitive manner in which his rape is investigated by the local police.

Male attitudes in general in the film are seen to be generated by a homophobia which is an unconscious response to insecurities in relation to sexuality, and John's and Tom's aggression can be interpreted as a projection of internal guilt in relation to their own transgression of norms.[12] Like a kaleidoscope shaken up to form strange and disturbing patterns, relationships in general in this film are blurred and tinged with transgression. All of these relationships are controlled by John, the narrative's 'bad father'. John is a regular visitor to Lana's home, but is not sexually involved with either her or her mother, although there had been an exchange of love-letters between Lana and John when she was thirteen years old and John was in prison. John is clearly still attracted to Lana and behaves possessively with regard to her. John has a six-year-old daughter, April, from a past relationship, towards whom he exhibits incestuous tendencies. The rape of Brandon by John is also of course a transgressive act, and a symbolic reimposition by force of the feminine gender on Brandon to protect John's own heterosexuality, which he unconsciously perceives to be under threat. John's homoerotic bond with both Tom and Brandon suggests a repressed homosexuality, and the associated guilt expresses itself in homophobic violence directed externally towards Brandon. To view Brandon as a lesbian rather than a transsexual is less threatening to male heterosexual identity. The sexual character of their attack on Brandon is at once a symbolic rejection of homosexuality, and through their rape of Teena, a symbolic reassertion of the heterosexual norm. What the men do to Teena is designed to restore the binary fixity that Brandon's behaviour threatens.

The absence of any positive paternal role models in Lana's extended family has deleterious effects on the psychological health of both the men and the women in these communities, and may therefore be a root cause of the male gender insecurities. All of the characters in the narrative – Lana, Brandon, Tom, Candace and even Lana's mother – appear to be locked into an abusive relationship with John, to whom they relate as to a father. In this extended family and, by implication, in the wider community, 'bad fathers' substitute for 'good ones', as young fatherless males engage in male-bonding rituals that encourage a subculture of machismo and violence (fights in bars, drag-racing).

The persisting insecurities and accompanying violence can be also analysed psychoanalytically as the product of a castration complex, itself a symptom of the unsatisfactory resolution of the Oedipal struggle between father and son. *Boys* illustrates well the theme of what Eugene Monick calls male rage. In Monick's Jungian perspective, male rage is the product of castration anxiety, a violent reaction against any threat to the phallos (sic), defined as a man's 'creative power' and the 'governing symbol of masculinity' (see p. 82):

> Whether or not a man 'should' feel so strongly about himself is not the issue here. Rage is an arc of emotion which by-passes intermediate and more rational anger, drawing its archetypal power from the depth of the masculine instinctual life force ... Rage is a last resort. Often its force is proportionate to the intensity of anger that has been repressed ... Rage is impacted, stored up, 'pressure-cooked'

primal anger. Once a survival threshold level of threat to phallos [sic] is perceived by a male – wherever that threshold may be for a given man – the rage response ... is automatic.

(Monick, 1991: 9, 17 and 99)

Monick readily acknowledges that all recipients of male rage are victims, and that nothing can justify abuse, beatings or murder. His agenda is to point up the connection between male rage and castration as a widespread societal phenomenon.

In *Boys*, it is significantly not the female 'victims' of Brandon's deception who are 'enraged', but the young and aggressively macho male members of their families. The intensity of this anger does appear to suggest a deep-seated anxiety related not only to their sexuality but also to their gender, which Brandon's example is unconsciously perceived to destabilize. It is, precisely, the collapse of a distinction between sexuality and gender that arouses anxiety, especially (though not exclusively) in the male characters of this film. A fear of being feminized is for Monick the underlying source of their rage. As a defence against the threat of castration that Brandon represents as a biological woman taking a man's place with another woman, John and Tom commit a symbolic act of castration against him, not only by raping him but also by exposing to Lana the castrated condition he shares with all women when they force her to look at Brandon's naked genitals.[13] Monick's Jungian analysis helps us to understand that this violence is an extreme response to castration anxiety pervading a culture that at bottom is still rooted in patriarchal ways of thinking.

The Wizard of Oz

Notwithstanding this irresistible reading of the film in terms of a rage stemming from homophobia rather than transgender, it is just possible to read the confusion over Brandon's sexual and gender identity in more positive terms. In counterpoint to the brutal violence of the film's climax and the hostile reality from which it emerges is a fantasy world in which all dreams can be fulfilled, all identities are possible, and all types of relationship thinkable. Ironically based on real events, *Boys* actually situates itself on the one hand between its pedagogical mission to expose homophobic violence and its sources and an enchanting 'Wizard of Oz' space on the other. This imaginary space is inhabited by Brandon, a likeable 'Billy Liar' who manages to convince himself as well as those around him that his imagination is a version of reality, to the extent that the boundary between the two becomes blurred, at least for a temporary period. Lana's repression of the evidence that Brandon is a woman may be interpreted in terms of a preference to maintain a pleasurable distance from reality. When Lana visits Brandon in prison, and he tells her he is a hermaphrodite, Lana's response suggests a refusal to base her feelings for him on sexual identity: 'I don't care if you're half monkey or half ape, I'm getting you out of here!' This linguistic disavowal is more clearly enunciated by Lana in the film's climax, when John and Tom are demanding to verify Brandon's sex: 'I know you're a guy!' she exclaims. Lana's disavowal of Brandon's true sex may be rooted in her own unconscious attraction to the feminine, as suggested by her fondness for 'cow' images. On the other hand, as Halberstam argues, Lana displays a 'willingness to see what is not there (a condition of all fantasy) but also a refusal to privilege the literal over the figurative (Brandon's genitalia over Brandon's gender presentation). The female gaze, in this scene, makes possible an alternative vision of time, space and embodiment' (Halberstam, 2001: 295). In any event, their relationship is marked by an intentional blurring of categories such as 'heterosexual', 'homosexual', 'masculine' and 'feminine' that invites the spectator to 'bracket off' the whole question of sexuality and gender in relation to sexual desire. Brandon himself is portrayed as a dreamer, forever fleeing reality and responsibility for his actions. This aspect of his character is encapsulated in his unrealisable ambitions to 'make it' in Graceland, or to join his non-existent sister who, he claims, is a model in Hollywood. The theme of escape into an imaginary world in which all socially-constructed boundaries dissolve and anything is possible is archetypally American in a cinematic context. After their love-making, Lana gazes up at the starry night sky and like Dorothy in *The Wizard of Oz*, fantasises about 'beaming ourselves out there!'[14]

How, then, might we sum up the film's representation of transgender? On the negative side, Brandon Teena, as played by Hilary Swank, is not an eroticised figure. Any eroticism in the film is generated by the girls Brandon seduces, not by Brandon himself who is too masculinised to appeal to a heterosexual male spectator (or lesbian?). Even the director has described the actress playing him, Hilary Swank, as 'androgynous-looking' (see Director's Commentary). Insufficiently masculine to be sexually attractive to most heterosexual women, the character of Brandon runs the risk of stereotyping female-to-male transsexuals as androgynous or asexual, or, at best, as appealing only to 'femme' lesbian spectators.

Almost all of the sexual excitement is generated by Chloë Sevigny as Lana Tisdel in love-making scenes between the two. The pretty and nubile Sevigny performs orgasmic pleasure exquisitely, an overhead camera shot of her facial expressions implicitly inviting the heterosexual male or homosexual female spectator to identify with the Hilary Swank character, as Lana's naked body is eroticised and objectified, with a fetishistic focus on her breasts. The eroticisation of Lana rather than Brandon helps to recuperate the film for a mainstream audience by reinforcing conventional binarisms (male spectator – female character).

The film thus simultaneously generates sympathy for the gender-confused Brandon (whom the narrative turns into a tragic victim) while reassuring the audience that their own sex/gender identities remain intact. We have seen how the 'lesbianisation' of Brandon and Lana in the final love-making scene evacuates the otherness of transsexuality, domesticating Brandon for a sexual politics that feels more comfortable with non-phallic sex between two biological females than with sex between a young woman and a female-to-male transsexual.[15] Above all, this aspect of the representation of transgender in this film underscores the need to find language for classifications of gender beyond male and female, and of sexuality beyond hetero and homo (Willox, 2003: 421, makes a similar point).

On a thematic level, some might regret the over-emphasis on an imaginary as the only locus in which sexual and gender deviation may safely exist, an imaginary that is here seen to clash violently with a hostile real world in which castration fear constantly pulls individuals back to collective norms. The imaginary in this film is a hopeless utopia, at best a temporary refuge from the real. In contrast, Butler has shown how the imaginary can serve a progressive gender politics, and, as I shall argue in my concluding chapter, the imaginary might indeed also offer ways forward to those for whom traditional sex and gender roles are an inadequate expression of their identity.

6
Walking on the Wild Side: Shemale Internet Pornography

Numerous studies have been published to date, many by gay and feminist scholars, on the nature and effects of pornographic representations. Very little attention, however, has been focused by scholars on the Internet, perhaps because it is still a relatively new medium, but above all, I think, because the Internet remains an unordered and chaotic space, Internet material defying definition, challenging conventional categories of authorship, genre and form. Such a space can appear daunting, its contents lacking the specificity required for critical investigation. It is understandable, then, that many in the academic community would seek to avoid any contact with the Internet, even as an object of study in itself. The view is often heard expressed – and in many respects it is a legitimate one – that Internet material is unoriginal and unexciting in both form and content, and so unworthy of critical interest. What little attention has been devoted to Internet pornography concentrates on images of men and/or women who can broadly speaking be described as straight or gay, engaged in activities associated with these binary sexual identities. Those few who have turned their critical gaze to Internet porn have shown little if any interest in Internet sites representing transsexuals.[1] As far as I know, the only critic to date to have devoted any serious effort to the subject of transgender in pornography is Laura Kipnis, whose work is of undoubted value and insight, but her focus is pictorials and personal ads in transvestite magazines[2] rather than transsexual or 'tranny' porn on the Internet, and she is less interested in transvestites as pornographic objects than as subjects that transgress stereotyped norms.[3] Much of Kipnis's work is nevertheless of relevance to the study of transsexual porn, and I shall refer to it from time to time here.

The male-to-female transsexual porn object is a relatively recent phenomenon. Indeed, opportunities for both men and women to transform their bodies in any kind of permanent fashion have been available only since the early twentieth century, while the World Wide Web, which has enabled the dissemination of transsexual pornography across the world in ways unthinkable in the past, has existed for a much shorter period of time. It would seem helpful to proceed by first sketching the history of the two technologies which have made possible the creation of this new and powerful pornographic object. (For the history of the Internet, see Mac Bride, 2001; Naughton, 1999; and Berners-Lee, 2000.)

The Internet is the hardware base (computers and connections between them, as well as the software that makes communication possible) upon which the World Wide Web is built. The host computers are owned and run by a variety of different institutions, including government agencies, businesses, universities and other organisations. There is therefore no single organism that owns or controls the Internet, which is partly why it is practically impossible to regulate. The history of the Internet dates back to the 1940s, when the US military were interested in creating a communications technology that would survive nuclear war, but the commercial and informational potential of the Internet was not realised until the development of the personal computer in the 1990s.

Concern about the dissemination of pornographic images on the Net arose in the mid-1990s. In the summer of 1995 *Time* magazine printed a story about the threat of 'cyberporn', which claimed that the Internet was dominated by pornography. Although the article and the research behind it were subsequently discredited, the allegations led to attempts to control the Internet in the United States through legislation.[4] As a result, The Communications Decency Act was introduced but following challenges by civil rights groups the act was eventually thrown out as unconstitutional.

It is undeniable that many forms of pornography are easily accessible on the Internet but the nature of sites accessed and numbers of 'hits' are extremely difficult to quantify because such information derives from those who own and manage the sites themselves and who therefore have a vested interest in artificially inflating access figures. It is also not possible to count the number of times files are downloaded since the Net only measures how many people are given the opportunity to download, not how many actually do so (see Naughton, 1999: 33). Yet, on the basis of claims made by porn sites themselves and of an impressionistic evaluation of the ever burgeoning numbers of 'tranny' sites as evidenced by results thrown up by search engines, 'shemale' Internet pornography can be said to be a significant and growing phenomenon. As with all forms of pornography, the rapid growth of Internet technology in the space of just a few years has itself led to a similarly rapid growth in such material.[5] And because anyone with a personal computer can access any site on the World Wide Web, this pornography knows no national or ethnic frontiers and is genuinely universal.

With the assistance of female hormones and sometimes surgical intervention, male-to-female transsexuals have for some time been able to acquire breasts, to flesh out their hips and buttocks into a more rounded feminine shape, and to get rid of facial and bodily hair so that their skin acquires a more feminine smoothness, although it is only over the past decade that Internet technology has afforded such individuals (and the pornographers who exploit them) the means to transform themselves into valuable erotic objects. (See Chapter 2 for the history of gender reassignment technology in the twentieth century.) The pre-op transsexuals that make up the overwhelming majority of transsexual models represented in Internet pornography, however, have retained their male genitals, greatly enhancing their erotic appeal (see later).[6] In fact, the opportunities for mass exposure and therefore high levels of remuneration that the Internet and, in some cases, prostitution provide are arguably the main incentive for many young and attractive pre-op male-to-female transsexuals to remain pre-op, although the expense of reassignment surgery may also prove a deterrent. Whatever the reasons for the preponderance of pre-op male-to-female transsexuals, it is the latter's uncertain or ambiguous status that has been found by some to be politically problematic.

What troubles gays about transsexuals is that their very existence threatens the notion of fixed and specific sexual orientations. As Leo Bersani observes, 'It is not possible to be gay-affirmative, or politically effective as gays, if gayness has no specificity' (Bersani, 1995: 61). Although little has been written about porn images of transsexuality, we are bound to assume that they would receive the same negative reception from the gay community as transgendered persons have done in society and for similar reasons. Judith Butler's argument against fixed and unambiguous gender identity which implicitly favours transgender without referring to it explicitly, is itself criticised by Bersani on these grounds:

> As an assault on *any* coherent identity, it forecloses the possibility of a gay or lesbian specificity (erasing along the way the very discipline – gay and lesbian studies – within which the assault is made): resistance to the heterosexual matrix is reduced to more or less naughty imitations of that matrix.
>
> (Ibid.: 48)

Moreover, as Kipnis observes, feminists have often expressed resentment that the transvestite male – and the same might surely be said of the pre-op male-to-female transsexual – may play at being a woman while retaining all the privileges of male power, as symbolised by the phallus. Hence, some feminist theorists of gender are highly suspicious of transgender, fearing that transgendered males in particular are producing negative caricatures of femininity and are fundamentally hostile to women. (See Kipnis, 1996: 88; see also Chapter 1 for discussion of Queer Theory's hostile reactions to transsexuality.)

More crucially in the context of this pornography, the phallic focus that the pre-op transsexual simultaneously embodies and invites keeps both viewing subject and viewed object trapped in a phallicist economy that is politically unacceptable to those feminist and lesbian groups seeking to transcend phallogocentrism to achieve what Judith Butler calls a 'postgenital sexuality' (see Butler, 1999: 39).[7] Transsexual pornography is typically constructed around a number of binary oppositions that might be seen as reinforcing and reflecting the male-female binarism of heterosexist culture.

All of this helps to explain why this form of pornography has remained virtually invisible to those researching the representations of sexuality and gender in pornographic media. Anti-pornography feminists such as Andrea Dworkin and Catherine MacKinnon, for example, whose main aim is to show the abuse and degradation of women represented in pornography produced by and for heterosexual men, or lesbian and gay commentators whose interest understandably lies principally in pornographic material aimed at their own communities, have shown little or no interest in transsexual pornography. (See Hughes et al., 1998, for a less partisan collection of essays in this area by lesbian and gay, as well as straight critics.) In either case, this pornography defies the categorisation and definition that their arguments demand. 'Shemale' porn disrupts some common assumptions about what porn is, especially the anti-porn feminist view that porn represents the graphic sexual abuse of women for the pleasures of heterosexual men, although, as we shall see later, the abusive rhetoric accompanying shemale porn is comparable to that found in more mainstream porn sites depicting biological women.[8]

There is little doubt, on the other hand, that transsexual pornography defies the conventional categories of gender classification. The bodies portrayed in 'tranny' porn sites appear to belong to at least three gender categories, from transvestite males, to pre-op male-to-female transsexuals with breasts and penises, to post-op transsexuals with breasts and vaginas. The pre-op transsexual is a model of gender subversion, transcending the binary system of gender far more effectively than the drag-artist or the gay man or woman. For what are we to call the pre-op tranny? – no longer just a 'he' and not yet quite a 'she', the 'chick with a dick' hovers confusingly and in many cases indefinitely between the masculine and the feminine. Unlike the post-op transsexual who has chosen a penis (female-to-male) or a vagina (male-to-female) as his/her means to bodily fulfilment, pre-op transsexual remains suspended between the sexes, between 'doing real' and 'being real' in Butler's terms, and as such, cannot be said to be reinforcing hegemonic binarism. (For Butler, post-op transsexuality – *being* a woman/man – is playing the hegemonic game, in which heterosexuality is the dominant player: see Chapter 1, 'Queer Theory', and Prosser, 1998: 48.) Indeed, the 'chick with a dick' inspires fear in some, precisely because (s)he is worryingly, perilously impossible to classify in normative categories of gender/sex/sexuality. If, as Luce Irigaray claims, woman is the sex that is not one, the pre-op transsexual is the sex that is both, an overdetermined gender cluster that Janus-like faces simultaneously into the masculine and the feminine (see Irigaray, *This Sex Which Is Not One*).

As regards sexuality, the shemale can be active or passive or both, heterosexual (attracted to men), homosexual (attracted to women), bisexual (attracted to both), narcissistically attracted to other shemales, or a mixture of all of these (some photosets depict more than one transsexual, either alone or with one or two males or biological females; here, the shemales may engage in sex with each other, with the males or biological females, or with all three). Indeed, this brand of pornography is disturbing because, unlike any other, it undermines and disrupts the viewer's (and that includes the critic's) sense of his or her own sexual identity. The shemale is infuriatingly 'in between', subverting all fixed norms, and transgressing the boundaries that conventionally demarcate sexual desire.[9]

Because of the literal *becoming* of the male-to-female pre-op transsexual, it seems that this figure disrupts the hegemony of 'compulsory heterosexuality'. When Wittig wrote of the lesbian as 'the only concept I know of which is beyond the categories of sex', one can only conclude that this assertion was born either of ignorance or of personal prejudice (quoted by Butler, 1999: 26).

The polymorphous nature of the shemale's erotic attractions manifests itself clearly in her excessive and emphatic physicality. Images of the shemale emphasise her open orifices and rotundities (mouth, penis, anus, breasts, belly, 'bubble ass'), making her in Bakhtinian terms a manifestation of the grotesque body, which destabilises all traditional boundaries:

> All these convexities and orifices have a common characteristic; it is within them that the confines between bodies and between the body and the world are overcome: there is an interchange and an interorientation. This is why the main events in the life of the grotesque body, the acts of the bodily drama, take place in this sphere. Eating, drinking, defecating and other elimination (sweating, blowing the nose, sneezing) as well as copulation, pregnancy, dismemberment, swallowing up of another body – all of these acts are performed on the confines of the outer world ...
>
> (Bakhtin, 1968: 317; quoted by
> Stallybrass and White, 1986: 65)

The shemale also serves Butler's arguments against the normative regulation of sexual and gender identities by undermining the presupposition of a causal relationship between gender and sexual desire: as mentioned above, shemale pornography displays transsexuals engaging in sex acts with men, women and other transsexuals (anal penetration but also fellatio and cunnilingus). It is now received wisdom that because a man wants to be a woman, this does not mean that (s)he sexually desires only men, so that a male-to-female trans-sexual may think of herself and behave as a lesbian. More than any other identity category, the shemale represents the possibility of the liberation of both gender and desire from binary or fixed norms. The transgressivity of the transsexual is therefore politically progressive, but it also, as we shall see below, plays a significant role in the tranny's success as a pornographic object of male desire.

For these reasons alone, Queer Theorists ought to take transsexual pornography far more seriously than they have done hitherto.[10] In its emphasis on the constructedness of gender and sexuality and its drive to escape the binarism of fixed heterosexual or homosexual positions, Queer Theory seems perfectly suited to the analysis of transsexual pornography and its effects. In spite of the difficulty of escaping the binary matrix of conventional sexual and gender roles, Butler's analysis of gender helps us to see how the transsexual object disrupts this binarism in one important respect: by appealing to a '*trans*itional' category of sexual orientation somewhere between the hetero and the homo. This is a new category, not synonymous with bisexuality, a sexual category created by new hormonal drugs, but also by its very representation in pornographic images and in the language created to describe and define them. As for the word 'she-male', it may be seen less as a word that privileges the masculine than as a linguistic oxymoron that simultaneously reflects – but by its very impossibility challenges – binary thinking, collapsing the divide between the masculine and the feminine. It is in this sense that pre-op transsexuality can be viewed positively as 'queer', in that it is at odds with all norms, whether of a dominant heterosexuality or a gay/lesbian identity. If this form of porn is simultaneously exciting and disturbing, it is in part because the phallic woman that the transsexual represents challenges the fixity of our own sexual identity.

In exploring the modes and metaphors of shemale pornography on the Internet, it is therefore the construction of the viewer within the pornography itself as male that is of particular interest. This is not, of course, to exclude the possibility of women viewing this pornog-raphy, but my concern here is with the visual and verbal imagery (the photosets and their accompanying verbal text) that explicitly target heterosexual men.[11] These culturally constructed images have little to do with any transgender or transsexual reality but are essentially fantasy products, chemically, surgically and fictively designed to appeal to largely unconscious desires. Analysis of the nature of these desires suggests that the attractions of this pornography are, above all, attributable to its transgessive character, inviting a repositioning and redefinition of sexual desire in the light of the appeal of shemale pornography and transsexual prostitutes to heterosexual males.

Most Internet shemale porn shows cross-dressed men and pre-op transsexuals, always referred to as 'she', often in lingerie and various states of undress to begin with (some are fully clothed, others may be naked but hide their genitals between their legs initially), but the photosets usually follow the pattern of a striptease, quickly leading to the uncovering of the penis, which may at first be flaccid and then may become erect. Some sites show stills from movies depicting 'cum shots' (ejaculation) as a finale.

Like the films examined in earlier chapters, transsexual pornography plays on the tension between concealing and revealing to generate maximum excitement in the viewer. The gradual unveiling of the phallus and its capabilities is sometimes playfully depicted as a pleasant surprise for the male viewer who may be represented in the scenario as an unsuspecting 'straight guy' who is tricked or enticed into sexual relations with a 'tranny'. The following, for instance, is not untypical: 'Could you believe that she has balls? We send out hot shemales to pick up unexpecting [sic] guys. Of course the guys don't know they are shemales! How will they react? Visit *Tranny Surprise*...'

By the same token, the verbal rhetoric of many sites often appeals to the 'bi-curious' though heterosexually identified male viewer: 'Are you curious about shemales?' 'Why not try the best of both worlds?' This rhetoric sometimes appears to exaggerate the masculinity of its target customer by positioning him as a violent 'macho' man. In the following accompanying text to be found in *LadyboyGuide*, for instance, the customer is implicitly invited to identify with the aggressive male lover of a passive transsexual: 'Wang is completely obedient and complied to my every command without a word. Even when I ripped her ass open, she just turned her head to look behind her and then beamed at me, wide eyes [sic].' Other sites seek to position the prospective customer as a solidly (and reassuringly) 'normal', upright and by implication, heterosexual male:

> Looking for something different to fulfil your fantasies? This is an exclusive opportunity to spend time with a gorgeous, feminine, 'shemale'.
> It's time to put all those taboos aside.
> Your secret desires are shared by many, healthy, upscale, professional men, just like you, who are interested in meeting a Sexy Pre-Op Transsexual.
>
> (Internet ad for transsexual escort)

Some photos have a sadomasochistic character (leather corsets, whips, face-masks and so on), and other types of fantasy scenarios are enacted, featuring the leather-clad dominatrix or the flirtatious schoolgirl. Facial expressions range through all familiar female stereotypes: raunchy, innocent, ecstatic, the starlet, the slut, the shy virgin, the 'good ole girl', and so on. Whatever the variations, however, the phallus is always the central and final focus of this pornography, represented as the most powerful term in the binary oppositions that help to frame and define it. The visual focus in these images frequently switches from female clothing to male genitals, from breasts to penis, from stereotypical female physical qualities such as pretty features, smooth and hairless skin, girlishly long hair and hourglass curves to the aggressive masculinity of large testicles and rampant erection. Indeed, it is largely from these contrastive juxtapositions that the shemale's erotic power stems. The rhetoric of accompanying verbal commentaries is frequently structured around a similar binarism, as the following examples taken from different shemale Internet sites clearly demonstrate: 'Want a woman but still ache for a man? Come to *Transsexuals*. We can make your fantasy come to life!' 'These women each have a package in their panties.' Moreover, the very names of many of these sites foreground this binarism: 'Shemales', 'Chicks with Dicks', 'Girls with Balls', 'HeGirls', 'Transgirl', 'Pretty Girls with Big Dicks'. From the perspective of a progressive gender politics, it might be argued that the positioning of the male viewer as a 'curious heterosexual' reinforces homophobia by implying the undesirability of the homosexual position.[12]

On the other hand, this privileging of the heterosexist model is, one might say, inevitable. As Butler has recognised in relation to the lesbian body, it is perhaps not possible for the transsexual body to be constructed entirely outside the heterosexuality it might at the same time be said to subvert.[13] In pornography in particular, both the gay and lesbian and the transsexual body are constructed by discourses dominant in society as a whole that privilege masculinity and phallocentrism. In a more obvious way than the gay or lesbian, however, the shemale constructs herself through hormone treatment and surgery, and to that extent the shemale escapes hegemonic cultural discourses (which may be said nowadays to include socially acceptable concepts of gayness) to achieve a measure of autonomy and self-definition. Nevertheless, given this phallocentrism, how are we to explain male desire for the transsexual erotic object? Does this object appeal to a repressed or disavowed homosexuality, or are more complex erotic mechanisms involved?

Wanting it all

The vast majority of transsexuals appearing on Internet porn sites are 'passable' women, and indeed, when judged according to conventional western criteria of feminine beauty, many are stunningly attractive. We are a long way from the ludicrous caricature of woman that is the pantomime dame or the outrageously attired drag-queen. The pre-op transsexual model is typically young (between eighteen and thirty), girlishly pretty, slim but curvaceous, with a smooth, toned and often tanned skin. In some exceptional cases, the model has worked in the mainstream glamour industry, passing herself off successfully (and very profitably) as a biological female. Many sites depict European and American shemales, both black and white, but Asian 'ladyboys' and Brazilian transsexuals appear to have a particularly high profile.[14] Clearly, it would be beyond the scope of this study to account for the varying sexual tastes and preferences of individual viewers with regard to differences of race and colour. What follows, therefore, is an attempt to analyse the generalities of attraction to shemales. Psychoanalytic theory presupposes the existence of universal unconscious desires transcending ethnic and racial differences.

The shemale appeals directly to two fundamental aspects of male sexual desire: promiscuity and the search for novelty. All of the elements of the shemale's attraction for heterosexual males fall, therefore, into either or both of these overlapping categories.

If shemale porn is a popular form of Internet porn, as indicated at the outset, it is probably because the shemale represents and reflects back to the male viewer the polymorphous perversity of his own desire. The transsexual, then, combines the attractions of femininity with the promiscuity and sexual availability of the masculine. The stereotypical sexual voracity of men is thus transplanted, as it were, into women, conventionally perceived as passive and slow to awaken.

One might say, in fact, that the shemale unconsciously represents the masculinisation and colonisation of the foreign land, the dark continent that, for Freud, is woman. If the pre-op Internet shemale has acquired through hormones and surgery the physical shape of a woman to match the mental and psychological attributes of femininity that she doubtless already possessed, she is also represented as retaining enough physical, psychological and symbolic traits of male sexuality to be identifiably same as well as excitingly other. 'Woman' is thus tamed; the inaccessible, unapproachable and ultimately incomprehensible feminine is made ever available and totally comprehensible thanks to the reassuring presence of the indispensible and omnipotent phallus. The shemale can pleasure a man better than any woman, the rhetoric has it, since she combines all the attractions of femininity with a unique understanding of the male body that only another male can possess. Shemale Internet sites often attempt to exploit this stereotyped view that only another 'man' knows what really turns a man on: 'These shemales can suck you off better than your wife.'[15]

At the same time, as with many porn images of biological women, the shemale offers an opportunity to express a powerful unconscious frustration with the maddeningly coquettish female object of male desire. The metaphorical language of shemale porn expresses degradation of the feminine as part of a process of erotic overfeminisation and at the same time, a settling of scores with the desired but castrating woman who exploits her sexual power over men. Terms such as 'sluts', 'whores', and 'bitches' are used in many sites to describe the transsexual models depicted. In this perspective, the shemale image is, therefore, vulnerable to analysis as the simultaneous expression of desire and hatred for the feminine, just like any other pornographic image that represents women as a potential object of male violence or contempt. Feminists might well argue here that the transsexual is, in this sense, an unconscious substitute for all women, a male effigy of the feminine that can be burnt at the phallic stake. At the same time, the transsexual's ambivalent gender status suggests that the motivations for this verbal and sometimes physical violence (see earlier) are more complex: in the transsexual scenario, the abuse is more ironic than serious, aimed at enhancing the erotic power of the shemale by emphasising her sexual appetites and drawing attention to her 'femaleness', albeit in ostensibly negative terms.

Both erection and, above all, ejaculation are as ubiquitous in straight as in shemale pornography, which perhaps suggests that the motivation for such displays in the straight scenario is less the satisfaction of the viewer's homoerotic desires than of a more complex unconscious need. This question might seem less clear-cut in the case of shemale porn, in that the viewer of this phallus-centred pornography may arguably be responding to latent homosexual urges. On the other hand, homosexuals are, after all, sexually attracted to attributes of masculinity (muscular physique, body hair, Adam's apple) of which even the pre-op transsexual model has rid herself. In case the male 'heterosexual' viewer does harbour homophobic anxiety about his own sexuality, this is neutralised by the model's excessive femininity, as exhibited in her bodily postures, facial expressions, and figure-hugging clothes.

If the pre-op transsexual is vastly more popular among Internet spectators than post-ops, then, it must be because the continued presence of the male genitals serves a more complex function than the simple satisfaction of homosexual or even bisexual urges. Drawing upon the Freudian theory of castration anxiety in all males, Linda Williams offers an explanation for the importance of what in the porn industry is known as 'the money-shot', that is, the fully visible ejaculation of semen. Williams sees the money-shot, an essential component of every hard-core movie, as a fetishistic figure of female lack, reassuring men, calming their castration fears (Linda Williams, 1990: 116). We remember that all fetishes are, for Freud, a substitute for the phallus that the female has lost and, as such, a means of assuaging male castration anxiety (Freud, 'Fetishism': 345–57). In this sense, desire for the shemale may be said to be, at least partly, fetishistic in nature. Moreover, for Freud, a fetish 'saves the fetishist from being a homosexual by endowing women with the characteristic which makes them tolerable as sexual objects' (ibid.: 353).

The male's unconscious fear of castration gives rise to a need for visual evidence of 'intactness' with which the male viewer unconsciously identifies, and in the shemale scenario, this evidence is not merely peripheral, as in heterosexual porn, but occupies centre stage where Irigaray's 'nothing to see' of the woman is filled by the 'look-at-me-ness' of the male erection ('l'horreur du rien-à-voir de la femme': Irigaray, 1977: 25). The fearsome threat of the *vagina dentata* has in the shemale been replaced by the reassuring familiarity of the phallus. In the unconscious perspective identified by Freud, then, the transsexual is not a man, chemically equipped with the attributes of a woman, but a woman to whom the lost penis has been restored. Hence, the constant focus in transsexual porn on the penis, its size, power and availability, both active and passive ('Imagine being fucked by your girlfriend!' 'These bitches love being sucked dry'). At the same time, the male viewer may somewhat paradoxically be made to feel inferior by the well-endowed transsexuals he encounters, and indeed, this sense of sexual inferiority is often encouraged by accompanying verbal messages – for example, 'Her dick is bigger than yours'. Indeed, some photosets are actually accompanied by advertisements for penis enlargement pills!

Linked to the need for visual signs of intactness is perhaps the satisfaction of a desire to see visual evidence of the other's arousal. Such a desire is not limited to twenty-first century visual pornography: Peter Cryle identifies it in the emphasis on erection and discharge to be found in the erotic fiction of eighteenth-century France. The commonplace that women are known to dissimulate, faking orgasm in particular to please their male partners, leads the men in these novels and the male readers whom they represent to require verification of female pleasure:

> A woman's desire is manifest in her erect clitoris, available for examination in a way that is parallel, if quantitatively inferior to a man's ... What climactic eroticism needs and desires is proof. It finds this proof readily in the bodies of men, and exacts it in kind from the bodies of women.
>
> (Cryle, 2001: 154 and 157)

In the most literal of senses, then, the shemale porn consumer wants it all: the feminine *and* the masculine, the breasts *and* the penis, visible and incontrovertible signs of *jouissance* from the uncastrated woman. The penis plays a crucial role in the arousal of the spectator – not necessarily because the latter is actually homosexual but because of the shocking and simultaneously exciting contrast it represents. The juxtaposition (all-important in visual porn) of male erection with female breasts and other archetypally feminine features incarnates an impossible fantasy of sexual totality that offers the male viewer complete sexual satisfaction, not simply because the transsexual image contains the attributes of both sexes, but because, as already noted, the viewer is offered in fantasy the sexual skills of another 'male'.

From a psychoanalytic point of view, this demand for total satisfaction is the expression of an unconscious yearning for the lost maternal phallus and an unconscious desire to return to pre-Oedipal unity with the mother. Collapsing both sameness and difference, the shemale represents the prelapsarian fantasy of the original undivided being, a utopian state that Monique Wittig nevertheless sees gender as destroying: 'Gender is an ontological impossibility because it tries to accomplish the division of Being. But Being as being is not divided' (Wittig, 81; quoted by Bersani, 1985: 189 n.19). For Joyce McDougall, similarly, the fantasy of the hermaphrodite, as old as the cultural history of mankind, is linked to a primordial desire to abolish the difference that separates self from other:

> I want to maintain here that the hermaphroditic ideal has its roots in the ideal of a unity of child with maternal breast. The search for an ideal state in which lack does not exist proves that the breast is already lost, that is, already perceived as being the essence of an Other. Thus, the bisexual illusion in all its manifestations is constructed upon the ramparts of sexual difference, but its underlying basis is located in the primordial relationship, in the still present desire to abolish this separation from the Other, to deny this impossible alterity.
>
> (McDougall, 1973: 410–11; my translation)

McDougall argues that the desire to be the other sex whilst retaining one's own sexuality is a universal unconscious desire (ibid.: 417). Desire for the transsexual, then (McDougall was writing well before the advent of the hormone treatment that has to a large extent made possible the transsexual's 'becoming' in the late twentieth and twenty-first century) is perhaps a displaced fantasy desire to *be* transsexual oneself, to regain that lost state of undifferentiation that we all enjoyed in the mother's womb (see ibid.: 413–14). The transsexual's penis and breasts that the viewer wants to suck and so literally introject are all maternal objects, the former being an unconscious metaphorical displacement for the mother's lost phallus, as well as a third nipple from which milk can be made to flow, a symbolic union and absorption of material sustenance, maternal love and sexual sensations that have their origins in the physical stimulations of the uterus.

As both male and female, the shemale in Lacanian terms both *has* and *is* the phallus. In Lacan's rereading of Freud's Oedipal phase, the male infant goes from *being* the phallus that the mother lacks to *having* the phallus by identifying with the father. (On being and having the phallus, see also *The Crying Game* in Chapter 5.) The pre-op transsexual clearly still has the phallus (not because she still possesses a penis – the phallus is more a signifier than a real object – but because, as a biological man, she retains male authority and power, or what Lacan calls 'The Law of the Father').[16] But at the same time, in feminising herself, in transforming herself into an erotic object of male desire, the shemale again *becomes* the phallus that (s)he was in the pre-Oedipal phase, when as an infant, (s)he tried to identify with the phallus as the mother's object of desire. In a Lacanian perspective, this is precisely what the fetishist, and in particular, the transvestite does, and in this respect, the pre-op transsexual is vulnerable to the same analysis. Quoting Lacan, Benvenuto and Kennedy provide a clear and concise summary of this process:

> The infant's main means of obtaining satisfaction is by identifying himself with the mother's object of desire – his desire is then the desire of the Other. To please her, to keep her love (or so he thinks) he must at one level *be* the phallus. He informs the mother that he can make up to her what she lacks, and he will be, as it were, the 'metonymy' of the phallus, replacing the desired phallus by himself. It is around this lure that the fetishist articulates his relation to his fetishistic objects (such as bits of clothing, shoes, etc.) which are symbols of the woman's phallus in so far as it is absent, and with which he identifies. The transvestite identifies with the phallus as hidden under the mother's clothes – he identifies with a woman who has a hidden phallus.

According to Lacan, the perversions seem to play a never-ending imaginary game, where the phallus is neither completely present nor absent: 'The whole problem of the perversions consists in conceiving how the child, in his relation to the mother, a relation constituted in analysis not by his vital dependence on her, but by his dependence on her love, that is to say, by the desire for her desire, identifies himself with the imaginary object of this desire, in so far as the mother herself symbolizes it in the phallus.'

(Benvenuto and Kennedy, 1986: 132–3; quoting Lacan, *Écrits*, 197–8)

In her own commentary on Lacanian psychoanalysis and its relation to gender, Butler stresses the link between being the phallus and the desire to rediscover a pre-gendered existence when self and (m)other were inseparable: 'To be the Phallus is to "embody" the Phallus as the place to which it penetrates, but also to signify the promise of a return to the preindividuated jouissance that characterizes the undifferentiated relation to the mother' (Butler, 1999: 203 n.13). To desire the one who both is and has the phallus is therefore to identify simultaneously with the masculine and the feminine positions as described by Lacan, an impossible situation symbolic of an unconscious yearning to become again the unsexed foetus, to be reunited with the mother in the fullness of the womb before gender differentiation occurred.[17] If, as we saw above, the 'mother's' penis is superior in size to that of the awestruck 'infant' viewer, this is as it should be in the hierarchy of the mother–child dyad.

Desiring the shemale may, then, after all, be an unconscious substitute for desiring the mother. In this respect, the shemale is a perfect representation of the phallic mother fantasy that counters male castration anxiety. The photosets of shemale sites appear typically to play a game with the viewer, as we have already seen, teasing him with a gradual striptease leading to a sudden and shocking unveiling of the phallus, as the beautiful 'girl' with feminine curves and soft skin is dramatically revealed to be genitally and often priapically male.[18] This game is of course known by all to be a pretence, the kind of ritualistic repetition that Freud identifies as an unconscious meaningful ritual. This is the *fort!da!* game, which both Freud and Lacan link with the origins of language, the latter identifying language itself as a substitute for the lost object of the mother's body (see Lacan,

1977b). This game of repetition crucially provides the child, and for Freud the agent of any creative activity, with the means of mastering a potentially painful memory. This is ultimately the role of all objects, but it is a function fulfilled perfectly by the Internet website, over which the viewer has the illusion of total control and to which he returns again and again. (See Chapter 1 for a description of the *fort!da!* game, as observed by Freud, and discussion of its relevance to the theme of unveiling in transgender narratives.)

The shock of the new

If this *fort!da!* game compels the viewing subject to repeat it endlessly in the unconscious hope of making the lost maternal object present again, it is because it is paradoxically novel and exciting each and every time it is played. The play between the hidden and the visible that constitutes desire's enigmatic object, and the shock of discovery are therefore central components of the metaphors of shemale porn. Roland Barthes's *S/Z* may once again prove useful as comparison here. (I have already exploited the relevance of *S/Z* in Chapter 3 in discussion of *Victor/Victoria*.) Barthes's 'hermeneutic' code, served by any phrase or sentence that helps to create mystery or enigma and so excite the reader's curiosity, may be applied to the first images in the shemale photoset. It is by adroitly manipulating this code in *Sarrasine* that Balzac is able to suggest to the reader (as to the eponymous hero) that La Zambinella is a woman, while simultaneously hinting that the opposite might in fact be the case. Like Balzac's hero, the reader is intended to be shocked and yet, at the same time, (s)he is curiously excited by the eventual discovery of the truth which, we are given to believe, (s)he may unconsciously have guessed at all along. Similarly, the shemale photoset initially performs not just the illusion of femininity but the suspension of disbelief by third parties, whether visually present in the images or implied in accompanying verbal text. This performance, as already indicated, leads to a final revelation of the phallus, which any males present in the images appear to find shocking ... and arousing. Yet, as in the Balzac story, rendered even more erotic by Barthes's own gradual and teasing unveiling, the viewer plays a game with himself, a willing accomplice in an erotic game of hide-and-seek. The finale is always shocking, but the shock was expected right from the start. And if, like Balzac's Sarrasine, the viewer discovers that the object of his desire is not what he thought it was, then he is compelled to acknowledge that he is not who he thought he was.

This pleasant half-expected shock – a sense of that 'familiar strangeness' that Freud identifies as associated with repetition and the repression of desires in the unconscious – derives much of its erotic impact from the revelation of contrastive juxtapositions (Freud, 'The Uncanny'). We saw earlier how an emphasis on such binary oppositions might be considered politically regressive, and yet, an essential element of the shemale's erotic power stems from them: breasts/balls, chicks/dicks, pretty girl/raging erection, smooth skin/stiff prick. These oxymorons create an uncertainty that is both reassuring and troubling, generating a thrill of pleasure in perversity, the sense of infringing those social and sexual taboos that defend both collective and individual identities, though without any associated moral or ethical guilt. They also help to generate an arousing sense of the transgression of limits defined by our culture. For Foucault, transgression is precisely the experience of such limits, outside of any ethical considerations: 'It is likely that transgression has its entire space in the line it crosses' (Foucault, 1963). More than any other, the pre-op transsexual inhabits this line between genders, and desire for the transsexual object is, therefore, a unique example of Foucault's concept of transgression as a liminal activity.

In conclusion, it seems important to reiterate that, by its very nature, the Internet is a fantasy realm, and that Internet pornography belongs, maybe more than any other pornographic medium, to fantasy alone. The vast majority of those who look at shemale images are unlikely, after all, to have any real contact with transsexuals. Fantasy allows the subject to free itself of sexual and gender identities in a manner that would prove difficult or impossible in the real world. By challenging received ideas concerning the nature of sexual desire and its relationship with fixed gender positions, these 'chicks with dicks' might in the end be shown to have rendered a vital service to the cause of an ongoing sexual and gender revolution. Far from being peripheral to contemporary debates about the representation of sexuality, transsexual pornography is of direct relevance, on a political and philosophical level, to the interests of all working in the field. Provocative, disturbing, even repulsive for some, the fantasy images that we have been considering are clearly not high art, but they are complex cultural phenomena that deserve far more critical attention.

7
Representation and Reality

Along with advances in surgical interventions, transsexuals have largely taken the place of cross-dressers in film dramas and documentaries. This is not the case with the comedies we have considered. As befitting its ludic aims, the comic genre inclines more to the portrayal of cross-dressing as a temporary disguise rather than as symptom of a more permanent and profound gender identity crisis. However, none of these is recent, the latest, *Mrs Doubtfire*, having appeared in the early 1990s. There have been no mainstream film comedies featuring cross-dressers since *Mrs Doubtfire*. In contrast, filmic, DVD and Internet portrayals of transsexuals who have undergone or would like to undergo a degree of surgical reassignment have increased, a fact that both reflects the higher profile of transsexuals in the media generally, and is evidence of a continuing fascination and anxiety which are focused more and more on the ever greater scientific possibilities and permutations of physical transformation. Other representations occupy the entirely negative vehicle of the thriller, or else find expression in the uneasy mix of comedy and drama, manifestation of the ambivalent reactions to transgender that we have identified throughout history.[1]

Overall, we have seen how the dominant filmic images of transgender from the 1950s to the end of the 1990s have in the end tended to reinforce stereotypical thinking on the subject. The intelligently written comedies of this period have been shown to contain a residual normativity that neutralised their more progressive features. The mixed-genre productions exhibit a greater ambivalence: ostensibly aiming to educate their audience into adopting more tolerant attitudes to transgender, these films have nevertheless been shown to reinforce the same stereotypes at unconscious levels, while the thriller genre has found an easy scapegoat in the ostensible strangeness of the transgendered.

On the other hand, despite the problems of objectification and of a phallicism inherent in the images of pre-op male-to-female transsexuals, Internet shemale pornography has paradoxically been shown to help liberate conventional notions of sexuality and gender, trapped within the artificial boundaries constructed by the binary system. It is ironic, although perhaps not entirely surprising, that pornography should prove more progressive than mainstream cinema, although the Internet is admittedly a very recent phenomenon, existing only since the early 1990s, while the majority of the films we have considered here were made in earlier, less enlightened times. Assuming that Internet pornography is a first primitive step in the positive direction of a virtual reality, we shall examine two related perspectives in this brief concluding chapter: the impact of the representation of transgender on concepts of gender and sexuality in the 'real', and what this implies for the future of desire. In other words, how does erotic fascination with transgender impact on our definitions and perceptions of sexual positioning and sexual desire?

Baudrillard and the dissolution of the real

So-called 'reality' TV shows take 'real' people as their subject in a variety of different situations, though the activities and situations they engage in are far from real. On UK television, soap-operas like *Coronation Street* and *Eastenders* which are set in working-class communities pride themselves on their gritty realism, and yet the tightly-knit communities they depict ceased to exist long ago. Significant sections of their viewers, on the other hand, believe in their reality to the point of sending wreaths to the studios when characters die, and to an even greater extent, the behaviours they represent have a demonstrable influence on the behaviour of viewers. Moreover, social pedagogy has increasingly dictated storylines in recent years. The sympathetic depiction of gays and, in the case of *Coronation Street*, of a transsexual character, best exemplify this level of interaction between television fiction and the reality it both reflects and impacts upon (see Chapter 1). As artists and poets have always known, representation influences how we see reality.[2] In a sea of images, representation has in so many respects conditioned our view of the real to the point where it can actually replace it. It is in this sense that one might say that all is performance now, so that Butler's implicit distinction between 'real' and 'performative' ceases to have meaning. The supremacy of the signifier (Lacan) and of metaphor (Barthes) has thus become the supremacy of representation over reality, and nowhere is this more true than in the realms of sexuality and gender, the two single most important dimensions of human life, and most essential to the maintenance of the symbolic order, and yet the two dimensions best suited to construction in the imaginary.[3]

The increasing dominance of the imaginary brings greater freedom for individuals to define themselves along sexual/gender continuums which themselves merge into and diverge from each other, waves rather than lines, spiralling between limits pushed ever further across boundaries long since forgotten. At the same time, the sense of transgression experienced in the crossing of boundaries lingers on as a Derridean trace, and as we have seen in our corpus, these developments meet with resistance from the (symbolic) law which seeks to reassert itself while appearing to appease the ever greater demand for the removal of boundaries. This ambivalence expresses itself in terms of an uncertainty, a vacillation between fear and fascination, between eroticisation and demonisation. The push towards the imaginary (mother) is held back by symbolic restraint (father). All of this is conducted beyond a real that, if it can be said to exist at all in a world in which biology is itself so often subject to imaginary desire, has little relevance to representation.

All of these trends are compatible with Jean Baudrillard's postmodern analysis of contemporary culture and his prophetic visions of the future. Much of Baudrillard's later work focused on new media, new technologies and cybernetics, and his theories are tailor-made for a study of filmic and computer-based images. In addition, many of the themes and motifs which we have identified in the representations of transgender examined in this book are also key notions in Baudrillard's postmodern view of the world. With the aid of Jean Baudrillard's postmodern vision of a real structured by a technological imaginary, I shall suggest how his theories may help to illuminate the relationship of cinematic and Internet images with reality, and the future of sexuality and gender as products of this relationship, and how, in an ideal future scenario, definitions and perceptions of sexuality and desire might continue to evolve. It is hazardous to predict any aspect of the future.

However, during the course of this book, we have unearthed some clues as to the potential forms and directions for the representation of sexual desire in the wake of the demolition of all fixed essences and boundaries that Baudrillard himself predicted over twenty years ago. That we have not yet reached this point is abundantly clear from my limited survey of films, but this does not prevent us from mapping out an ideal blueprint for the future.

Baudrillard's work constitutes an analysis of contemporary western culture that offers an interesting and oddly appropriate model for the mapping of future sexualities and genders. In Baudrillard's postmodern view, the model or code structures social reality. The effect of this is the erosion of distinctions between the model and the real, between representation and reality, and the impossibility of any direct access to the real, so that the 'real' as such disappears to be replaced by simulacra or simulations of reality:

> Today abstraction is no longer that of the map, the double, the mirror, or the concept. Simulation is no longer that of a territory, a referential being, or a substance. It is the generation by models of a real without origin or reality: a hyperreal. The territory no longer precedes the map, nor does it survive it. It is nevertheless the map that precedes the territory – *precession of simulacra* – that engenders the territory ... It is the real, and not the map, whose vestiges persist here and there in the deserts ... *The desert of the real itself.*
> (Baudrillard, 1994: 1)

In *Simulacra and Simulation*, Baudrillard identifies three orders of simulation:

1. A first-order simulation is one in which an imperfect representation is rendered (for example, a novel, painting or map).
2. A second-order simulation is one that so perfectly resembles reality that it could be taken for reality itself (for example, a plastic replica, exact in every respect, of the Eiffel Tower).
3. A third-order simulation is one that no longer has any basis in reality. This virtual reality, completely unconnected to reality itself, is what Baudrillard calls hyperreality, which the media of our consumer society help to construct.

Media representations thus refer primarily to other media representations rather than to the outside world (we have seen to what extent both thrillers and comedies with a transgender theme constantly refer to previous examples of the genre). The emphasis in my corpus has been on an imaginary universe, which moulds the spectator's view of transgender, just as in the world of media spectacles and simulations described by Baudrillard, the model or simulation comes first: 'Simulation is characterized by a *precession of the model*, of all the models based on the merest fact – the models come first, their circulation, like that of the bomb, constitutes the genuine magnetic field of the event' (ibid.: 16).

In this postmodern world, everything becomes undecidable: 'The medium itself is no longer identifiable as such, and the confusion of the medium and the message (McLuhan) is the first great formula of this new era' (ibid.: 30).[4] This undecidability makes it increasingly hard to distinguish true from false. What, we are bound to ask, are the implications of Baudrillard's theory of hyperreality and simulacra for the evolution of sexual desire?

The future of desire

It seems possible to apply Baudrillard's model to representations of sexuality with some accuracy. Taking Baudrillard's three stages in turn, the evolution of attitudes to sexuality can be broadly described as follows:

1. Sexual images are constructed/perceived as being an inferior substitute for 'the real thing'.
2. Pornography as representation slowly takes the place of 'real sex' which ceases to exist as such. The representation of sex in the imaginary scenarios of film and internet porn offers a satisfaction that 'real sex' can never do.
3. Gradually, these representations will in the future become disconnected from the real entirely, as virtual sex entirely replaces sex in the real.

The first two stages seem nowhere as well exemplified as in contemporary screen pornography, in which the represented object of desire is a fantasy construct. Both photographic and screen images are notoriously capable of pleasantly deceiving the viewer's eye, where a flesh and blood encounter with the human being(s) in front of the lens might prove deeply disappointing. The curious 'realness' of these representations, the 'insistence of the referent' which Roland Barthes in *Camera Lucida* identifies in the photographic image itself blinds the viewer to the fact of the referent's absence – the real body is no more present in the pornographic image than it is in any other form of (mediated) representation. The third and final stage of virtual or cyber-sex, wholly self-generating and dependent exclusively on constructed models rather than on photographic images of real people, is already beginning to appear possible, given the speed of technological advance (see below). But what has Baudrillard had to say about his theory's impact on sexuality, and what are the political implications of such developments?

In spite of his privileging of the imaginary over the real, and his prediction that all binaries will eventually crumble, much of Baudrillard's thinking on sexuality proper makes gloomy reading for those who would welcome a sea-change in this area, and indeed, my own analysis of transgender in mainstream cinema would seem to support his pessimistic vision. In a study entitled 'Fashion or the Enchanted Fairy Land of the Code' (in *L'échange symbolique et la mort* [Symbolic Exchange and Death]), Baudrillard applies his notions of simulation and the code to fashion, but also to the body as an object of design. Designing the body as a fashion object in itself is for him a characteristic feature of modernity. Together with the body, sexuality too becomes an object of simulation, determined by models (Kellner, 1989: 97). In his essay, 'The Body or the Carnality of Signs' (in *L'échange symbolique et la mort*), Baudrillard also views the body as marked by the signs of fashion and sexuality. Here, the implications are decidedly negative from the viewpoint of a progressive sexual politics and of individual freedom, since this body is inserted into a system of sexual exchange value 'organized entirely around the fetishization of the phallus as the general equivalent' (*L'échange symbolique et la mort*, 155; trans. Kellner, 99). While he frequently attacks Freudian theory, Baudrillard nevertheless broadly accepts Freud's notion of phallic dominance, insisting on the ubiquity in our culture of fetishistic displays of the phallus to alleviate castration anxiety: 'Fashion, publicity, nude-look, nude theatre, strip-tease: everywhere, it's the scenodrama of erection and castration' (ibid., 155; trans. Kellner, 99). He goes on to interpret various phenomena in these terms, including make-up, gloves, ties, stockings, striptease, and nudity:

> The line of the stocking across the thigh: the erotic power of this image does not come from its proximity to real sex and its positive

promise ... but from an apprehension of sex (the panicked recognition of castration) which is arrested upon the mise en scène of castration – this inoffensive mark of the line of the stocking ... and the naked thigh and metonymically the entire body, becomes through this caesura a phallic effigy, a fetish object of contemplation and of manipulation stripped of all menace.

(Ibid., 156; trans. Kellner, 99)

This is indeed a depressing scenario, since it totally excludes sexual desire, interpreting sexuality, including transsexuality, instead as a system of signs in which castration is the dominant one, and we have noted in preceding chapters the negative effects of castration fear in representations of transgender.

Above all, the body in its materiality tends to disappear in this postmodern vision, in which the signifier is all, and the referent has no solidity. In fact, this view is merely the culmination of a long western philosophical tradition. Since the Renaissance, the body has become less and less significant for philosophers.[5] Prosser cites a number of postmodernists who appear to celebrate the advent of bodiless sex: 'for Arthur and Marilouise Kroker transsexuality creates sex as it should be in our postmodern age, sex free from the body: "sex [that] has fled its roots in the consanguinity of nature, refused its imprisonment in the phallocentric orbit of gender" ' (Prosser, 1998: 14). The Krokers, Prosser maintains, 'read the transsexual's techno-surgery as the ultimate deconstruction of the sexed body ... glimpse a "new sexual horizon, post-male, post-female" ' (ibid.: 90). These extreme notions seem as unlikely as they are undesirable, from our current perspective at least.

There are, in any case, blatant contradictions in postmodern thought, taken as a whole, and Baudrillard himself elsewhere expresses more positive views of the evolution of sexuality, and implicitly, of gender. In *Forget Foucault*, for example, he heralds the collapse of the phallocratic empire: 'Today phallocracy is crumbling ... taking with it all forms of traditional sexuality' (Baudrillard, 1987: 57), whilst in *De la séduction* (On Seduction), he seizes upon cloning technology as facilitating new transformations of the body and sexuality. He sees cloning as offering a reproductive model that will separate sexuality from reproduction and make possible new kinds of body (and, by implication, new permutations of gender). A new kind of body, then, like that of the post-op transsexual, but a body nonetheless.

Baudrillard's pronouncements in this area have proven to be highly prophetic. The substitution of the signs of the real for the real (1984: 2), as he has pointed out, can already be seen at work at the heart of western culture, so that Disneyland (ibid.: 12–13), and so-called 'real' cities and countries (Los Angeles, Las Vegas, America) 'are no longer real, but belong to the hyperreal order and to the order of simulation' (ibid.: 12). Moreover, it is already clear from the current state of knowledge in the genetic sciences that gene manipulation could soon have the capacity to produce simulations of gender, made to order, whilst sexuality will be determined at will at a chosen point on a continuum. Given the now very real prospect of the conception and development of babies to term entirely in the laboratory, sexuality and reproduction will no longer have a necessary link. Sexuality will be cut loose, enjoying an unprecedented freedom to serve individual needs and desires. On the other hand, the child will no longer be caught up in the Oedipal drama, and psychoanalysis itself will become redundant: 'Father and Mother have disappeared to the profit of a matrix called a code. No more mother: a matrice' (*De la séduction*, 230; trans. Kellner, 101). Taking Baudrillard's analysis to its logical conclusion, it seems clear that the entire symbolic system may also disappear, and with it, the gender polarities (masculine/feminine) that found it.[6]

In conclusion, we can summarise the potentially positive consequences of Baudrillard's vision as follows:

- The continued explosion of binary polarities of sex/gender in a hyperreality tailor-made for each individual user.
- A menu of possibilities and potentialities to cater for all tastes, a remapping of identities as plural and limitless in the safety of hyperreal/cyberspace.[7]
- The subsuming of transgender in a plurality of sex/gender positions on a potentially unending continuum.
- The individualisation of sex/gender encounters through computer-generated simulations of sexual acts and the adoption of gender identities.
- The fragmentation of identities/sexualities in a radical decentring of societal/cultural interaction.

If Baudrillard is right, then any psychoanalytical projection of future cultural models will also be redundant. But as I write these concluding sentences in October 2005, such a paradise of individual freedom and choice has not quite yet arrived on earth. The symbolic order and the Oedipal struggle from which it emerges still control our lives. At the end of Chapter 2, I posed the problem inherent in any Freudian approach to aspects of human behaviour: how do we reconcile the unchanging responses of an unconscious formed in an Oedipal phase that repeats itself generation after generation, century upon century, with the hypothesis of a gradual dissolution of gender/sex/sexual fixity? We have established that, from the statues of Hermaphrodite sculptured by the ancients to recent films like *Boys Don't Cry* and *Cherry Falls*, the same mix of fear and fascination, of eroticism and repulsion structures our responses to transgender in the imaginary of our culture. Perhaps the answer to this apparent contradiction lies in how we deal with these unconscious responses, in strategies of reconciliation that change and evolve over time, varying according to the culture we inhabit. In a secular society, for example, we are far less likely to consider the sexual thrill associated with gender transgession as sinful, and are therefore less inclined to give in to guilt-induced repression. To believe that this is the positive direction in which sexuality will continue to evolve is, at least, an optimistic note on which to end this book. Representations in the form of models and simulacra may yet offer the potential for a total revolution in sexual behaviour and conceptions of sex and gender. Transsexuality, a hybrid product of the present binary system, defined by the very media images that depict it, is in this perspective only the beginning of a revolution that will transform our sexual habits in the west, leading to an explosion of multiple sexualities and genders beyond a reality that increasingly eludes meaningful definition.

Notes

1. Introduction

1. On the castrating effects on men of female laughter, see Hélène Cixous, 'The Laugh of the Medusa'. Castration as a metaphor refers to a man's deepest fear that his manhood might be lost or seriously compromised.
2. Endocrinology is defined as 'a new science that attempted to locate the essence of sex, gender, and sexuality in the secretions of the gonads' (Meyerowitz, 2002: 16).
3. Eve Kosofsky Sedgwick, among others, has recognised that transgender is a particularly good reason for developing a new theory of sexuality as distinct from gender (see Sedgwick, 1990: 37–8).
4. See Jagose (1996) for a useful overview of the subject.
5. Butler refers to Foucault's work on the nineteenth-century French hermaphrodite, Herculine Barbin, as demonstrating the inadequacy of conventional medico-legal discourse to account for the sexual practices of such people: 'Herculine is not an "identity", but the sexual impossibility of an identity . . . The linguistic conventions that produce intelligible gendered selves find their limit in Herculine precisely because she/he occasions a convergence and disorganization of the rules that govern sex/gender/desire' (Butler, 1999: 31).
6. In *Bodies that Matter: On the Discursive Limits of 'Sex'* (1993), Butler had also referred to the transsexual in a limited way as representing an ambivalence as regards sex.
7. Janice Raymond's lesbian feminist *The Transsexual Empire: the Making of the She-male* (1979) had argued that 'transsexuals are constructs of an evil phallocratic empire and were designed to invade women's spaces and appropriate women's power' (see Sandy Stone, 1991: 283).
8. For Judith Butler, Aretha Franklin's song reinforces the fiction of a natural or true gender identity, while simultaneously pointing to its constructedness: 'she seems at first to suggest that some natural potential of her biological sex is actualised by her participation in the cultural position of "woman" as object of heterosexual recognition. Something in her "sex" is thus expressed by her "gender" which is then fully known and consecrated within the heterosexual scene. There is no breakage, no discontinuity between "sex" as biological facticity and essence, or between gender and sexuality. Although Aretha appears to be all too glad to have her naturalness confirmed, she also seems fully and paradoxically mindful that confirmation is never guaranteed, that the effect of naturalness is only achieved as a consequence of that moment of heterosexual recognition. After all, Aretha sings, you make me feel *like* a natural woman, suggesting that this is a kind of metaphorical substitution, an act of imposture, a kind of sublime

and momentary participation in an ontological illusion produced by the mundane operation of heterosexual drag' (Butler, 1991: 27–8).
9. The word 'perversion' is regularly misused in this culture. In the UK, colloquial working-class discourses (those of tabloid newspapers, for example) frequently apply the term 'perv' or 'pervy' to what the popular culture regards as unacceptable expressions of sexuality, for example, the sexual attraction of an older man for a young woman, whereas 'perversion' in its strict psychological sense means 'deviation from the "normal" sexual act when this is defined as coitus with a person of the opposite sex directed towards the achievement of orgasm by means of genital penetration' (Laplanche and Pontalis, 1985: 306).
10. 'Under the hermeneutic code, we list the various (formal) terms by which an enigma can be distinguished, suggested, formulated, held in suspense, and finally disclosed' (Barthes, 1990: 19).
11. This and other related terms were developed by the French structuralist, Gérard Genette: for Genette, 'intradiegetic' describes a second-level narrator (or narratee), who is a character, telling (or listening to) a tale which is embedded in a primary narrative (see Genette, 1972: 238–41). However, I am using the term here in its literal sense of 'within the diegesis or primary narrative as opposed to outside it'.
12. In *S/Z*, Barthes sees the search for truth in realist literature as the completion of a sentence. In the dramatic theatre, according to Brecht, there is passionate interest in the dénouement. *Sarrasine* is a dramatic story, in which the dénouement is an unveiling: 'what constitutes the dénouement is the truth' (Barthes, 1990: 187). The sentence of truth is completed: 'truth is the predicate at last discovered, the subject at last provided with its complement' (ibid., 188). The subject, at least from an epic point of view, is constantly wandering in search of its predicate, and 'This temporary wandering of the predicate can be described in terms of a game. The dramatic narrative is a game with two players: the snare and the truth' (ibid.). Once the game is over, the drama has its dénouement, and the subject is united with its predicate, the discourse 'can do nothing more than fall silent' (ibid.).

2. Transgender in the historical imagination

1. The dangers of knowledge of the other sex is a common motif of the comedies discussed in Chapter 3.
2. As the title of Graille's book suggests, he is principally concerned with the representation of hermaphrodites in the discourses of the seventeenth and eighteenth centuries, but like my own, his study takes full account of an essential historical background, offering a unique exploration of the evolution of thinking about hermaphrodites in the mythical, medical and legal discourses of western culture since ancient times. Graille cites a number of similar cases of hermaphrodites executed for having used the forbidden sex, including that in the early 1600s of a Scottish maidservant

who was accused of making her master's daughter pregnant and was tortured and buried alive (see Graille, 2001: 107 ff.). Hermaphrodites are still persecuted by laws which forbid them from marrying or from entering the religious life (ibid.: 175 n.123).

3. John O'Brien's unpublished paper, 'Betwixt and Between: Hermaphroditism and Masculinity', also emphasises the role of the imagination in the perception of hermaphrodites in late sixteenth-century France, suggesting a historical continuity of this theme from the ancients through the medieval period to the European Renaissance. I am grateful to Professor O'Brien for allowing me access to his work.

4. See my *Sade: the Libertine Novels* and *The Marquis de Sade: a Very Short Introduction*.

5. For Marjorie Garber the codpiece from Renaissance theatre is a sign of gender indecisiveness, the mark of 'seeming', Lacan's third term interposed between 'having' and 'being' the phallus – the space, as Garber argues, occupied by the transvestite (see Garber, 1993: 122).

6. In eighteenth-century England, feminine men and masculine women, known as mollies and tommies respectively, were regarded as third and fourth genders (see Trumbach, 1991: 112–13; also Norton, 1992).

3.   Cross-dressing in film comedy

1. See Chapter 2 for discussion of the antiquity of this theme. The Hollywood comedy, *What Women Want* (2000), in which a man suddenly acquires the ability to read women's thoughts, bears testimony to the enduring appeal of this theme.

2. This phrase was coined by Adrienne Rich in 1978 in her enormously influential essay, 'Compulsory Heterosexuality and Lesbian Existence'. In it, Rich identifies heterosexuality as a 'political institution' which systematically works to the disadvantage of all women (see Jagose, 1996: 49–50, 53–4).

3. Lieberfeld and Sanders also hint at the carnivalesque role of Florida in the narrative: 'Whereas Chicago mainly is depicted in nightmares and noirish interiors, Florida is a romantic leisure land "by the beautiful sea", as the soundtrack informs us, where boundaries dissolve and transgression is the norm. Joe and Jerry, like disguised revelers during Carnival, are free to adopt identities distinct from their own. Participants in carnivalesque ritual are permitted, even expected, to temporarily lose control, to go "running wild" – which is *Some Like it Hot's* theme-song' (1998: 2).

4. Terry Eagleton also believes that Bakhtin's view of carnival is too positive: 'Carnival, after all, is a licensed affair in every sense, a permissible rupture of hegemony, a contained popular blow-off as disturbing and relatively ineffectual as a revolutionary work of art' (Eagleton, 1981: 148; quoted by Stallybrass and White, 1986: 13).

5. See Garber (1993: 6; quoting Showalter, 1983: 138) 'As Showalter points out, the success of the film comes primarily "from the masculine power disguised and veiled by the feminine costume".' Not all feminist critics have

condemned the film in such terms, a notable exception being Susan Dworkin (1983).

6. That this belief is deeply rooted in our popular culture is evidenced by the enormous success of John Gray's book, *Men are from Mars, Women are from Venus*.

7. Waller's argument is well made and my reader is referred to p. 3 of her article for a detailed analysis of the positioning of actors on screen.

8. Caroline Warman (2000: 94) links the unveiling of truth in Sade's fiction with the forbidden unveiling of the female body. Thus, revelation of truth is always, in a sense, an unconscious expression of male sexual desire for the naked female body.

9. The pantomime's farcical dame figure thrusts her gender-bending in the audience's face (literally in some cases!), in sharp contrast to the muted and disavowed ambivalence of the principal boy who is nevertheless clearly an eroticised object, while female singers in the nineteenth-century music halls frequently performed in men's clothes, mirroring the principal boy's gender undecidability and its erotic impact on the audience.

10. Cohan (1998: 51–5) himself gives a number of additional reasons for viewing this ending as 'not that fully recuperative'.

11. Garber (1993: 127) also makes the point that the image of Mrs Doubtfire urinating assuages castration-fear by presenting the visual image, lost since infancy, of a pre-Oedipal mother.

4. Psycho–trans

1. In *The Silence of the Lambs*, this revelation takes place a little earlier in the narrative than usual, presumably so that the killer's psychology can be explored in some detail.

2. The demonisation of the feminine-maternal in the thriller genre is well-documented by critics. Barbara Creed, for example, points out that the maternal figure is constructed as the monstrous feminine in *Psycho, Carrie* and *The Birds* (see Creed, 1996: 42). See also Williams (1996) on the castrating woman' gaze, Clover (1996) on gender in the slasher film, Doherty (1996) on gender in the *Aliens* trilogy, and Lindsey (1996) on feminine monstrosity in *Carrie*. Clover catalogues the main elements of slasher movies in a manner reminiscent of Propp's *Morphology of the Folktale*. She concludes that the killer in slasher movies is often a feminine male, and the heroine a masculine female. The monster, Clover claims, is thus constructed as feminine (Clover, 1996: especially 101–6).While acknowledging that there are notable exceptions, we might broadly agree with Clover's notion of the preponderance of a 'monstrous feminine' in the horror genre, given the femininity of monsters in human narratives from *Beowulf* to *The Exorcist* and *Alien*.

3. This self-reflexivity has more recently become a recognisable feature of the genre, as the *Scream* series of films demonstrates.

4. Clover (1996: 101) considers 'The identity-game' to be 'too patterned and too pervasive in the slasher film to be dismissed as supervenient. It would

seem instead to be an integral element of the particular brand of bodily sensation in which the genre trades.'

5. See 'phallic woman' discussion in *Psycho* section. Linda Williams also reads the mutilation of Kate as 'a form of symbolic castration on a body that is frightening to the male precisely because it cannot be castrated, has none of his own vulnerability. The problem, in other words, is that she is not castrated; the fantasy solution of the male psychopath and the film itself is symbolically to prove that she is' (Williams, 1996: 32).

6. Williams (1996: 28) similarly argues that woman is both victim and monster in *Psycho* and *Dressed to Kill*.

7. Insect metamorphosis irresistibly recalls Kafka's short-story, *Die Verwandlung* (Metamorphosis), in which the author's alter ego, Gregor Samsa, awakes one morning to discover that he has changed into an enormous beetle. Kafka's tale is a symbolic and metaphorical exploration of his own sense of alienation as a writer, and insect metamorphosis is thus associated in our cultural memory with highly negative emotions. With a slightly different emphasis, Žižek also traces this theme to Kafka (see ibid.: 173–4).

8. Garber observes that, in its depiction of the killer's horrific method of transforming himself into a woman, the film 'declares its anxieties about transvestism and transsexualism in astonishingly overt ways' (Garber, 1993: 116–17).

9. See Prosser (1998: 67): 'In that s/he seeks to align sex with gender identification; in that the somatic progression toward these goals of sexed embodiment constitutes the transsexual narrative, the transsexual does not approach the body as an immaterial provisional surround but, on the contrary, as the very "seat" of the self. For if the body were but a costume, consider: why the life quest to alter its contours?' (see also Chapter 1, 'Queer Theory').

10. See note 2.

11. Garber (1993: 116) describes the film as 'a fable of gender dysphoria gone spectacularly awry', while for Prosser (1998: 67–8), this film contains 'one of the most disturbing recent representations of the transsexual . . . The transphobic stereotype in *The Silence of the Lambs* is particularly noxious because it arrogates and psychopathologizes figures immanently significant to transsexual accounts, inscribing the somatic trouble of the transsexual into the transsexual as trouble for the social corpus.'

12. This film has to my knowledge attracted no academic interest to date.

13. Large swathes of American society still cling to a sexual morality founded in Christianity which forbids pre-marital sex.

14. This literal inscription of innocence on the body of the victim is an ironic inversion of the branding of thieves in centuries past.

15. In reinforcement of this theme, an overweight and 'geeky' boy at the school is similarly marked out as an outsider and ridiculed by his peer-group. The collective rejection and demonisation of the outsider is a familiar theme in modern literature – Albert Camus's *L'Étranger* perhaps offers the best-known example.

16. For a modern reading of Freud's theory of the murder of the father in the primal horde in relation to the incest taboo, see Girard (1988: Ch. 8,'Totem *and Taboo* and the Incest Prohibition', 193–222).
17. There are possible intertextual echoes here of Terry Southern's and Mason Hoffenberg's erotic novel, *Candy*, in which the eponymous heroine is wont to exclaim 'Oh, daddy!' on numerous occasions, as she recognises the man having sex with her as her father.
18. Psychoanalytical approaches to transvestism have tended to emphasise identification in the male-to-female transvestite with the phallic woman/ mother: Meyerowitz quotes the prominent psychoanalyst, Otto Fenichel's view that the male-to-female transvestite 'fantasises that the woman possesses a penis, and thus overcomes his castration anxiety, and identifies himself with the phallic woman' (Fenichel, 1953: 179; quoted by Meyerowitz, 2002: 104).

5. Drama queens and macho men

1. It is one of our main hypotheses that representation acts upon the real, that cinematic images, in this case, help to mould the views and perceptions of the social phenomena so represented: see Chapter 1.
2. The mirror and its function of blurring reality is also an important motif in *Dressed to Kill*: see Chapter 4, pp. 101–2 on Lacan's 'Mirror Stage' and its relevance to the question of identity and the imaginary.
3. Jennifer Wicke expresses surprise that so many claim to have been deceived by Dil's 'masquerade' (Wicke, 1997: 375). It is tempting to conclude that the degree of Dil's sexual attractiveness to the spectator is the crucial factor here.
4. For Lacan, women are the phallus but cannot have it, while for men the reverse is true: in the Oedipal phase, as reinterpreted by Lacan, the boy goes from being the phallus to having it, thereby separating himself from the mother and identifying with the father (see Lacan, 1956–7).
5. The importance the director attached to this *Fort!da!* game is demonstrated by his swearing the crew to secrecy when the 'revelation scene' was filmed.
6. Trickery is a common theme in shemale Internet pornography where in contrast, the discovery of the deception is seen as exciting rather than disturbing.
7. *Boys Don't Cry* also reverberates with erotic moments, but these tend to centre upon the character of Lana, rather than on that of Brandon, the female-to-male transsexual.
8. This film has attracted little academic interest to date, and although it is well-known for its drag-queen character, I have not found any serious secondary literature on the film relevant to the subject of transgender.
9. Similarly, the nineteenth-century French hermaphrodite Herculine Barbin's change of status from woman to man was viewed suspiciously by the populus; people thought pretending to be a girl was a feint to avoid conscription,

a pretext for being a Don Juan lusting after young virgins (see Foucault, 1980: 90).

10. This is a theme which we have found to be present in other films, especially the comedies, and which we shall find to be a salient characteristic of shemale porn (see Chapter 6).

11. Both Willox and White also regret that the final scenes appear to evacuate Brandon's transsexualism, while Halberstam argues that the 'lesbian scene' and the portrayal of Brandon's murder as the consequence of homophobic rage prevent the film from promoting transgender as a positive identity (Halberstam, 2001: 297–8). Taking a wholly different tack, Lisa Henderson reads the film primarily as about transgender, but through the optic of class, seeing the poverty and hopelessness of the poor white milieu in which Brandon lives and moves as bearing significantly on the tragic events that befall him and those around him (Henderson, 2001: 301–3).

12. Violence against gays and transgendered people is in fact often perpetrated by adolescent males who are not secure in their own sexuality. Those who are outraged by sexual deviation (homophobes) are often fighting something within themselves. A recent UK TV programme reported the results of a scientific experiment conducted in the psychology department of an American university, according to which homophobes were shown to be sexually aroused by gay videos, while the majority of non-homophobes, of those secure in their sexuality, were not aroused by such material (Channel 4: *Middle Sex*, 26 May 2005).

13. Halberstam (2001: 295) also considers this latter scene as about belittling Brandon in front of Lana by revealing his castratedness to her.

14. In her Director's Commentary on *Boys* (DVD version), the director refers to *The Wizard of Oz* as inspiration for the film's escapist themes.

15. The transsexual has posed serious problems for some gays and feminists in that (s)he implicitly accepts the rules of the binary game, thus remaining within the phallicist economy (see Chapter 1, 'Queer Theory').

6.   Walking on the wild side: shemale Internet pornography

1. Laurence O'Toole's detailed survey of pornographic media in *Pornocopia: Porn, Sex, Technology and Desire*, for example, includes a lengthy chapter on 'cyberspace', but makes no mention at all of transsexuals or the pornographic sites in which they are represented.

2. See Chapter 1 for definitions of 'transvestite' and 'male-to-female transsexual'. Female-to-male transsexuals are not found in Internet or any other kind of pornography, and are therefore not discussed here.

3. Laura Kipnis is one of the very few academic commentators on pornography centring on transgendered subjects. See, for example, her essay, 'Shemale Fantasies and the Aesthetics of Pornography'. Much of the material in this essay is reproduced in Chapter 2 of her excellent book, *Bound and Gagged: Pornography and the Politics of Fantasy in America*.

4. Marty Rimm, 'Marketing Pornography on the Information Superhighway', carried out at Carnegie-Mellon University. See Naughton (1999: 32–3): 'Critics pointed out that many of Rimm's statistics – for example, his claim that 83.5 per cent of the images stored on the Usenet newsgroups are pornographic – were nonsensical. Two acknowledged experts from Vandebilt University, Donna Hoffman and Thomas Novak, maintained that pornographic files represent less than one half of 1 per cent of all messages posted on the internet.'

5. As Naughton points out (1999: 34–5), the Net does not require the consumer to cross a 'shame' threshold when accessing pornography, since this can be done in the privacy of one's own home, and so the exponential rise in the consumption of porn on the Net is completely unfettered by any fear of moral or ethical stigmatisation. This reveals some unpalatable truths about human nature, which is perhaps why the issue of Internet porn provokes such heated responses.

6. Some images on these sites represent post-op transsexuals, but these are a very small minority. My analysis in this chapter is concerned with pre-op transsexuals alone, because it is the pre-op who overwhelmingly constitute the erotic object of choice. The pre-op might also be said to occupy the shifting middle ground between conventional gender and sex binaries (see Chapter 1).

7. 'Phallicist' and 'phallogocentrism' are terms derived from Freudian psychoanalysis and Derridean post-structuralism and designate a male orientation in the linguistic and cultural expressions of the west.

8. Compare Laura Mulvey's view in both 'Visual Pleasure and Narrative Cinema' and her later 'Afterthoughts' that biological women are the only possible erotic objects in cinema.

9. Prosser identifies 'inbetweenness' as an object of fear and as a motive for the killing of the pre-op transsexual in Jennie Livingston's film, *Paris is Burning* (1990): 'Her death is indexical of an order that cannot contain crossings, a body in transition off the map of three binary axes – sex (male or female), sexuality (heterosexual or homosexual), and race (of color or white): a light-skinned Latina transsexual body under construction as heterosexual and female. At work in Venus's murder is not fear of the same or the other but fear of bodily crossing, of the movement in between sameness and difference: not homo- but transphobia, where "trans" here signifies the multileveled status of her crossing. This interstitial space is not foregrounded in Butler's reading of Venus's death' (Prosser, 1998: 47). See also Butler's chapter on the film, 'Gender is Burning: Questions of Appropriation and Subversion' in *Bodies That Matter* (1993: 121–42). Butler uses the film to emphasise the ambivalent effects of transgender.

10. Although Butler does not refer to transsexuals in any detail in her seminal work on Queer Theory, *Gender Trouble*, she declares in her 1999 preface to the book that, were she to rewrite it 'under present circumstances', she would include in it a discussion of transgender and intersexuality (xxvi). Indeed, she has devoted a recent if brief essay to the subject, see Butler (1998)

11. The photosets are frequently made up of stills from shemale movies that can either be purchased on video or DVD, or downloaded from the Internet.
12. All of this confirms the power of norms to resist resignification. As Bersani points out, 'resignification cannot destroy; it merely presents to the dominant culture spectacles of politically impotent disrespect . . .' (Bersani, 1995: 51); and referring specifically to Judith Butler's positive view of drag as exemplifying the performativity of gender: 'These mimetic activities are too closely imbricated in the norms they continue' (ibid.).
13. In conceding this, Butler is at odds with Monique Wittig's view of lesbianism's politically subversive potential (see Bersani, 1995: 47).
14. In this context, the term 'Asian' is used in its North American sense to denote natives of Far-Eastern countries, and not those from the Indian subcontinent. Thailand in particular has a well-known reputation for transsexuals.
15. Similarly, lesbians often claim that another woman is more skilful than any man in pleasuring a woman.
16. As indicated earlier, this is also one of the reasons for gay and feminist hostility to transsexuals.
17. The psychoanalyst, Louise Kaplan argues that the transvestite also desires a position beyond sexual difference. For Kaplan, perversions are not just sexual pathologies, they are pathologies of gender role identity. What they represent is an inability to conform completely to the gender conventions and gender stereotypes of the dominant social order (see Kaplan, 1992: 9). Kaplan believes that transvestites are attracted to elaborate, theatrical forms of feminine display as a way of denying sexual difference.
18. This striptease of course also occurs at the level of each individual image as it gradually unfolds upon the computer screen from thumbnail to full-size picture. This happy coincidence, resulting from the nature of Internet technology itself, adds to the provocative effect of such images upon the viewer.

7. Representation and reality

1. In the mixed-genre category, a number of Pedro Almodovar's films, too, feature transvestites or transsexuals in a somewhat self-parodic and even farcical manner, the best known examples being *All about my Mother* (*Todo sobre mi madre*, 1999) and his most recent production, *Bad Education* (*La Mala Educacion*, 2004), although their portrayal is for the most part a positive and sympathetic one.
2. Indeed, for Plato, no direct access to any reality is possible, since all we ever see are shadowy images of that reality, like the images projected by the sun on to the wall of a cave. This idea has strongly influenced philosophical notions of reality in the modern era, from Cartesian doubt in the seventeenth century to phenomenology and post-structuralism in the twentieth. This is the principal theme of a recent BBC2 series, *How Art Created the World* (May–June, 2005). Programmes in this series have

shown how the first human images created narratives about life which themselves provided the structure for living itself, how militaristic societies of the ancient world used artistic imagery to manipulate and control their populations, and finally, how religious representations have determined our attitudes to death and the afterlife.

3. 'The replication of heterosexual constructs in non-heterosexual frames brings into relief the utterly constructed status of the so-called heterosexual original. Thus, gay is to straight *not* as copy is to original, but, rather, as copy is to copy' (Butler, 1993: 31).

4. In *Forget Baudrillard* (Baudrillard, 1987: 70–1) Baudrillard reiterates what he calls the 'crisis of representation', claiming that reality can no longer be represented, that the reality principle is collapsing with the dissolution of the subject. What's left is, for Baudrillard, a 'world ruled by reversibility and indetermination'.

5. Sade is a notable exception to this trend: see my *Sade: the Libertine Novels*, and *Marquis de Sade: a Very Short Introduction*.

6. In the 1990s, Camille Paglia also identified a move away from polarised sexualities as a solution to the tensions between men and women which are still ongoing in 2006 : 'Bisexuality is our best hope of escape from the animosities and false priorities of the current sex wars' (Paglia, 1994: 94).

7. We are reminded here of the declaration of intentions in the Introduction to Sade's *One Hundred and Twenty Days of Sodom* to offer readers a menu of 600 'passions' or perversions in the hope of catering for all tastes. Like Sade's narrator, the Internet in particular offers consumers of porn a personalised service, drawn from an unprecedented choice of perversions and scenarios, in the comfort of their own homes and of an individual imaginary free from guilt and embarrassment.

Bibliography

Books and articles

Althusser, Louis, 'Ideology and Ideological State Apparatuses', in *Lenin and Philosophy and Other Essays*, trans. Ben Brewster (New York: Monthly Review Press, 1971).

Austin, J. L., *How to Do Things With Words* (Oxford: Oxford University Press, 1962).

Babington, Bruce and Peter William Evans, *Affairs to Remember: the Hollywood Comedy of the Sexes* (Manchester: Manchester University Press, 1989).

Backus, Margot Gayle and James Doan, 'Riverine Crossings: Gender, Identity and the Reconstruction of National Mythic Narrative in *The Crying Game*', *Cultural Studies*, 15 (1), 2001, 173–91.

Bakhtin, Mikhail, *Rabelais and his World*, trans. H. Iswolsky (Bloomington, Ind.: Indiana University Press, 1984).

Barthes, Roland, *S/Z*, trans. Richard Miller (Oxford: Basil Blackwell, 1990); original French edition, Paris: Éditions du Seuil, 1973a.

Barthes, Roland, *Le Plaisir du texte* (Paris: Éditions du Seuil, 1973b); in English as *The Pleasure of the Text*, trans. Richard Miller (New York: Hill and Wang, 1975; London: Jonathan Cape, 1976).

Barthes, Roland, *La Chambre Claire: note sur la photographie* (Paris: Gallimard and Seuil, 1980); in English as *Camera Lucida: Reflections on Photography*, trans. Richard Howard (New York: Hill and Wang, 1981; London: Jonathan Cape, 1982).

Baudrillard, Jean, 'Fashion or the Enchanted Fairy Land of the Code', in *L'échange symbolique et la mort* (Paris: Gallimard, 1976).

Baudrillard, Jean, *Forget Foucault* (New York: Semiotext(e), 1987); originally published as *Oublier Foucault* (Paris: Éditions Galilée, 1977). Text also contains *Forget Baudrillard*.

Baudrillard, Jean, *De la séduction [On Seduction]* (Paris: Denoel-Gonthier, 1979).

Baudrillard, Jean, 'The Precession of Simulacra', in *Simulacra and Simulation* (Ann Arbor: The University of Michigan Press, 1994); original French edition, Paris: Éditions Galilée, 1981.

de Beauvoir, Simone, *The Second Sex* trans. and ed. H.M. Parshley (London: Picador Classics, Pan Books, 1988); original French edition, *Le Deuxième Sexe* (Paris: Gallimard, 1949).

Benjamin, Harry, *The Transsexual Phenomenon* (New York: Julian Press, 1966).

Benvenuto, Bice and Roger Kennedy, *The Works of Jacques Lacan: an Introduction* (London: Free Association Books, 1986).

Berners-Lee, Tim, *Weaving the Web: the Past, Present and Future of the World Wide Web* (London and New York: Texere, 2000).

Bersani, Leo, *Homos* (Cambridge, MA and London: Harvard University Press, 1995).

Bibliography 185

Bride, Mac, *The Internet* (UK: Teach Yourself Books, 2001).
Butler, Judith, *Bodies that Matter: On the Discursive Limits of 'Sex'* (New York: Routledge, 1993).
Butler, Judith, Afterword for 'Transgender in Latin America: Persons, Practices and Meanings', a special issue of the journal *Sexualities*, 5(3), 1998.
Butler, Judith, *Gender Trouble. Feminism and the Subversion of Identity* (New York and London: Routledge, 1999); first published 1990.
Cantarella, Eva, *Bisexuality in the Ancient World* (Newhaven and London: Yale University Press, 2002); first published in English translation, 1992.
Casanova, Giacomo, *Histoire de ma vie*, trans. Willard R. Trask, *History of my Life*, 6 vols (Baltimore: Johns Hopkins University Press, 1997).
Chion, Michel, 'The Impossible Embodiment', in *Everything You Always Wanted to Know about Lacan (But Were Afraid to Ask Hitchcock)*, ed. Slavoj Žižek (London/New York: Verso, 1992), pp. 195–207.
Cirlot, J. E., *A Dictionary of Symbols* (Routledge, 1993); translated from the Spanish, Routledge & Kegan Paul Ltd, 1962.
Cixous, Hélène, 'The Laugh of the Medusa', *Signs*, 1(4), 1975, 875–93.
Clarke, Jan, 'Female Cross-dressing on the Paris Stage, 1673–1715', *Forum for Modern Language Studies*, XXXV (3), 1999, 238–50.
Clover, Carol J., 'Her Body, Himself: Gender in the Slasher Film', in *The Dread of Difference*, ed. Thomas Schatz (Austin: University of Texas Press, 1996), pp. 66–113; first published in *Misogyny, Misandry, Misanthropy*, eds R. Howard Bloch and Frances Ferguson (Berkeley: University of California Press, 1989).
Cohan, Steve, ' "I think I could fall in love with him": *Victor/Victoria* and the "drag" of romantic comedy', in *Terms of Endearment: Hollywood Romantic Comedy of the 1980s and 1990s*, eds Peter William Evans and Celestine Deleyto (Edinburgh: Edinburgh University Press, 1998), pp. 37–56.
Creed, Barbara, 'Horror and the Monstrous-feminine: an Imaginary Abjection', in *The Dread of Difference*, ed. Thomas Schatz (Austin: University of Texas Press, 1996), pp. 35–65.
Cryle, Peter, *The Telling of the Act: Sexuality as Narrative in Eighteenth- and Nineteenth-century France* (London: Associated University Presses, 2001).
Delcourt, Marie, *Hermaphrodite: Myths and Rites of the Bisexual Figure in Classical Antiquity* (London: Studio Books, 1961).
Docter, Richard F., *Transvestites and Transsexuals: Toward a Theory of Cross-gender Behavior* (New York: Plenum Press, 1988).
Doherty, Thomas, 'Genre, Gender, and the Aliens Trilogy', in *The Dread of Difference*, ed. Thomas Schatz (Austin: University of Texas Press, 1996), pp. 181–99.
Dubois, Diane, 'Seeing the Female Body Differently: Gender Issues in *The Silence of the Lambs*', *Journal of Gender Studies*, 10(3), 2001, 297–310.
Dworkin, Andrea, *Pornography: Men Possessing Women* (London: The Women's Press Ltd, 1981).
Dworkin, Susan, 'The Behind the Scenes Story of the Movie That Helps Men Understand What It's Like to Be a Woman', *Ms Magazine* (March 1983), 39–42.

Eagleton, Terry, *Walter Benjamin: Towards a Revolutionary Criticism* (London: Verso, 1981).

Fenichel, Otto, 'The Psychology of Transvestism', in *The Collected Papers of Otto Fenichel* (New York: W.W. Norton, 1953); essay first published in 1930.

Foucault, Michel, 'Préface à la transgression', in *Critique*, nos 195–6 (1963), 751–69.

Foucault, Michel, *The History of Sexuality*, vol. 1, *An Introduction*, trans. Robert Hurley (Harmondsworth: Penguin, 1978); first published in French, *Histoire de la sexualité*, vol. 1 *La Volonté de savoir* (Paris: Éditions Gallimard, 1976).

Foucault, Michel, *Herculine Barbin. Being the Recently Discovered Memoirs of a Nineteenth-century French Hermaphrodite*, Introduced by Michel Foucault (Brighton: The Harvester Press, 1980); first published in French, *Herculine Barbin dite Alexina B.* (Paris: Gallimard, 1978).

Foucault, Michel, *Les Anormaux*, Cours au Collège de France, 1974–1975 (Paris: Hautes Études-Gallimard-Seuil, 1999).

Freud, Sigmund, 'The Uncanny' (1919), in *Art and Literature*, The Pelican Freud Library, Vol. 14 (London: Pelican Books, 1985), pp. 335–76.

Freud, Sigmund, 'Fetishism' (1927), in *Three Essays on Sexuality*, The Pelican Freud Library, Vol. 7 (London: Pelican Books, 1984), pp. 345–57.

Friday, Nancy, *My Secret Garden. Women's Sexual Fantasies* (London and New York: Quartet Books, 1976); first published in 1973.

Garber, Marjorie, *Vested Interests: Cross-dressing and Cultural Anxiety* (London: Penguin Books, 1993); first published in the USA by Routledge, 1992.

Genette, Gérard, *Figures III* (Paris: Éditions du Seuil, 1972).

Girard, René, *Violence and the Sacred*, trans. Patrick Gregory (London: The Athlone Press, 1988); original French edition, *La Violence et le Sacré* (Paris: Éditions Bernard Grasset, 1972).

Graille, Patrick, *Les Hermaphrodites aux XVIIe et XVIIIe siècles* (Paris, Les Belles Lettres, 2001).

Halberstam, Judith, 'Skinflick: Posthuman Gender in Jonathan Demme's *The Silence of the Lambs*', *Camera Obscura: a Journal of Feminism, Culture, and Media Studies*, 27, 1991, 5–35.

Halberstam, Judith, 'The Transgender Gaze in *Boys Don't Cry*', *Screen*, 42(3), 2001, 294–8.

Handler, Kirstin, 'Sexing *The Crying Game*: Difference, Identity, Ethics', *Film Quarterly*, 1994, 31–42.

Hanson, Helen, 'The Figure in Question: the Transvestite Character as a Narrative Strategy in *The Crying Game*', in *The Body's Perilous Pleasures*, ed. Michele Aaron (Edinburgh: Edinburgh University Press, 1999).

Henderson, Lisa, 'The Class Character of *Boys Don't Cry*', *Screen*, 42(3), 2001, 299–303.

Hill, John, 'Crossing the Water: Hybridity and Ethics in *The Crying Game*', *Textual Practice*, 12(1), 1998, 98–100.

Hirschfeld, Magnus, *Die Transvestiten* (1910).

Hughes, A., O. Heathcote and J. Williams (eds), *Gay Signatures. Gay and Lesbian Theory, Fiction and Film in France, 1945–1995* (Oxford: Berg, 1998).

Irigaray, Luce, 'Ce Corps qui n'en est pas un', in *Ce Sexe qui n'en est pas un* (Paris: Minuit, 1977); English translation *This Sex Which Is Not One* (Ithaca: Cornell University Press, 1985).

Jagose, Annamarie, *Queer Theory: an Introduction* (New York University Press, 1996).

Kaplan, Louise J., *Female Perversions. The Temptations of Emma Bovary* (New York: Anchor Books, 1992).

Kellner, Douglas, *Jean Baudrillard: From Marxism to Postmodernism and Beyond* (Cambridge, Polity Press, 1989).

Kipnis, Laura, 'She-male Fantasies and the Aesthetics of Pornography', in *Dirty Looks: Women, Pornography, Power*, eds Pamela Church Gibson and Roma Gibson (London: BFI Publishing, 1994), pp. 124–43.

Kipnis, Laura, *Bound and Gagged: Pornography and the Politics of Fantasy in America* (New York: Grove Press, 1996).

von Krafft-Ebing, Richard, *Psychopathia Sexualis* (London: Velvet Publications, 1997); first published 1877.

Kristeva, Julia, *Powers of Horror: an Essay on Abjection*, trans. Leon S. Roudiez (New York: Columbia University Press, 1982); originally published in French, *Pouvoirs de l'horreur* (Paris: Éditions du Seuil, 1980).

Kuhn, Annette, *The Power of the Image: Essays on Representation and Sexuality* (London: Routledge, 1985).

Laplanche, J. and J.-B. Pontalis, *The Language of Psycho-analysis* (London: The Hogarth Press & The Institute of Psycho-analysis, 1985).

Lemaire, Anika, *Jacques Lacan* (London: Routledge & Kegan Paul Ltd, 1977).

Lewis, Matthew, *The Monk* (Harmondsworth: Penguin Classics, 1998).

Lieberfeld, Daniel and Judith Sanders, 'Comedy and Identity in *Some Like it Hot*', *Journal of Popular Film and Television*, 26(3), 1 September 1998.

Lindsey, Shelley Stamp, 'Horror, Femininity and Carrie's Monstrous Puberty', in *The Dread of Difference*, ed. Thomas Schatz (Austin: University of Texas Press, 1996), pp. 279–95.

Lacan, Jacques, Seminars on 'The Formations of the Unconscious', summarised by Pontalis (Seminars, 1956–7), in *Bulletin de Psychologie*, 1956–7.

Lacan, Jacques, 'Aggressivity in Psychoanalysis', in *Ecrits*, trans. Alan Sheridan-Smith (London: Tavistock Publications, 1977a); first published in French as 'L' aggressivité en psychanalyse', in *Écrits* (Paris: Seuil, 1966).

Lacan, Jacques, 'The Seminar on *The Purloined Letter*', in *Ecrits*, trans. Alan Sheridan-Smith (London: Taristock Publications, 1977b); first published in French as 'Le Séminaire sur la lettre volée', *Écrits* (Paris: Seuil, 1966).

Lacan, Jacques, 'The insistence of the letter in the unconscious', *Ecrits*, trans. Alan Sheridan-Smith (London: Tavistock Publications, 1977c); first published in French as 'L'instance de la lettre dans l'inconscient', in *Écrits* (Paris: Seuil, 1966).

Love, Brenda, *Encyclopedia of Unusual Sexual Practices* (London: Greenwich Editions, 1999); first published 1992.

MacKinnon, Catherine, *Only Words* (London: HarperCollins, 1994).

Martinez, Maria Jesus, '*Some Like it Hot*: the Blurring of Gender Limits in a Film of the Fifties', *Barcelona English Language and Literature Studies (BELLS)* 9, 1998, 143–52.

McDougall, Joyce, 'L'idéal hermaphrodite et ses avatars', in *Bisexualité et différence des sexes*, publié sous la direction de J.-B. Pontalis (Paris: Éditions Gallimard, 1973), pp. 409–31.

Meyerowitz, Joanne, *How Sex Changed: a History of Transsexuality in the United States* (Cambridge, MA and London: Harvard University Press, 2002).

Milner, Max, *Freud et l'interprétation de la literature* (Paris: CDU et SEDES réunis, 1980).

Monick, Eugene, *Castration and the Male Gaze: the Phallic Wound*, Studies in Jungian Psychology by Jungian Analysts, General Editor Daryl Sharp (Toronto: Inner City Books, 1991).

Montero, Oscar, 'Lipstick Vogue: the Politics of Drag', *Radical America*, 22(1), 1988.

Moreau, François, *L'image littéraire* (Paris: CDU et SEDES réunis, 1982).

Mulvey, Laura, 'Visual Pleasure and Narrative Cinema', in *The Audience Studies Reader*, eds Will Brooker and Deborah Jermyn (London: Routledge, 2003), pp. 133–42; originally published in *Screen*, 16(3), 1975.

Munich, Adrienne Auslander, 'Tootsie's Gender Act', *Denver Quarterly*, 18(4), 1984, 108–18.

Naughton, John, *A Brief History of the Future. The Origins of the Internet* (London: Weidenfeld and Nicolson: Phoenix Paperbacks, 1999).

Nietzsche, Friedrich, *On the Genealogy of Morals*, trans. Walter Kaufmann (New York: Vintage, 1969).

Norton, Rictor, *Mother Clap's Molly House* (London: GMP Publishers, 1992).

O'Brien, John, 'Betwixt and Between: Hermaphroditism and Masculinity' (unpublished paper).

O'Toole, Laurence, *Pornocopia: Porn, Sex, Technology and Desire* (London: Serpent's Tail, 1998; updated in 1999).

Paglia, Camille, *Sexual Personae* (New York: Vintage Books, 1991).

Paglia, Camille, 'What a Drag: Marjorie Garber's *Vested Interests: Cross-Dressing and Cultural Anxiety*', in *Sex, Art and American Culture, Essays* (Harmondsworth: Penguin, 1992), pp. 96–100.

Paglia, Camille, *Vamps and Tramps* (New York: Vintage Books, 1994).

Phillips, John, *Sade: the Libertine Novels* (London and Sterling, Virginia: Pluto Press, 2001).

Phillips, John, *The Marquis de Sade: a Very Short Introduction* (Oxford: Oxford University Press, 2005).

Prosser, Jay, *Second Skins: the Body Narratives of Transsexuality* (New York: Columbia University Press, 1998).

Raymond, Janice, *The Transsexual Empire: the Making of the She-male* (1979); reissued with a new introduction on transgender (New York: Teacher's College Press, 1994).

Rich, Adrienne, 'Compulsory Heterosexuality and Lesbian Existence', in *Powers of Desire: the Politics of Sexuality*, eds Ann Snitow, Christine Stansell and Sharon Thompson (New York: Monthly Review Press, 1983); written in 1978 and first published in *Signs: Journal of Women in Culture and Society* in 1980.

Ricoeur, Paul, *La Métaphore Vive* (Paris: Éditions du Seuil, 1975).

Rimm, Marty, 'Marketing Pornography on the Information Superhighway', research carried out at Carnegie-Mellon University, and referred to by Naughton (1999: 32–3).

Robbins, Betty and Roger Myrick, 'The Function of the Fetish in *The Rocky Horror Picture Show* and *Priscilla, Queen of the Desert', Journal of Gender Studies*, 9(3), 2000, 269–80.

Roger, Philippe, *La Philosophie dans le pressoir* (Paris: Bernard Grasset, 1976).

de Sade, *Voyage d'Italie*, in *Oeuvres du Marquis de Sade*, vol. XVI, edited by Gilbert Lély (Paris: Cercle du livre précieux, 1966–7).

de Sade, *Histoire de Juliette, ou les Prospérités du vice*, in *Oeuvres Complètes*, eds Le Brun and Pauvert (Paris: Société Nouvelle des Éditions Pauvert, 1987), Vols 8 & 9; English translation: *Juliette*, trans. Austryn Wainhouse (London: Arrow Books Ltd, 1991 (1968)).

de Sade, *Les 120 Journées de Sodome* (Paris: P.O.L., 1992); English translation: *The One Hundred and Twenty Days of Sodom*, compiled and translated by Austryn Wainhouse and Richard Seaver (London: Arrow Books, 1990).

Schaeffer, Neil, *The Marquis de Sade. A Life* (Picador, 2001); first published 1999.

Sedgwick, Eve Kosofsky, *Epistemology of the Closet* (Berkeley: University of California Press, 1990).

Segal, Lynne, *Slow Motion: Changing Masculinities, Changing Men* (London: Virago, 1997).

Showalter, Elaine, 'Critical Cross-dressing: Male Feminists and the Woman of the Year', *Raritan*, 3(2), 1983.

Southern, Terry and Mason Hoffenberg, *Candy* (Paris: Olympia Press, 1958).

Stallybrass, Peter and Allon White, *The Politics and Poetics of Transgression* (Ithaca: Cornell University Press, 1986).

Stoller, Robert J., *Sex and Gender: On the Development of Masculinity and Femininity* (London: The Hogarth Press and the Institute of Psychoanalysis, 1968).

Stone, Sandy, 'The Empire Strikes Back: a Posttranssexual Manifesto', in *BodyGuards: the Cultural Politics of Gender Ambiguity*, eds Julia Epstein and Kristina Straub (London and New York: Routledge, 1991), pp. 280–304.

Tharp, Julie, 'The Transvestite as Monster', *Journal of Popular Film and Television*, 19(3), 1991, online version.

The Times Higher, 'Why should a John be a Joan?', 8 October 1999, 19.

Tincknell, Estella and Deborah Chambers, 'Performing the Crisis: Fathering, Gender, and Representation in two 1990s' Films', *Journal of Popular Film and Television*, 29(4), 2002, 7.

Trumbach, Randolph, 'London's Sapphists: From Three Sexes to Four Genders in the Making of Modern Culture', in *BodyGuards: the Cultural Politics of Gender Ambiguity*, eds Julia Epstein and Kristina Straub (New York: Routledge, 1991).

Waller, Margaret, 'Academic Tootsie: the Denial of Difference and the Difference it Makes', *Diacritics*, Spring 1987, 2–20.

Warman, Caroline, 'The Jewels of Virtue: Sade's Claim to the Legacy of Materialism', *Paragraph, a Journal of Critical Theory*, 23(1), March 2000 (special issue on Sade, edited by John Phillips), 87–97.

Warner, Marina, *Managing Monsters: Six Myths of Our Time*, The Reith Lectures, 1994 (Vintage Books, 1994).

White, Patricia, 'Girls Still Cry', *Screen*, 42(2), 2001, 217–21.

Whittle, Stephen, *The Transgender Debate. The Crisis Surrounding Gender Identity* (Reading, UK: South Street Press, 2000).

Wicke, Jennifer, 'Double-cross-dressing: the Politics of a Genre', *Annals of Scholarship: an International Quarterly in the Humanities and Social Sciences*, 11(4), 1997, 359–77.

Williams, Albert, '*Victor/Victoria*: a New Queen on the Scene', *American Theatre*, 12(9), 1995, 15.

Williams, Linda, *Hard Core: Power, Pleasure, and the Frenzy of the Visible* (London: Pandora Press, 1990).

Williams, Linda, 'When the Woman Looks', in *The Dread of Difference*, ed. Thomas Schatz (Austin: University of Texas Press, 1996), pp. 15–34; first published in *Re-Vision: Essays in Feminist Film Criticism*, ed. Mary Ann Doane, Patricia Mellencamp and Linda Williams (Frederick, Md.: University Publications/American Film Institute, 1983), pp. 83–99.

Willox, Annabelle, 'Branding Teena: (Mis)Representations in the Media', *Sexualities*, 6(3/4), 2003, 407–26.

Wittig, Monique, *Straight Mind*; quoted by Bersani, (1995: 189 n.19).

Wood, Robin, *Hollywood from Vietnam to Reagan* (New York: Columbia University Press, 1986).

Žižek, Slavoj, 'In His Bold Gaze My Ruin Is Writ Large', in *Everything You Always Wanted to Know about Lacan (But Were Afraid to Ask Hitchcock)*, ed. Slavoj Žižek (London/New York: Verso, 1992), pp. 211–72.

Filmography (in chronological order)

Magic (Richard Attenborough, 1978); based on the 'Ventriloquist Dummy' segment of *Dead of Night* (1945)

Some Like it Hot (Billy Wilder, 1959)

Psycho (Alfred Hitchcock, 1960)

The Rocky Horror Picture Show (Lou Adler, 1975)

Kramer versus Kramer (Robert Benton, 1979)

Dressed to Kill (Brian de Palma, 1980)

Tootsie (Sydney Pollack, 1982)

Victor/Victoria (Blake Edwards, 1982)

The Silence of the Lambs (Jonathan Demme, 1991)

Mrs Doubtfire (Chris Columbus, 1993)

The Crying Game (Neil Jordan, 1993)

The Adventures of Priscilla, Queen of the Desert (Stephan Elliott, 1994)

Midnight in the Garden of Good and Evil (Clint Eastwood, 1997)

Boys Don't Cry (Kimberly Peirce, 1999)

Director's Commentary on *Boys Don't Cry* (available on the DVD edition)

Todo sobre mi madre/[All about my Mother] (Pedro Almodovar, 1999)

What Women Want (Nancy Meyers, 2000)

Cherry Falls (Geoffrey Wright, 2000)
Minority Report (Steven Spielberg, 2002)
La Mala Educacion [Bad Education] (Pedro Almodovar, 2004)

Television and Internet

Coronation Street (Granada Television)
Middle Sex (Channel 4), 26th May, 2005
BBC2 series, *How Art Created the World* (May–June, 2005)
Internet shemale pornography sites

Index

Adventures of Priscilla, Queen of the Desert, The, 7, 126–34
Almodovar, Pedro, 182 n.1
Althusser, Louis, 27–8,
  interpellation, theory of, 28
androgyneity/the androgyne, 8,
  32–5,
  of names in *The Crying Game*, 119
  see also bisexuality
Asian 'ladyboys', 156, 182 n.14
Austin, J.L.,
  speech-act theory, 12

Bakhtin,
  carnivalesque, 60, 65, 176 n.4
  hybridisation, 17
  grotesque body, 152
Balzac, Honoré de,
  Sarrasine, 23–4, 26, 27, 49, 72–4,
    75, 163: *see also* Barthes, *S/Z*
Barthes, Roland, 2, 20, 21,
  Camera Lucida, 169–70
  hermeneutic code, 19, 163, 175
    n.10
  proairetic code, 135
  symbolic code, 135
  S/Z, 23–4, 26, 72–4, 75, 163, 175
    n.12
Baudrillard, Jean, 14, 15, 16, 27–9,
  60, 166–72,
  'Fashion or the Enchanted Fairy
    Land of the Code', 170
  Forget Baudrillard, 183 n.4
  Forget Foucault, 171
  hyperrreal, 172
  On Seduction, 171
  simulacra, theory of, 28, 168–9
  'The Body or the Carnality of
    Signs', 170
Beauvoir, Simone de, 2, 12
Benjamin, Harry, 10

Benvenuto, Bice and Kennedy,
  Roger, 6, 161–2
Berners-Lee, Tim, 148
Bersani, Leo, 149, 150, 182 n.12
Big Brother, 1
binary thinking, 32–4
bisexuality, 8, 34,
Boys Don't Cry, 27, 138–46, 179 n.7
Brazilian transsexuals, 156
Bride, Mac, 148
Butler, Judith, 122, 128, 140, 146,
  150, 151, 153, 156, 162, 174
  n.5, 174–5 n.8, 183 n.3,
  *Bodies that Matter: On the Discursive
    Limits of 'Sex'*, 174 n.6, 181 n.9
  Gender Trouble, 11, 12, 13, 181 n.10
  performativity, theory of gender
    as, 13–14, 63, 65, 72, 105,
    125, 127, 182 n.12

Camus, Albert,
  L'Étranger, 178 n.15
Cantarella, Eva, 34
Carrie, 96
Casanova, Giacomo,
  Histoire de ma vie, 42
castration anxiety/complex, 7, 18,
  23–4, 28, 73, 76, 82–3, 158, 162,
  170–1,
  motifs in *The Adventures of Priscilla,
    Queen of the Desert*, 131
  motifs in *Boys Don't Cry*, 142–4:
    see also homophobia
  motifs in *The Crying Game*, 124–5
  motifs in *Dressed To Kill*, 99–100
  motifs in *Mrs Doubtfire*, 177 n.11
  motifs in *The Silence of the Lambs*,
    105
  motifs in *Psycho*, 92, 94
catharsis, 18
Cauldwell, Dr David O., 10

Cherry Falls, 107–14
Chion, Michel, 88–9, 91
Cirlot, J.E., 104
Cixous, Hélène, 174 n.1
Clarke, Jan, 46–7
closure,
  parody of, 77–81
Clover, Carol J., 95, 177 n.2, 177 n.4
Cohan, Steve, 74, 78, 177 n.10
compulsory heterosexuality, 55
Coronation Street, 1, 15–16, 25–6, 166
Creed, Barbara, 177 n.2
cross-dressing, 44–50, 51–2,
  in film comedies, 51–84
  in the Middle Ages, 44–5
  in the nineteenth century, 45
  in Roman times, 34, 44
  in thrillers, 85–114
  see also transvestism
Crying Game, The, 26–7, 116–26
Cryle, Peter, 159

death's-head moth, 103–4
deception, theme of,
  in *The Crying Game*, 125–6
  in Internet pornography, 179 n.6
  in the progress narrative, 52 ff.
  see also veiling/unveiling
Delcourt, Marie, 33, 34, 35, 37
Descartes, René, 31
dislocation,
  theme of in *Psycho*, 87 ff., 94
Doane, Mary Anne, 129
Docter, Richard F., 9
Doherty, Thomas, 177 n.2
Donahue, Phil, 98
drag, 9, 13, 66, 77, 127 ff., 137,
  parody of in *Victor/Victoria*, 71–2
  as performative, 128–9
Dressed to Kill, 94–102
Dubois, Diane, 105, 106
Dworkin, Andrea, 150
Dworkin, Susan, 177 n.5

Eagleton, Terry, 176 n.4
Eliot, T.S., 112–13

Fenichel, Otto, 179 n.18
Foster, Jody, gay identification with,
  106
Foucault, Michel, 2, 20, 27, 31, 41,
  Herculine Barbin, 42–4, 174 n.5,
  179–80 n.9
  Les Anormaux, 37–8
  transgression, theory of, 164
Franklin, Aretha, 15, 174–5 n.8
Freud, Sigmund,
  fetishism, 91, 99, 158: *see also*
  castration anxiety/complex,
  motifs in *Dressed To Kill*
  'Fort!da!' game, 22–3, 76–7, 162–3,
  179 n.5
  incest prohibition, 179 n.16: *see
  also* Girard
  Oedipus complex, 93–4, 109,
  124–5
  repetition compulsion, 31, 162–3
  the Uncanny, 89–90, 93, 137, 164
Friday, Nancy, 139

Garber, Marjorie, 2–4, 7, 8, 9, 53,
  54, 95, 96, 128, 138, 176 n.5,
  177 n.11, 178 n.8,
  progress narrative, theory of, 52–3,
  56, 57, 69
  on *The Silence of the Lambs*, 178 n.11
gender, 7–1, 12,
  see also sex; sexuality
gender dysphoria, 9,
  see also transsexuals
Genette, Gérard, 175 n.11
Girard, René,
  Violence and the Sacred, 110–11,
  179 n.16
Graille, Patrick, 39, 175–6 n.2
Gray, John,
  *Men are from Mars, Women are from
  Venus*, 177 n.6

Halberstam, Judith, 105, 145, 180
  n.11, 180 n.13
Hamburger, Dr Christian, 10
Handler, Kirstin, 8, 121, 123

Hanson, Helen, 119
Henderson, Lisa, 180 n.11
Hermaphrodite, Greek god, 36–7,
  40–1
hermaphrodites, 8, 35–44, 160,
  175–6 n.2
Hill, John, 119, 122
Hirschfeld, Magnus, 8–9, 45
Hitchcock, Alfred, 86–7
Hoffman, Donna, 181 n.4
homophobia, 67, 74, 76, 137, 140,
  142–4, 180 n.12
homosexuality, 10, 45, 111
How Art Created the World, 182–3 n.2

Internet, 147–9, 181 n.5
  porn, 183 n.7
intersexuality, 8, 38–9
Irigaray, Luce, 151, 159

Jagose, Annamarie, 174 n.4, 176 n.2
Jorgensen, Christine, 10
Jung, Carl,
  collective unconscious, theory of,
  31

Kafka, Georg,
  Die Verwandlung, 178 n.7
Kaplan, Louise, 182 n.17
Kipnis, Laura, 147–8, 150,
  'She-male Fantasies and the
    Aesthetics of Pornography',
    180 n.3
knowledge of other sex,
  dangers of, 43
  forbidden knowledge, 54–5
Krafft-Ebing, Richard von, 45
Kristeva, Julia,
  abject, theory of, 17–18
Kroker, Arthur and Marilouise, 171
Kuhn, Annette, 57

Lacan, Jacques, 179 n.4,
  Father's Law, 5–6, 21–2, 28, 80–1,
    86, 107, 111, 161, 176 n.5
  fetishism, 161–2

Imaginary Order, 6, 28, 84
  mirror stage, 101–2, 179 n.2
  Name of the Father, 74
  Symbolic Order, 6, 28, 84, 107,
    111, 172, 173
  Real Order, 6
  urinary segregation, theory of,
    24–6
  see also Freud, repetition
    compulsion and *'fort!da!'*
    game
Laplanche, J. and Pontalis, J.-B., 175
  n.9
Lemaire, Anika, 22–3
lesbianism, in *Boys Don't Cry*, 146
Lewis, Matthew,
  The Monk, 48
Lieberfeld, D. and Sanders, J., 56, 57,
  59, 176 n.3
Lindsey, Shelley Stamp, 95, 177 n.2
Livingston, Jennie,
  Paris is Burning, 181 n.9
Livy, 36
Love, Brenda, 9

MacKinnon, Catherine, 150
Magic, 90
Martinez, Maria Jesus, 57
McDougall, Joyce, 160–1
Meyerowitz, Joanne, 174 n.2, 179
  n.18
*Midnight in the Garden of Good and
  Evil*, 134–8
Minority Report, 28
misrecognition, 19, 101
mollies and tommies, 176 n.6
molly houses, 45,
  see also homosexuality
Money, John, 39
money shot, 125, 158
Monick, Eugene, 82, 91, 143–44,
  see also castration complex
Moreau, François, 130
Mrs Doubtfire, 79–84
Mulvey, Laura, 64, 97, 120, 181 n.8
Munich, Adrienne Auslander, 65

Nietzsche, 12
normativity
  in comedies, 165
  in popular culture, 15–16
Novak, Thomas, 181 n.4
Naughton, John, 148, 181 n.4, 181 n.5

O'Brien, John, 176 n.3
O'Toole, Laurence,
  Pornocopia: Porn, Sex, Technology and Desire, 180 n.1

Paglia, Camille, 3–4, 48–9, 128, 183 n.6
pantomime dame, 66, 177 n.9,
  see also drag
performance, 54, 70–1,
  see also Butler, performativity
perversion, 182 n.17,
  definitions of, 175 n.9
phallicism/phallogocentrism, 181 n. 7
phallic mother, 91–4
phallic woman, 123
Plato, 32–3, 34, 110, 182 n. 2
popular culture, 27–8
postmodernism, *see Baudrillard*
pre-oedipal unity with the mother, 160
Propp, Vladimir,
  Morphology of the Folktale, 177 n.2
Prosser, Jay, 13, 171, 178 n.9, 181 n.9
Psycho, 86–94,
  see also Hitchcock

Queer Theory, 11–14, 181 n.10,
  see also Butler

Raymond, Janice,
  The Transsexual Empire: the Making of the She-male, 174 n.7
representation, influence on reality, 166–7
Rich, Adrienne, 176, n.2

Ricoeur, Paul, 130
Rimm, Marty,
  'Marketing Pornography on the Information Superhighway', 181 n.4
Robbins, Betty and Myrick, Roger, 129, 131, 132
Rocky Horror Picture Show, The, 1
Roger, Philippe, 41

Sade, D.A.F., Marquis de, 183 n.5,
  on hermaphrodites, 39–42
  Juliette, 39–41, 48
  The 120 Days of Sodom, 41, 183 n.7
  Voyages d'Italie, 40, 41
scorpions, in *The Crying Game*, 122–4
Sedgwick, Eve Kosofsky, 11, 174 n.3
Segal, Lynne, 127
self-reflexivity/referentiality,
  in *Victor/Victoria*, 70
  in *Psycho*, 87
sex, 7–11,
  see also gender; sexuality
sexual politics,
  in *Boys Don't Cry*, 141–2
sexuality, 7–11, 14–15
Shakespeare, 46, 70
shemales,
  internet pornography, 147–64, 166
  male-to-female, pre-op, 14
  see also transsexuals
Showalter, Elaine, 176 n.5
signifier, incessant movement of,
  dominance of, 24–7
Silence of the Lambs, The, 102–7
sodomy, 38
Some Like it Hot, 56–61
Southern, Terry and Hoffenberg, Mason,
  Candy, 179 n.17
specular images, 101, 117, 121,
  see also Lacan, mirror stage
Stallybrass, P. and White, A., 17, 152
Stoller, Robert, 138
Studlar, Gaylyn, 129

196   *Index*

Tharp, Julie, 103, 106
Tincknell, Estella and Chambers,
    Deborah, 129, 131, 132, 134
Tiresias, 37
Tootsie, 61–8
transgender, 11,
    in film drama, 115–46
    historical survey of, 30–50
transgression,
    temporary, 55–6
transsexualism, 9, 10, 14,
    in *Dressed to Kill*, 97–100
    on the Internet, 147–64, 181 n.6
    see also Boys Don't Cry
transvestism, 8–9, 17, 182 n.17,
    on stage and in literature, 46–50
Trumbach, Randolph, 176 n.6

urinary segregation, 55, 82–3,
    see also Lacan

vagina dentata, 159
veiling/unveiling, 18–24, 53–4,
    76–7, 83, 117–18, 125–6,
    see also deception
Victor/Victoria, 26–7, 68–79

Waller, Margaret, 64, 177 n.7
Warman, Caroline, 177 n.8
Warner, Marina, 15, 86
What Women Want, 176 n.1
White, Patricia, 180 n.11
Whittle, Stephen, 8, 9, 45
Wicke, Jennifer, 57–8, 79, 119, 179 n.3
Williams, Albert, 68–9
Williams, Linda, 158, 177 n.2, 178
    n.5, 178 n.6
Willox, Annabelle, 103, 146, 180 n.11
Wittig, Monique, 12, 152, 160, 182
    n.13
Wizard of oz, The,
    theme in *Boys Don't Cry*, 144–6,
    180 n.14
Wood, Robin, 69
World Wide Web, 148

Žižek, Slavoj, 88–9, 103, 178 n.7

CPI Antony Rowe
Chippenham, UK
2016-12-27 13:41